W9-AFH-437

The Present Past

THE PRESENT PAST

AN INTRODUCTION TO
ANTHROPOLOGY FOR ARCHAEOLOGISTS

Ian Hodder

PICA PRESS   NEW YORK

For the joy of little Greg

Published in the United States of America in 1983 by
PICA PRESS
Distributed by Universe Books
381 Park Avenue South, New York, N.Y. 10016

82 83 84 85 86/10 9 8 7 6 5 4 3 2 1

Printed in Great Britain

Library of Congress Cataloging in Publication Data
Hodder, Ian
    The present past.

    Bibliography: p.
    Includes index.
    1. Ethnoarchaeology.   I. Title.
CC79.E85H63 1983   930.1   82-17437
ISBN 0-87663-736-5

Contents

Acknowledgements 6

List of Illustrations 7

Preface 9

1 The use of analogy 11
Problems with analogies 12   The proper use of
analogy 16   Context 24   Conclusion 27

2 Ethnoarchaeology 28
Relations with experimental approaches in
archaeology 29   History of the use of ethnographic
analogies in archaeology 31   Ethnoarchaeological
field methods 41

**3 The formation of the archaeological
  record** 47
Post-deposition 47   Deposition 56   Conclusion 65

4 Technology and production 68
Formal analogies 68   Relational analogies based on
natural processes 72   Cross-cultural relationships
85   Relational analogies and cultural context
89   Conclusion 92

5 Subsistence strategies 93
Hunters and gatherers 93   Pastoralists 104
Agriculturalists 106   Bones and seeds 111
Conclusion 113

6 Social organisation 117
Settlement 117   Burial 139   Exchange 146   Levels
of societal complexity 152   Conclusion 157

7 Ritual 159
Conclusion 171

8 Art, decoration and style 173
Art 173   Decoration 182   Style 191   Conclusion 195

9 Looking at ourselves 197

**10 Conclusion : archaeological
   anthropology 210**
Interpreting the past 210   A theory of material
culture 212

Bibliography 217

Index 233

Acknowledgements

The following publishers are acknowledged for permission to reproduce the
illustrations appearing in this book.

Academic Press: fig. 22 from Steensberg A. 1980 *New Guinea gardens*.
George Allen and Unwin: fig. 41c from Heyerdahl T. and Ferdon E.N. (eds) 1961
Archaeology of Easter Island. Volume 1.
Athlone Press: fig. 41d from Evans J.D. 1971 *The prehistoric antiquities of the Maltese
Islands: a survey*.
Barrie and Jenkins: figs 35, 36 and 37 from Rapoport A. (ed.) 1969 *Shelter and
Society*.
Cambridge University Press: fig. 29 from Hugh Jones C. 1979 *From the milk river*.
Chapman and Hall Ltd.: fig. 16 from Clark J.G.D. 1952 *Prehistoric Europe: the
economic basis*.
Jonathan Cape: fig. 41b from Renfrew A.C. *Before Civilisation. The radiocarbon
revolution and prehistoric Europe*.
Hutchinson: fig. 39b from Phillips P. 1975 *Early farmers of West Mediterranean Europe*.
International African Institute: figs 33 and 34 from *Africa* Volume 50.
International Louis Leakey Memorial Institute for African Prehistory: fig. 21 from
Leakey R.E. and Ogot B.A. (eds) 1980 *Proceedings of the 8th Panafrican Congress of
Prehistory and Quaternary Studies*.
Kroeber Anthropological Society: fig. 11 from *Kroeber Anthropological Society Papers*,
Volume 37.
Michigan Discussions in Anthropology: fig. 28 from Smiley F.E. *et al* (eds) 1980 *The
archaeological correlates of hunter gatherer*.
Prehistoric Society: from the *Proceedings of the Prehistoric Society*, figs 2a and 3a from
Volume 6, fig. 27 from Volume 5, fig. 3 from Volume 37, fig. 5 from Volume 32,
fig. 40 from Volume 44.
Prentice Hall: fig. 41a from Sahlins M.D. 1968 *Tribesmen*.
Rex Features Ltd.: fig. 47 from York P. 1980 *Style Wars*.
Society of Antiquaries: fig. 39c from *Antiquaries Journal*, Volume 51.
Thames and Hudson: fig. 1a from Megaw J.V.S. (ed.) 1976 *To illustrate the
monuments*; figs 5 and 6 from Willey G.R. and Sabloff J.A. 1974 *A history of American
Archaeology*; figs 42 and 43 from Clark J.G.D. 1967 *The Stone Age hunters*.

I wish also to thank Francoise for her help in surveying the relevant literature and
for her advice. Parts of the typescript for this book were produced while a visiting
Professor at the Van Giffen Institute of Pre- and Proto-history of the University of
Amsterdam, and my debt to the patience and generosity of the members of that
Institute is warmly acknowledged.

The illustrations

		page
1	Archaeological and ethnographic stone axes	12–13
2	Circles of post-holes and round houses	15
3	The interpretation of four-post arrangements as granaries	17
4	Relationship between computer simulation, experimental archaeology and ethnoarchaeology	30
5	Burial ceremony of south-eastern American Indians	36
6	Major John Wesley Powell consulting an Indian, near the Grand Canyon	37
7	Hut collapse in Baringo district, Kenya	48–9
8	Pulling out posts in Mbunda village, western Zambia	50
9	Mud wall decay in Ghana	51
10	Pits in various stages of infill, western Zambia	52–3
11	Disposal of bones by scavengers and natural agencies	55
12	Interior of abandoned hut, Baringo district of Kenya	57
13	A broken pot used to collect rainwater, from western Zambia	57
14	Gypsy encampment in east of England	63
15	Interior of two Mesakin Nuba compounds where dirt and refuse are allowed	66
16	Clark's comparison of wooden arrowheads	69
17	Different types of arrowheads, used by Lozi groups in western Zambia	69
18	Iron age artifacts termed 'weaving combs'	70
19	Hair comb from Kenya	71
20	Making clay pots in Baringo district, Kenya	73–7
21	Ethnographic and archaeological evidence of iron smelting	78
22	Stone axes from contemporary New Guinea and Neolithic Denmark	80
23	House construction in Baringo district, Kenya	81–4
24	Njemps house in Baringo district, Kenya	85
25	Contemporary artifacts from Baringo district, Kenya	87
26	Uniform artifacts of the Tugen, Baringo area, Kenya	89
27	Typical camps and house types among Wikmunkan tribe, Australia	98–9
28	Wikmunkan seasonal use of the environment	102–3
29	Pirá-paraná long house	115
30	Different structures based on posts in a square	118–9
31	Granaries around edge of Lozi village, western Zambia	121
32	Pots produced by women in Lozi village, western Zambia	129–31

33 Symbolic dimensions of the Swazi homestead 133
34 Schematic summary of Swazi symbolic dimensions 135
35 The Pueblo 136
36 The Hogan 137
37 Schematic depiction of structural differences
between Hogan and Pueblo 138
38 Axes from main quarries in New Guinea Highlands 148–9
39 Artifacts and behaviour termed 'ritual' by archaeologists 160–3
40 Neolithic causewayed-camp in east England 165
41 Easter Island as an analogy for prehistoric Europe 168–70
42 Palaeolithic cave painting from Ariège 175
43 Bison from Ariège 177
44 Historical analogy for a rock painting in South Africa 180–1
45 Examples of Nuba decoration 186–8
46 Child play in refuse 200–1
47 Johnny Rotten 205

Jacket illustration
Modern Baka pottery manufacture in Western
Equatoria. The decoration is made with the broken
ends of straws and is carried out prior to completing
the lip of the pot. All the objects around the potter are
used in the potting processes. (Reproduced by kind
permission of David Phillipson, Museum of
Archaeology and Anthropology, Cambridge)

Preface

The past is the present in the sense that our reconstructions of the meaning of data from the past are based on analogies with the world around us. The aim of this book is to achieve a more comprehensive review than is at present available of the use of ethnographic data and anthropological concepts by archaeologists. However, I have not attempted to refer to every relevant piece of work. Even if that would have been possible, though I doubt it given the vast area of study involved, the concern has been more to provide a critical appraisal of the use of analogy in archaeology by the assessment of a representative range of examples. The purpose has been to make a number of simple points in, as far as I can, an accessible manner.

All archaeology is based on analogy and the process of analogical reasoning can be explicit and rigorous. But we cannot, as has often been claimed, strictly *test* the analogies and the hypotheses which result from their use. Archaeologists cannot *prove* or *falsify* their hypotheses on independent data. All they can achieve is a demonstration that one hypothesis or analogy is better or worse than another, both theoretically and in relation to data. In Chapter 1, a range of ways of supporting or criticising analogies which are applied to archaeological data is discussed.

Our 'choice' of what is a pursuasive analogy depends at least partly on our own preconceptions. This statement does not imply that theories are unaffected by data because they clearly are. But it does imply that our knowledge of the past is based on the present and that the task of the rigorous and conscientious archaeologist is to remove the scales of assumptions and to achieve critical self-knowledge, particularly in relation to ideologies of material culture – the material archaeologists dig up from the past. Archaeological anthropology, a generalising science of human culture, is concerned to examine material culture in modern western societies and traditional non-industrialised societies in order that through interpreting these data we may achieve a greater knowledge of ourselves and more accurate reconstructions of the past.

I would hope that the term 'the present past' would also refer to a current view of the role of archaeology. The discipline is defined not so much by its concern with the past and with chronological change since this is also the domain of historians. Rather, it is distinguished by its preoccupation with material culture. Our aim as archaeologists, as members of society and as writers of the past, is to achieve critical self-awareness in relation to material culture. Such a programme of research does not involve confusing our methods with our aims. Rather, the programme is concerned to identify, in dissatisfaction with the evolutionary approaches seeking laws of societal change, new aims for archaeology.

1   The use of analogy

When an archaeologist digs an object out of the ground and says 'this is an axe', how does he know? He may have dated the site from which the object comes to millenia before the first written records, so how does he know it is an axe? The answer is, really, that he doesn't. All he can do is make a reasonable guess based on the fact that the object he has in his hand from the past looks like axes he has seen in his own or in other contemporary societies. In the first half of the nineteenth century, the Danish scientist P.W. Lund sent back polished stone axes from Brazil to be compared with Danish antiquities (*fig. 1a*). This information supported early Scandinavian archaeologists such as Nilsson in their notion that similar artifacts found on their soil were indeed 'primitive' axes. Polished stone objects found widely in Europe (*fig. 1b*) have the shapes of axes with sharp edges; they are called axes on analogy with modern objects.

To support the axe interpretation the archaeologist might examine the edge of the artifact with a microscope to show that it has traces of wear from cutting; he might conduct experiments to show that it is possible to cut down a tree with such an object; and he could conduct pollen studies of the environment of the prehistoric site where the object was found to show that trees had been cut down in the vicinity. Yet all these subsidiary studies are developed to support or weaken the initial analogy.

Much the same could be said for nearly every other interpretation that the archaeologist makes about the past. He is rarely shown directly what prehistoric objects were used for. He has to guess, using analogies. So, when he finds a circle of post holes in the ground and says 'this is a house', he is influenced by evidence of modern round houses lived in by many Africans and American Indians (*fig. 2*).

Many such interpretations may seem obvious to the archaeologist and he may be unaware that he is using an analogy at all. It needs no specialist knowledge to describe an object as an axe, pin, dagger, sword, shield or helmet. And the notion that circles of post-holes indicate houses is so deeply enshrined in archaeological teaching that the archaeologist may not question the ethnographic origin of the idea. Other uses of ethnographic analogies are more conscious and calculated. When an attempt is made to reconstruct from fragments of archaeological evidence the organisation of prehistoric social relations, exchange, burial ritual and ideologies, the archaeologist searches among traditional societies today, in Africa, Asia and America, or in historic Europe, for suitable parallels and analogies.

1 Archaeological and ethnographic stone axes. **a** Polished axes from Brazil sent by Lund to the Royal Society of Northern Antiquaries in Copenhagen (Klindt-Jensen 1976). **b** Neolithic stone axe from Cambridgeshire, England

So, in nearly every interpretation he makes of the past, the archaeologist has to draw on knowledge of his own or other contemporary societies in order to clothe the skeleton remains from the past in the flesh and blood of living, functioning and acting people. The drawing of analogies would thus seem to play a central role in archaeological reasoning. Yet recently, many archaeologists have tried to diminish the use of analogies because they are unreliable, unscientific and limiting. Why is this?

Problems with analogies

An interpretation of the past using an analogy is thought to be unreliable because, if things and societies in the present and past are similar in some aspects, this does not necessarily mean they are similar in others. As an example of this difficulty we might take Grahame Clark's (1954) reconstruction of life at the Mesolithic site of Star Carr

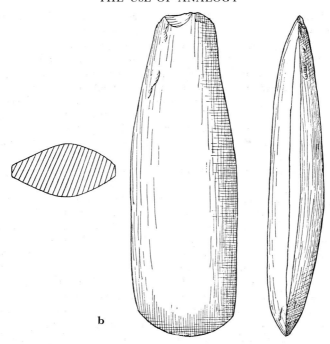

b

in Yorkshire, England. Clark suggests (1954, 10–12) that the evidence of skin-working at Star Carr argues for the presence of women on analogy with the hunting peoples of North America and Greenland. Amongst the Caribou Eskimos women are mainly responsible for flaying the kill and preparing the skins for use, and Clark suggests the same for his Mesolithic hunter-gatherers from Yorkshire. On the basis of the presence of women, Clark further postulates the number of people living at Star Carr, and the form of subdivision of labour. The environment, technology and hunting-gathering economy of the Star Carr inhabitants and the Eskimos are, very vaguely and broadly, comparable. But are these general similarities in some spheres sufficient to allow us to infer correlations in others? There seems no reason to suppose that skin working amongst modern Eskimos and at 7200 BC Star Carr was carried out by the same sex just because they both had broadly the same economy and environment. Clark's interpretation seems highly unreliable.

Clark, in the Star Carr example, seems to be assuming a deterministic 'uniformitarianism'; he supposes that societies and cultures similar in some aspects are uniformly similar. Such a view is unreliable, especially given the great spans of time over which the comparisons are being made and given the great diversity of present-day cultural forms.

Clark happened to use the North American Eskimos, but he could have chosen other societies where men prepare the skins.

If analogies are unreliable, they must also be unscientific. Or so the argument goes. It has been implied by many archaeologists recently that we can never check or prove analogies because we can always find alternative analogies which would fit the data from the past equally well. Because similarities in some aspects do not necessarily, certainly or logically imply similarities in others, we can never prove interpretations such as Grahame Clark's at Star Carr. Such archaeological interpretation is seen as subjective story-writing, pure speculation without any scientific basis.

While it will be explained below why charges of unreliability and anti-science are only really relevant to the misuse of analogy, a charge that analogical reasoning limits and restricts our knowledge of the past also needs to be considered. It seems logically to be the case that, if we interpret the past by analogy to the present, we can never find out about forms of society and culture which do not exist today (Dalton 1981). We are limited in our interpretation to our knowledge of present-day societies. Since these societies, industrialised and non-industrialised, represent a highly specialised set of interlinked economic, social and cultural adaptations, it seems unlikely that they adequately represent the full range of social forms that existed in the past. So we would never be able to understand the full variety of prehistoric societies. Anyway, what would be the point of repeating our knowledge of contemporary societies by tagging labels on to societies in the past?

The various criticisms of the use of analogy in archaeology have led to some extreme statements rejecting analogical reasoning in archaeological interpretation. Freeman (1968, 262) claimed that 'the most serious failings in present models for interpreting archaeological evidence are directly related to the fact that they incorporate numerous analogies with modern groups'. While few archaeologists would now go as far as Freeman, it is widely accepted that the use of analogies should be limited. Ucko (1969) has indicated the possible pitfalls in interpreting past burial practices using analogies, and Binford (1967) has indicated that analogical reasoning is of little value unless associated with a rigorous, scientific testing procedure. Tringham (1978, 185) also suggests that we should try and move away from discovering analogies which can be fitted to archaeological data, while Gould (1978a) has attempted to move 'beyond analogy'. I will try to show that these assessments of the value of analogy in archaeology are clouded by a misconception of the nature and proper use of analogy. It will then be possible to reassess the supposed unreliable, unscientific and limiting features of analogies.

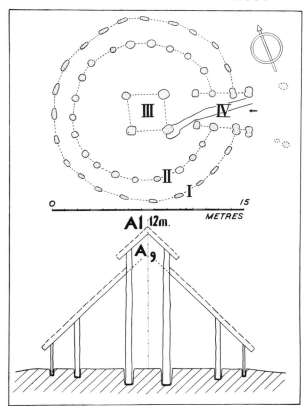

2 Circles of post-holes and round houses. **a** Circles of post holes from the Iron Age site of Little Woodbury, England, reconstructed by Bersu (1940). **b** A modern round house in Kenya

The proper use of analogy

As a form of inference, 'analogy' can be defined as the 'transportation of information from one object to another on the basis of some relation of comparability between them' (Umeov 1970; Wylie 1980). The proper use of such analogies has been discussed by philosophers of science (Hesse 1974; Copi 1954; Umeov 1970) and from their work we can draw some general conclusions (see Wylie 1980).

A distinction can be made between *formal* and *relational* analogies. According to a formal analogy it is suggested that, if two objects or situations have some common properties, they probably also have other similarities. Such analogies are weak in that the observed association of characteristics of the objects or situations may be fortuitous or accidental. So other analogies, of the relational kind, seek to determine some natural or cultural link between the different aspects in the analogy. The various things associated within the analogy are said to be interdependent and not accidentally linked.

There is in fact a continuum of variation from the more formal to the more relational analogy. Unfortunately, most archaeological uses of analogy have tended to cluster at the more formal end of the scale. Clark's interpretation at Star Carr is really a formal analogy in that the Mesolithic site and the Eskimos are said to be similar in certain aspects (environment, technology and economy) and are 'therefore' similar in other aspects (women do the skin preparation). No link is suggested by Clark between the two parts of his analogy; we are not told why females prepare skins in such environments, technologies and economies. Other examples abound. In the late Iron Age in southern England, four or six post-holes are frequently found on hillforts and settlement sites arranged in a square averaging 3m by 3m. Analogies with contemporary and recent societies suggested to Bersu (1940) that these post-holes contained posts holding up granaries with raised floors (*fig. 3*). The formal similarity in the square of posts in past and present agricultural societies was taken as indicating a similar above-ground function.

How can such formal analogies be strengthened? Most obviously, the more similarities that can be identified between the two situations being compared, the more likely are other similarities to be expected. A formal analogy becomes more reasonable as the number of similarities increases. At some point, the volume and detail of comparable points become so great that it is unreasonable to suppose differences in the few aspects for which comparability is unknown. So, in the Star Carr example, if we could list a very large number of ways in which the prehistoric site was a replica of a modern Eskimo site, similarities in the 'unknowns', including who prepared the skins, might be thought to be expected. Similarities between the 'squareness' of post-hole arrangements in past and present sites could be augmented by examining the detailed dimensions of the post-holes, their

16

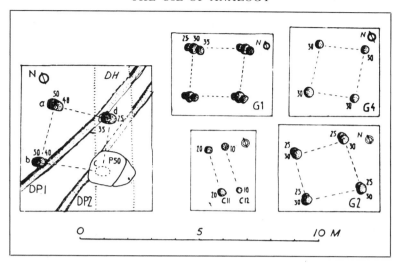

3 The interpretation of four-post arrangements as granaries.
a Arrangements of four post-holes at the Iron Age site at Little
Woodbury, England (Bersu 1940).   **b** A modern raised granary and store
of the Tugen in Kenya. For other modern examples see *fig. 30.*

widths and depths, by considering the soil conditions, the presence of vermin and damp which might cause the above-ground storage of grain to be necessary, and by searching for evidence of grain in the post-holes. As the number of similarities between past post-hole arrangements and present above-ground granaries increases, the interpretation of the Iron Age feature in terms of a granary becomes more acceptable

One way in which the number of formal similarities between a past and present situation can be increased is by comparing a recent archaeological site with modern sites in the same area. Thus, in North America it is sometimes possible to interpret prehistoric palaeo-Indian sites on the basis of analogy with modern or historically recorded surviving Indian groups in the same vicinity. In Africa, also, continuity between archaeological and ethnographic data can frequently be assumed. Such comparisons make up what is called the *direct historical approach* in archaeology. Where continuity between the past and present can be assumed, it is easier to acknowledge many formal similarities between the information being compared.

If the direct historical approach cannot be followed, formal analogies can be further strengthened by a very different strategy. Rather than simply increasing the number of similarities between the source and the subject of the analogy, the range of instances in which various characteristics of the analogy are associated can be emphasised. Thus, if it could be shown that, whatever the environment or economy, skin working was always carried out by women, then Clark's interpretation at Star Carr would have greater validity. Similarly, if it could be shown that patterns of post-holes with particular detailed dimensions were, in modern and historical examples, always associated with above-ground granaries, then the Iron Age interpretation would be more believable. In fact, neither of these two correlations can be made. Yet it remains possible to substantiate the use of an analogy by demonstrating its wide range. In recent archaeology, such wide-ranging statements, valid across different cultures and environments, have sometimes been declared *cross-cultural laws*.

Schiffer, one of the main exponents of the development of cross-cultural laws, or 'correlates', has provided many examples. He describes (1978, 233) the law taken from Yellen's detailed ethnographic studies that the diversity of maintenance activities performed at a settlement varies directly with the length of occupation'. Thus the 'law', which in this case is little more than an expression of association, states that the longer a group of people stays in the same place, the more different types of activities it will perform. Schiffer (ibid., 244) shows that this observation has been made independently in a range of very different situations. In suggesting the credibility of the analogy, appeal is made to the great range of societies and cultures where the suggested relationship between length of occupation and number of activities holds true.

A third aspect of the strengthening of formal analogies can be identified. The conclusions drawn from the analogy should not be too ambitious in relation to the number of similarities between the source and subject. In Clark's example, very little attention is paid to listing the similarities between Star Carr and Eskimo hunters and yet the interpretations made are highly ambitious. However, a cautious and modest interpretation based on a large number of correspondences may be seen to be more acceptable.

However much we might reinforce our analogies by increasing the number and range of similarities between past and present objects and situations, comparisons made at the formal end of the scale will always remain shrouded in unreliability and will always remain easy prey for ridicule and for charges of anti-science. In particular, it will always be possible to provide examples where the suggested association or correlation breaks down. The depressing tone of Ucko's (1969) article on analogies for the interpretation of burial remains derives from the ease with which he can show that various aspects of burial, such as cremation, the body lying looking to the east, or the presence of rich graves, may mean very different things in different societies. The recent archaeological literature abounds with 'cautionary tales' which show how easily archaeologists can make mistakes in using particular analogies since alternative interpretations can be found. Archaeologists have delighted in visiting recently abandoned camps, interpreting the remains as archaeologists, and then asking the inhabitants of the site what actually occurred there. Invariably, the archaeologists' interpretations are shown to be wrong.

All such pessimism and caution derive from an overemphasis on formal as opposed to relational analogies. Of course, different analogies can be found to fit the same set of archaeological data if we simply look for formal similarities in the arrangement of post-holes and if we simply list associations of traits. Analogies, from wherever they are derived, must be deemed to be relevant to the subject of study in the past. I have applied Central Place Theory, derived from modern locational studies of the arrangement of towns in Germany, to Roman Britain. This use of analogy has been rightly criticised (Hodder 1975) because it is irrelevant to pre-industrialised societies such as existed in Roman Britain.

Relational analogies are thus concerned to demonstrate that similarities between past and present situations are relevant to the 'unknowns' that are being interpreted, whereas the differences that can be observed do not really matter; they are not really relevant because there is little link between what is different and what is suggested as being the same. Archaeological uses of analogy often do imply, although they rarely state, some necessary relationship between the various aspects of the analogies. But the relationships that are suggested are nearly always functional. Examination of four-post above-ground granaries indicates that they may function to keep out vermin and to keep the grain dry. The longer a site is occupied, the more functions are necessarily carried out there and so a wider range of debris and waste products is found.

The attempts which have been made in archaeology to use and develop relational analogies have aimed to define the contexts in which different properties of societies and cultures are functionally interdependent. It is thought to be possible to demonstrate that 'in certain conditions C, if A, then necessarily B'. The supposition is made that the material culture which the archaeologist digs up functioned in a particular way. So if, in the past, a group of people had a certain style of life, then material culture was used in particular ways; material culture patterning can be predicted because of its functional relationships with other aspects of life.

For many, the existence of such predictable functional links has meant that analogies can be scientifically tested against archaeological data. It is suggested (e.g. Gould 1978; Tringham 1978) that we can find present-day analogies for our data from the past, but that the unreliability of these analogies can be decreased by 'testing' their consequences in the material remains. This widely held illusion that the charge of anti-science can be avoided by a particular form of 'testing' of analogy against data derives from Binford's much quoted example of the use of analogy in archaeology. It is worth briefly considering Binford's (1967) account in order to demonstrate the false character of the claims for the 'hypothetico-deductive' testing of analogies and in order to show the nature of relational analogies.

Binford discusses the interpretation of 'smudge pits', 'caches', small pits filled with carbonised corncobs in Mississipian sites and dated from AD 470 until recent times. He describes their archaeological distribution, shape and size, and he then lists ethnographic examples of similar pits which are used for smoking hides. He demonstrates that the archaeological and ethnographic pits occur in approximately the same region in North America, that they have the same form, and that there is possible continuity between the archaeological and ethnographic examples (so the direct historical approach is being used). Binford proposes that the archaeological pits were used for hide smoking.

It is of interest to note that, up to this point in Binford's analysis, he has used a largely formal analogy. The relationship between the archaeological pits and hide smoking is based on the formal similarity of the sizes, shapes and contents of the ethnographic pits, on the formal similarity in their distribution, and presumably on other similarities implied by the continuity of societies through time. But Binford then says that he can 'test' his interpretation by drawing deductively a set of secondary expectations.

The deductive predictions are based on functional links between hide smoking and other aspects of life. Binford suggests that other activities involved in hide smoking might be identified archaeologically in the vicinity of the 'smudge pits'. He notes that, ethnographically, hide smoking was carried out in a spring and summer 'base camp' so that the 'smudge pits' should occur, archaeologically, in sites occupied during these seasons. In addition, in the ethnographic cases, hide smoking was women's work, so stylistic variation in 'smudge pits' should vary directly with variation in other female-produced items such as pots.

Binford presents his secondary predictions as testable hypotheses within the framework of a scientific deductive and positivist explanation, breaking away from subjective interpretations which use analogies. But in view of the discussion above it is apparent that Binford, in the second part of his analysis, has simply shown how the formal analogy could be supported by increasing the number of similarities. It could also be claimed that various functional links are being assumed between hide smoking and other activities. By searching for such additional and functionally relevant similarities between the past and present situations which are being compared, Binford strengthens his interpretation and moves towards a relational analogy.

Binford's interpretation of 'smudge pits' is not a good example of the use of the hypothetico-deductive method. If a true deductive argument had been followed there would have to be some logically necessary link (Binford 1972, 70 calls it a logico-deductive argument) between his predictions and the use of 'smudge pits' as hide smoking facilities. But no such logical necessity can be demonstrated in this instance. For example, it does not seem at all logical to me that all artifacts, including 'smudge pits', associated with women should show the same stylistic variation. It would need to be explained to me *why* pots made by women should be linked in an argument to 'smudge pits' made by women. In other words, I would search for a relational analogy which examined more adequately the relevant causal links between the different parts of the analogy. When archaeologists claim a 'logically deduced' argument, they are usually simply imposing their own assumptions on the data. In a relational analogy all the linking arguments must be examined in relation to a clearly defined and explained cultural context, in which the various functional activities take their place. More generally, archaeologists need to examine why one variable (such as pot variation) is relevant to another (such as smudge pits) when using an analogy. There must be greater concern with causal relationships rather than simply with associations. But our assessment of cause and relevance is always likely to be influenced by our own cultural and personal preconceptions. The use by archaeologists of the hypothetico-deductive method recognised this problem of subjectivity and tried to overcome the biasses by rigorous testing of hypotheses against data. But this notion is misconstrued because, as well as considering the data, we consider or assume causal relationships lying behind the data.

If Binford was really using a logico-deductive argument, we would expect the secondary predictions to lead to valid independent tests of the initial proposition that 'smudge pits' were used for hide smoking. In fact, the second tests of data are not independent of the first. The identification of other activities involved in hide smoking near the 'smudge pits' would support the analogy, but they do not 'test' the proposition. The archaeologists' interpretation of tools as used for hide smoking activities may itself be influenced by the proposition that is to be tested. In addition, no matter how many times pits and tools are found in association, the pits may still have been used for some other purpose, with the hide smoking activities carried out around them. We need to know much more of the cultural framework within which these various activities were carried out and why they were associated together. The analogy can be supported by examining the cultural interdependence between the different aspects of data, but it cannot be 'tested' on independent data. The whole process of inference is one of building up an edifice of hypotheses, adding one to another and moving beyond the data in order to explain them. In such a procedure there is always the possibility of error, incorrect assumptions, faulty logic, biassed observation and so on. We cannot prove or disprove, partly because our predictions and expectations (the 'test') may themselves be incorrectly construed, but also because there are no independent data, and a great deal of subjectivity is involved.

I have discussed little the disproof of theories, and yet refutation is seen by many archaeologists as an important aspect of their scientific methods, derived from Karl Popper. But in my view one cannot disprove in an absolute sense in archaeology any more than one can prove. I have shown how we can support a hypothesis by considering (a) relevance, (b) generality, (c) goodness-of-fit (number of similarities between object and analogy). Many archaeologists would agree that one cannot prove a hypothesis because other hypothetical processes could produce the same observed pattern. But they would say we can disprove a hypothesis if the predictions of the hypothesis are not verified in empirical data. However, the prediction is itself based on a hypothesis which may be incorrect. Any disproof is itself a hypothesis. For example, say I have made the hypothesis that, on analogy with modern societies and environments, a past shell-collecting society concentrated on the larger and more nutritious shell type A in order to maximise the resource potential in the environment. Consider the situation in which I find that on the prehistoric site there is mostly the smaller shell type B and few shells of type A. Can I say I have disproved the maximisation hypothesis? Clearly not, since there may be other reasons why few type A shells were found on the site. Type A shells may have been discarded elsewhere even though they were the most abundant species collected. The general problem here is that the predictions are not necessary outcomes of the behavioural hypothesis. In Binford's smudge pit example, if the styles of pots made by women do not correlate with the styles of pits, the hypothesis that the pits were used for hide smoking is not disproved. The hypothesis may, if the reader accepts Binford's assumptions about the causes of stylistic variability, be weakened but not disproved since the hypotheses (that the pits were for hide smoking and that women made the pits and the pots) may be correct but the prediction (that the styles of pits and pots should correlate) may be incorrect. The archaeologist can never test the validity of the predictions themselves because there are no data available from the past concerning the relationship between material culture and human activity. In the shell-collecting example, we could never be certain that shells of a certain type had been deposited in such a way that archaeologists would find them. So, although we can support or weaken hypotheses by arguments of relevance, generality and goodness-of-fit, we cannot test or refute in any absolute or final way.

The 'smudge pits' example does illustrate that it would be possible to be rigorous in the use of analogies if the number and range of similarities are great and if relationships between the different aspects of the analogy could be adequately specified. After the publication of Binford's interpretation of the pits as for hide smoking, Munsen (1969) suggested an alternative hypothesis that they were used in the smudging of ceramics. In his reply to Munsen's suggestion, Binford (1972) rightly indicated that it would be possible to differentiate between the two interpretations by examining other linked aspects of the use of the pits for the two alternative functions. Thus, by examining the causal relationships in a particular cultural context between the pits and other activities which also might be identifiable in the archaeological record, it becomes possible to differentiate between competing analogies.

Relational analogies and the notion of the context of the things being compared can now be seen to be essential aspects of the proper use of analogy in archaeology. We can avoid the charges of unreliability and anti-science by increasing the number and range of points of comparison between past and present, but also by identifying the relevance of the comparisons. We have to understand the variables which are relevant to the interpretation of particular features of cultural evidence; we must have a better idea of the links between the properties we are interested in and their context. As I have already indicated, the links and the contexts in which archaeologists have recently been most interested concern function. What I wish to do now is develop the idea, to be examined more fully later in this book, that the notion of context must include not only function, but also the ideational realm.

Context

It may be helpful to begin with an example. We shall see in Chapters 3 and 5 that many archaeologists have recently attempted to make generalisations about the way people living in settlements organise and deposit their refuse. Schiffer (1976) and Binford (1978), for example, have suggested several cross-cultural relationships between discard behaviour and size of site, length of occupation, amount of effort put into making a tool, and so on. For example, it has been suggested that, with longer and more intense occupation on a site, there is more secondary removal and clearance of refuse away from activity areas. This is a functional relationship concerned with the need to keep areas habitable and clean, and with the likelihood of secondary kicking and removal as population densities increase. Now, while the theoretical statements concerning such cross-cultural gene-ralisations do note the importance of describing the conditions under which the relationship holds, in practice the conditions, the context, are not well defined. The 'law' is supposed to be universal, or the context is simply pushed off to the side under the heading 'other things being equal' (Binford 1976). There is rarely any analysis of what the 'other things' might be except in so far as analysis is made of technological, economic and environmental constraints. We have already seen how dangerous it is to assume that aspects of the material environment are sufficient to define a context for the relationship between variables.

In the studies of refuse, no emphasis has been placed on how peoples' attitudes to dirt and rubbish might affect the functional relationships between discard patterns and site size and occupation intensity. Yet there are many anthropological studies, which will be discussed in Chapter 5, that demonstrate how our conceptions of what is dirt and our concern with keeping things clean are very much dependent on local frameworks of meaning. Attitudes to refuse vary from society to society, and from group to group within societies; just consider the dirt and rubbish piling up around a gypsy camp site in England and the offence that is given to many of the hygienic, sparkling pillars of non-gypsy society; or the contrived dirtiness and dishevelled aspect of hippies breaking away from the attitudes, standards and interests of their middle-class parents who are concerned with tidiness, manners and impeccably clean self-presentation. There can be no simple functional links between refuse and types of site, lengths of occupation or forms of society, because attitudes and conceptions intervene.

The notion of context, then, must concern both functional and ideological aspects of life. In developing the use of analogy in archaeology the emphasis must be on examining *all* the different aspects of context which might impinge upon particular characteristics of material culture. But this more developed notion of context implies that every context is unique. The framework of meaning within which we carry out day-to-day actions is a unique combination of ideas, strategies and attitudes. And the symbolism given to material culture within such a meaningful context is likely to be peculiar to that context.

In the discussion of relational analogies it was suggested that it is possible to answer the criticisms that analogies are unreliable and unscientific. But a third problem with analogies was also identified in the first part of this chapter: analogies from the present limit our understanding of the past. The emphasis on the unique nature of each context aggravates the problem. If each context in which material culture is used represents a peculiar arrangement of meanings and ideas and personal strategies, how can we ever use a present context to interpret evidence from the past?

This is not such a difficult question to answer as it might seem at first sight. The problem of the contextual nature of material culture patterning can be examined in two ways. First, each unique cultural context is assembled from general principles of meaning and symbolism, which are often used in comparable ways. Thus, in many societies dirt is used as a symbol of rejection of the control and authority of dominant groups. So, Gypsies use dirt to contradict the non-Gypsy society in which they live in much the same way as hippies use dirt and disorder to defy the generation and society of their parents. One aim of the development of the use of analogies is to increase our understanding of how aspects of material culture patterning such as dirt and disorder can be used in personal and group strategies. The general principles of material symbolism must be examined. But in developing generalisations about symbolism it is essential to pay particular attention to the links with other variables, and to the conditions under which a particular type of symbolism might be used. Clearly not all minority groups use dirt as a part of their rejection of authority. We need to examine carefully what other factors are relevant and how they are linked. If we know a lot about how aspects of material culture (such as dirt or burial) are used and given meaning, if we know a lot about the links between material culture and its functional and meaningful context, then we can interpret new situations, unique cultural arrangements beyond present-day experience. We can interpret how the new cultural 'whole' has been assembled from general principles which are well understood.

Second, in all uses of analogy it is necessary to define what aspects of the things being compared are similar, dissimilar or of uncertain likeness. The aim is to throw light on what is not known (the uncertain likeness) by demonstrating the strength and relevance of the positive analogy, while showing that the negative likenesses are of limited consequence. So, all analogical reasoning accepts that there will be some differences between the things being compared. We can set the past beside the present even if some aspects of the contexts do differ. Indeed, Gould (1978) has suggested a 'contrastive' approach which moves 'beyond analogy'. He indicates that we can use modern situations as base lines *against* which to compare evidence from the past. In fact Gould's contrasts do not lead to a different approach; they are an integral part of the use of analogy.

It is important, then, to be able to decide whether the differences between a past and present situation are enough to invalidate the use of a particular positive analogy. In making such a decision it is essential to understand the factors which link variables of material culture to their context, as suggested in the first point above. For example, I have compared the use of material culture to mark ethnic group distinctions in modern Kenya and Iron Age Britain (Blackmore, Braithwaite and Hodder 1979) even though the pattern of annual rainfall differs considerably in the two places. I feel it is valid to make such a comparison because my studies of ethnic group expression identified no direct link to rainfall patterns. However, it would be invalid to draw analogies from the Kenyan area in order to interpret Iron Age farming practices in Britain, since rainfall regime and agricultural systems are closely linked. Depending on the analogy being made, different aspects of context are more, or less, relevant to an assessment of the validity of the analogy and interpretation.

It is possible to interpret the manipulation of material items in a unique context in the past by (a) referring to general principles of symbolism and to generalisations about the links between those principles and the context in which they are used, and by (b) carefully using selected analogies for different aspects of the evidence, identifying similarities and differences, and gradually building up from bits and pieces to an understanding of how the whole picture is composed.

In my answer to the problem of how to use analogies if each situation, past and present, is unique, it has become evident that two types of analogy are necessary; (a) it is valid to suggest general theories about the relationship between material culture and social and economic aspects of life as long as the links to context are understood; (b) with that general theoretical knowledge, it is possible to assess which aspects of each particular analogy are relevant. The use of relational analogies depends on a good theoretical framework within which one can identify what is relevant in a particular case.

Examples of the peculiar and particular nature of modern material culture patterning are important as archaeologists carefully select analogies to build up, from bits and pieces, to an assessment of the whole in each context. An interest in the particular as opposed to the general is also essential since the traditional societies that remain for us to study today are often highly specialised to particular environments and ways of life. Indeed it is probable that types of society which were common in the past are represented by only one or a few examples today. Particular modes of manipulation of material culture may be extremely rare today. There will always be a place for the unique and the odd, even if only to provide a contrast.

Conclusion

On the whole the criticisms that have been made of the use of analogy in archaeology should be restricted to its misuse. Interpretation with the aid of analogies is unreliable and non-rigorous when the similarities between the things being compared are few in number and when the relevance of the comparison cannot be adequately demonstrated. The proper use of analogy in archaeology must pay special attention to context; that is, to the functional and ideological framework within which material items are used in everyday life. Most recent discussions of analogy in archaeology have considered cross-cultural laws which note the co-occurrence of different aspects of material culture and society. Such studies pay too little attention to when and why covariation occurs. It is necessary to examine not only the *existence* and *strength* of covariation, but also its *nature* and cause. It is only when archaeologists understand more fully the conditions and context in which certain things hold true that the use of analogies can be seen to be reliable and rigorous.

Several archaeologists have recently attempted to diminish the role of analogies by suggesting that analogies should simply be used for the forming of propositions about the past. The real guts of a scientific archaeology is then said to be in the deduction of the consequences of the proposition and in the testing of those implications in independent archaeological evidence. In fact, the nearest the archaeologist can get to a rigorous method is the careful use of a relational analogy. The analogy is situated within its relevant context.

For the moment it is difficult to see how archaeologists might break away from their dependence on analogies with the present; or why they should want to do so. I have tried to show in this chapter the importance of analogy in archaeology, and I have attempted to demonstrate that the use of present analogies does not entirely limit our interpretations of the past. While it is true that all our interpretations of human behaviour and thought are affected by the society in which we live, it is also true that we can comprehend different societies, cultures and economies in other parts of the world, and that we can use this additional information in describing and explaining the past. As archaeologists our dependence on other societies, other behaviour and ways of thought always has been, and remains, immense. The links with ethnography and anthropology are close, as Chapter 2 shows.

2 Ethnoarchaeology

An important source of analogies, although as we shall see not the only source, is difficult to label since almost every word which is commonly used brings with it offence. But I hope that, if I talk of traditional, less-industrialised contemporary societies, my meaning will be understood. In the last 25 years archaeologists have begun to carry out field studies amongst traditional societies in order to answer questions of archaeological interpretation and in order to develop and examine analogies. It is this type of work which is called ethnoarchaeology.

First, some definitions. Although the word 'ethnoarchaeology' was used in 1900 by Fewkes, it has only recently become a popular term. Yet there is a divergence of opinion as to its meaning. Gould (1978b) and Stiles (1977) define it as the comparison of ethnographic and archaeological data. This definition seems hopelessly broad, especially if one accepts that all archaeological interpretation involves making analogies with present-day societies. Nearly all archaeological interpretation could then be described as ethnoarchaeology. Stanislawski (1974), on the other hand, defines ethnoarchaeology as being a field study and it is easier to concur with such a viewpoint. Ethnoarchaeology is the collection of original ethnographic data in order to aid archaeological interpretation. This second definition coincides more closely with current usage than does the first. The armchair archaeologist leafing through ethnographic tomes is less likely to retort 'I am doing some ethnoarchaeology', than is an archaeologist conducting his own ethnographic field research.

There is often confusion about the relationship between ethnography, ethnology and anthropology and it is perhaps necessary to clarify these terms. Ethnography is the analytical study of contemporary ethnic groups; an examination of their material, social and linguistic characteristics. Ethnology, on the other hand, is the development of theories about the relationships between the characteristics of ethnic groups and about why they change. Ethnology has tended to be concerned with simpler, non-literate peoples, so leaving the more complex industrialised societies to sociology, geography, etc. Anthropology is a wider set of sciences, which in North America includes archaeology, but which in Britain does not, concerned with the study of man, usually simpler, less industrialised man. It is a generalising discipline which includes both ethnography and ethnology. For further definitions and distinctions between European and American terminologies the reader is referred to Rouse (1972)

Relations with experimental approaches in archaeology

Contemporary traditional societies are not the only source of analogies for the archaeologist. Analogies can also be derived from studies of material culture in our own, highly industrialised societies as will be shown in Chapter 9, and such work is also called ethnoarchaeology. But in our own societies archaeologists can also set up artificial experiments in order to draw further analogies with the past. Both experimental archaeology (Coles 1973; 1979) and computer simulation (Hodder 1978b) are concerned to test the feasibility of particular archaeological interpretations. They differ from ethnoarchaeology in several ways. In the first place, an experiment such as firing pots in a kiln in order to see what methods and kilns could have been used in the past can be truly experimental in that different trials can be made, the conditions and temperature in the kiln can be accurately monitored and recorded, and variables can be controlled. The simulation of a hypothesised process of prehistoric exchange on the computer can be even more carefully controlled, with huge numbers of different trials being 'run' and the effects of different variables carefully examined and experimented with. In an ethnoarchaeological study, on the other hand, there is little experimental control. One is above all an observer and an asker of questions; one cannot try this and that and see what happens.

What ethnoarchaeology loses in experimental control it gains in 'realism'. The ethnoarchaeologist does not study an artificial environment that he has created (although we shall see in the discussion of field methods that some qualification is needed here). He can fit the firing of pottery in a kiln into its total social, cultural and economic context, and he can observe all the possibly relevant variables. The experimental archaeologist, on the other hand, has created an artificial situation, even though trying to duplicate as closely as possible the prehistoric information. The experimental archaeologist tries to learn and implement craft techniques to which he is unaccustomed and which his society has long forgotten. Apart from these practical difficulties, the experiment is carried out in a vacuum so that links with the social, cultural and ideological aspects of life are difficult to identify. While he may be able to examine the effects of technological and natural variables in his experiments, the experimental archaeologist is at a loss to assess the broader context which, in Chapter 1, was suggested as being of such importance. Computer simulation is totally artificial. Any analogies that derive from such work depend entirely on the assumptions that the archaeologist has fed into the computer. The working of the computed model depends on the second-hand ethnographic and experimental information.

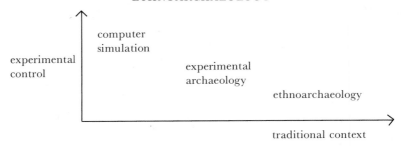

4 Some aspects of the relationship between computer simulation, experimental archaeology and ethnoarchaeology

Experimental archaeology involves the carrying out of experiments in order to test beliefs about archaeological data. We have seen that it is less realistic, but more controlled than ethnoarchaeology. But ethnoarchaeology has one possible additional advantage over its rival. It can be claimed to be less ethnocentric. Any experiment carried out within our own society is bound by the assumptions and knowledge of that society. The extent to which we can broaden our ideas about the past by conducting experiments in modern Western society is limited. Ethnoarchaeology, on the other hand, is able more radically to confront the Western archaeologist with alternative behaviour. The ethnocentric bias can more readily be broken. However, there is a danger that we substitute one type of ethnocentricism with another, and I have already shown in Chapter 1 that analogies must not be taken over wholesale from one modern traditional society to a prehistoric society. There is a need for careful selection and control of analogies.

Attempts have been made by some archaeologists to combine the advantages of ethnoarchaeology and experimental archaeology by carrying out limited but controlled experiments in traditional contexts. One example is the experiment conducted by White and Thomas (1972) in which native New Guineans were asked to carry out experiments in stone tool manufacture. Duna-speaking people from the Central Highlands of Papua-New Guinea were asked by the ethnoarchaeologists to make traditional stone tools and the variation in form of the tools made by men in different parishes could then be analysed. Such an experiment carried out by ethnoarchaeologists has the advantage that the analysis, and the discovery of the variables which are thought to have most affect on tool variation, can be controlled and sufficiently large samples can be obtained. But there are also disadvantages. In particular, the ethnoarchaeologist is no longer an observer of traditional behaviour. He isolates activities from their context and he intrudes himself starkly onto the scene. He brings an artificiality and the context, normally such an important constituent of ethnoarchaeological work, is eroded. We end up knowing very little about the conditions under which the relationships identified by White and Thomas might hold true, so that it is difficult to use their results in other contexts.

Experimental archaeology is of greatest value in understanding how things could have been made and used, and in identifying the natural properties of materials such as flint when flaked by man or stone when used to cut down trees. But in answering 'why' questions which seek to relate technologies and economies to broader social and cultural contexts, the approach is limited.

History of the use of ethnographic analogies in archaeology

Ethnoarchaeology has been given a more restricted definition than the general use of ethnographic analogies. But it is necessary to chart, even if sketchily, the history of the use made by archaeologists of ethnography and anthropology in order to assess the present importance and purpose of ethnoarchaeology. The past use of ethnographic analogies can be followed in both Europe and America.

In Europe, the Renaissance revival of interest in the Classical world and its literature led to an awareness of ancient societies existing prior to literary civilisations. Indeed the earliest ethnographies which were to prove of service to archaeologists may well have been the accounts of Caesar and Tacitus, who in *De Bello Gallico* and the *Germania* described the native inhabitants of France, England and the lower Rhine area. But at the same time as the increasing interest in early ethnographies led to a picture of a barbarous past, pictures of a very different kind from the contemporary world were also arousing attention.

Explorations beyond the known world introduced the sixteenth-century European to altogether novel cultures. John White, the Elizabethan explorer in Virginia, described and illustrated the villages, ceremonies, arrowhead manufacture and the hunting and farming activities of the Indians of Pomeiock. Some of his watercolours were printed in de Bry's (1590) edition of Harriot's *Brief and true report of the new found land of Virginia*. But de Bry also attached to the volume the first representation of past Britons as other than Tudors, Romans or mythical heroes. The pictures were accompanied by the following caption. 'The painter of whow I have had the first of the Inhabitants of Virginia, give me allso thees 5 Figures fallowinge, fownde as hy did assured my in a colld English cronicle, the which I wold well sett to the ende of thees first Figures, for to showe how that the Inhabitants of the great Bretannie have been in times past as sauuage as those of Virginia' (from Orme 1973, 488). So here an ethnographic parallel was used in order to add information to what was known about the past. In 1611 John Speed referred to the Virginians in supporting his theory that the

Ancient Britons went naked. Again ethnography was used to shock the civilised members of seventeenth-century society about their primitive past.

Another instance in which ethnography was used to change romantic and mythical interpretations of the past was in the debate about early stone implements. In the mid-seventeenth century Aldrovandus described stone tools as 'due to an admixture of a certain exhalation of thunder and lightening with metallic matter, chiefly in dark clouds, which is coagulated by the circumfused moisture and conglutinated into a mass (like flour with water) and subsequently indurated by heat, like a brick', and at about the same time Tollius suggested that chipped flints were 'generated in the sky by a fulgurous exhalation conglobed in a cloud by the circumposed humour' (Daniel 1950, 26). Other interpretations of early stone tools were that they were thunderbolts or elf arrows. Such theories were put to an end in Oxford by Dr Robert Plot and his father-in-law Dugdale and his assistant Lhwyd in 1686, 1656 and 1713 respectively, incorporating the aid of ethnographic parallels. By 1800, John Frere could describe Palaeolithic hand axes as 'weapons of war'.

In the eighteenth century many parallels were built between ethnographies and the European past, as is clear from the titles of J.T. Lafitau's 1724 Paris publication *Moeurs des Sauvages Amériquains, Comparées aux Moeurs des Premiers Temps*, and J.Kraft's 1760 Copenhagen publication *Brief account of the principal institutions, customs and ideas of the Savage Peoples illustrating the human origin and evolution generally* (Klindt – Jensen 1976). Lafitau had been a French missionary in Canada and he drew parallels between Indians and the Bible and classical literature. Kraft's more general work was translated into German and Dutch, but remained largely unnoticed by archaeologists. He explicitly drew parallels between stone tools found in the soil in Europe, and primitive stages of man, on analogy with existing primitive societies.

All these instances of the use of ethnographic parallels in the sixteenth to eighteenth centuries were concerned with making simple formal analogies for the immediate purposes of clarification and for the derivation of alternative interpretations. A lack of concern with the dangers of ethnographic parallels continued in the nineteenth century with the exception of such archaeologists as Nilsson in Denmark and Pitt Rivers in England.

Nilsson in *Primitive Inhabitants of Scandinavia* (1843) used a 'comparative method' by which prehistoric artifacts were compared with formally and functionally identical objects used by modern peoples. He claimed that by using the comparative method archaeology ought to be able 'to collect the remains of human races long since passed away, and of the works which they have left behind, to draw a parallel between them and similar ones which still exist on earth, and thus cut out a way to the knowledge of the circumstances which have been, by comparing them with those which still exist'. But he also noted that care was needed in the use of ethnographic analogies. 'Similarities such as the presence of similar stone arrows in Scania and Tierra del Fuego do not always prove one and the same origin' (quoted by Daniel 1950, 49). The same caution is evident in Pitt Rivers' important and independent development of the use of ethnographic comparisons. General Pitt Rivers' involvement in the army led to an interest in the development and improvement of the rifle. His careful classification of categories and forms of rifle was followed by careful collections of a wide range of weapons, boats, musical instruments, religious symbols and so on. In arranging his material, Pitt Rivers was more concerned with types than their country of origin. Archaeological and ethnographic material could be compared, side by side. Yet, like Nilsson, he was wary of discussing only formal parallels. In making an analogy it was necessary to demonstrate functional as well as formal identity. This concern with function extends the context of the formal similarity and moves towards a relational analogy.

Orme (1973, 487) suggests that the work of Wilson (1851), Evans (1860), Christy and Lartet (1875) in recognising and identifying artifacts used comparisons with the material culture of contemporary traditional groups, while the more general interpretations of Lubbock (1865) and Tylor (1865) also relied heavily on ethnography. In 1870, Sir John Lubbock wrote in *The Origin of Civilisation and the Primitive Condition of Man* that 'the weapons and implements now used by the lower races of men throw much light on the signification and use of those discovered in ancient tumuli, or in the drift gravels: . . . a knowledge of modern savages and their modes of life enables us more accurately to picture, and more vividly to conceive, the manners and customs of our ancestors in bygone ages'. The influence of ethnography on archaeology in the second half of the nineteenth century increased as part of two additional developments. The first was the reference, in interpretations of the past, to the folklore survivals of 'primitive' antecedants (Daniel 1950, 185). Second, the 'culture' concept began to replace the previous emphasis on dividing archaeological material into epochs. The European school of 'anthropogeographers' started by Ratzel and his pupil Frobenius described cultural areas in West Africa and in Melanesia. The work of German ethnologists came to have a great impact on the development of the culture concept in archaeology as it was later to be adopted by Childe. Indeed, Daniel (1950, 246) has described the organisation of prehistory into cultures as the anthropological attitude to prehistory.

Though the debt to ethnography and anthropology in the second half of the nineteenth century was large, the cautions of Nilsson and Pitt Rivers went generally unheeded. Formal parallels were applied with little attention to context and the dangers were little discussed.

The trend of increasing links with anthropology continued in the first half of the twentieth century with, for example, the journal *Annals of Archaeology and Anthropology* first issued in 1908 under the auspices of the University of Liverpool Institute of Archaeology, but the increase in quantity was not always associated with an increase in quality.

The first issue of *Antiquity* (1927) included an article by Raymond Firth on Maori hillforts which was intended to aid British prehistorians in the interpretation of their own Iron Age earthworks. While the place of hillforts in Maori society is well discussed, comparisons with English hillforts are scanty and formal, based on such features as the size and shape of ramparts. Thomson, in his 1939 study of the Wik Munkan Aborigines of the Cape York Peninsula of Australia, recognised that the archaeologist would be confused and possibly misled by the surviving material culture. The Aborigines lead such different lives in the different seasons of the year that the archaeologist might be fooled into thinking the different assemblages were produced by separate peoples. In addition, Thomson noted that very little would survive to be found by archaeologists anyway. This is the first example of a pessimistic, negative type of analogy which became common later as 'cautionary tales'. Most such cautions have the characteristic that they are little concerned with the context which leads to the particular material remains: in the Australian example the context is highly specialised and generalisation would be difficult (see discussion in Chapter 5).

Parallels with societies closer at hand seemed to avoid some of these problems. In his report of the excavations at Skara Brae, a Neolithic settlement on the Orkney Islands, Childe (1931) used analogies with recent inhabitants of the northern isles in his interpretation of the functions of beds and other features inside the huts. Clark (1952) also used a wealth of information from recent and modern Scandinavian societies in order to provide formal analogies for prehistoric tools. But in the same book many formal comparisons were made over great distances to the Eskimos and tribes of Canada and North America, as was also seen (Chapter 1) in his account of the Star Carr site. More recently, a visit by Grahame Clark to Australasia led to an article (1965) comparing, with some concern for context and relevance, the axe trade there with the distribution of Neolithic axes in Britain. It was suggested, on the basis of the similarities of the axes, their very wide distributions, and the simple level of societies, that the Neolithic axes were traded by ceremonial gift exchange, much the same as in New Guinea and Australia.

An increasing concern with relevance and context has continued in the careful and informed analogies drawn in the more recent work of, for example, David (1971; 1972) and Rowlands (1971; 1976). But the emphasis on formal comparisons still remains. Clarke (1968) used evidence from Californian Indians to suggest that links could be set up between the forms of regional artifact distributions and linguistic groupings, while other formal comparisons of cultural distributions have been made by Hodder (1978a). Such formal studies are now decreasing in frequency as warnings are made (e.g. Ucko 1969) and assessments published (Orme 1973; 1974; 1981). The strength of the link between archaeology, anthropology and ethnography has now reached a new peak in England and continental Europe with ethnographic archaeology posts in three departments of archaeology in English universities, several archaeology and anthropology joint degrees, numerous courses, and a host of articles, many of which will be referenced in the pages which follow. Nevertheless the fuss over the conscious rapprochment between archaeology and anthropology in Britain is slight when compared with the call to arms that has emanated from North American publications over the last 25 years. Indeed much of the recently increased popularity of ethnography for archaeologists in England and Europe must be seen as a result of influence from the other side of the Atlantic.

In America, the presence of living Indian societies in areas where excavations were being undertaken helped to make archaeologists aware of the possibilities of using the present to interpret the past. In a much more direct way than in Europe, American archaeologists have always been able to make use of ethnohistory and modern ethnographic accounts. An example of the early use of ethnography in America is provided by the resolution of the 'moundbuilders' controversy. By the late eighteenth century, a large number of mounds or ruins had been discovered in Ohio and in other frontier areas. Any idea that these monuments could have been built by the Indian 'savages' was rejected, and a 'lost race' was imagined which had been replaced by the Indians. The nature and origin of the lost race of moundbuilders were the subject of much fanciful speculation until finally, in the late nineteenth century, the myth was laid to rest by the work of Cyrus Thomas. Major John Wesley Powell (the first explorer to descend the Grand Canyon rapids of the Colorado River in a boat; see *fig. 6*) was Director of the Bureau of Ethnology and he picked Thomas to carry out research into the mounds in the 1880s and 1890s. Through Thomas' excavations and comparisons of the excavated material with contemporary Indian material culture in the same areas, Powell and Thomas were able to suggest that the moundbuilders were the same people as the modern 'savages'.

This direct historical approach, used by Thomas to throw light on archaeological information, was part of a more general emphasis on continuity. Around the turn of the century a number of studies (Fewkes 1893; Hodge 1897; Kroeber 1916) tried to use archaeological evidence to test Indian oral traditions or to find sites associated with particular clan myths. Analogies based on continuity in local areas were an important part of the ethnic identification of cultural

35

5 An important early European view of the south-eastern American Indians is provided in the illustrations of Jacques Le Moyne, who accompanied the French settlers to north-eastern Florida in the 1560s. This drawing shows a burial ceremony with the grave or small burial mound outlined in arrows and topped by a conch-shell drinking vessel. The mourners surround the mound, and in the background is a palisaded village. Pictures such as this were either unknown to or ignored by early writers on the Moundbuilder controversy (Willey and Sabloff 1974)

complexes throughout the early part of the twentieth century in North America. In particular, W.D. Strong (1935) and J.H. Steward (1942) developed the direct historical approach as a distinct procedure within archaeological interpretation.

Although the same emphasis on using continuity to support analogies is still seen in more recent American work (for example in the 'smudge pit' study discussed in Chapter 1), there has been an increasing concern over the last 30 years with generalisation, as part of the conscious expansion of what came to be termed 'anthropological archaeology'. In 1948 (p. 6) Taylor described the archaeologist as a 'Jekyll and Hyde, claiming to "do" history but "be" an anthropologist'. The use of direct, continuous analogies was more clearly associated with a historical emphasis, and the new concern with making general statements about man, society, ecological relationships and systems which has lasted to the present day, eschewed emphases on historical frameworks and sought to embrace more

6 Major John Wesley Powell consulting an Indian on the Kaibab Plateau, near the Grand Canyon of the Colorado River in northern Arizona (Willey and Sabloff 1974)

closely the generalising science of man. Associated with this development has been a decreasing concern with causal relationships within particular contexts when using ethnographic analogies. The aim has been to build and use general comparative analogies. Interpretations of the past are obtained through broadly comparative and quasi-universal generalisations about human cultural behaviour, rather than being confined to a specific historical context (Willey and Sabloff 1974, 207). But this view has not gone without its critics in America. According to Anderson (1969), 'logical analysis of form depends as much on perception of the object, which is conditioned by cultural background, as by any universal principles'. Those recent studies which do examine context and which use relational analogies have been more concerned with the functional and ecological context than with the realm of ideas.

It was in this more recent period, as 'anthropological archaeology' became taken up as the battle cry of the 'new archaeologists' (Meggers 1968; Longacre 1970) that ethnoarchaeology became defined as a distinct area of research. We have already seen that the word was used as early as 1900 by Fewkes, but it was in the '50s and '60s that the main development occurred. Various definitions and outlines of ethnoarchaeology and the equivalent terms 'action' or 'living' archaeology were suggested by Kleindienst and Watson (1956) and Ascher (1962) and specific studies appeared (Thompson 1958, Oswalt and Van Stone 1967). The *Man the Hunter* symposium (Lee and De Vore 1968) was important in bringing a large amount of information and general statements about hunter-gatherers to the notice of archaeologists, while in the same year the collection of essays edited by the Binfords included important ethnoarchaeological studies (e.g by Longacre and Ayres). Since then the number of studies, definitions and books has greatly increased (Donnan and Clewlow 1974; Stiles 1977; Yellen 1977; Ingersoll, Yellen and MacDonald 1977; Gould 1978b; 1980; Binford 1978; Kramer 1979). But it is important to realise that this rash of ethnoarchaeological work is not characterised by a uniformity of approach. Variation in views on definitions was described at the beginning of this chapter. There is also still considerable variation in the emphasis placed on context and relevance. For example, Wilmsen's (1979; 1980) careful study of the particular Bushman cultural and historical context and the patterning of material remains contrasts with Schiffer's (1978) call for the generation of cross-cultural 'laws'. While some studies are interested in only the ecological and functionally adaptive context within which material residues are produced (e.g. Binford 1978), others are concerned to examine the cognitive basis of behaviour (e.g. Hardin 1979).

There is also variation in views about the part played by ethnographic analogies in archaeological interpretation. Oddly, much of the recent ethnoarchaeological fervour has occurred at a time when the dominant consensus among American archaeologists has been that the role of analogy should be limited. Several archaeologists have emphasised that explanation should proceed by the testing of deductive hypotheses. The analogy derived from ethnoarchaeology is seen as playing only a small initial role in suggesting the hypothesis. In Chapter 1 we saw why this view is misleading. In fact, archaeologists do and can proceed rigorously by the careful use of relational analogies and it is not necessary to set up this procedure as 'hypothetico-deductive'.

The increase in ethnoarchaeology is a product of the anthropological emphasis in American archaeology, and of the growing interest in the formulation of cross-cultural generalisations about human behaviour. Ethnoarchaeology is also seen to provide particular hypotheses to be tested deductively against archaeological data. Whether carried out by Americans or Europeans, and however it is used, ethnoarchaeology now has a number of important functions. First, it became clear, as archaeologists turned more and more to social anthropologists for advice and inspiration, that existing ethnographic studies were inadequate. Ethnographers had rarely collected the type of data on material residues that is most relevant for archaeologists. They had concentrated on aspects of social and linguistic variability, and on general accounts of cultural material. Few ethnographic studies provided detailed information on the locations of settlements, size and shape variation of artifacts, or disposal processes. In particular, questions concerning the depositional and post-depositional processes which result in distributions of artifacts and features on archaeological sites could not be answered using existing ethnographic studies. The increased interest in such questions in the last ten years (e.g. Schiffer 1976) has been one further factor encouraging the recent rise to importance of ethnoarchaeology. It became necessary for the archaeologist to collect his own ethnographic information, and in fact most ethnoarchaeology is today carried out by people trained as archaeologists, not by ethnographers or social anthropologists.

A second important function that ethnoarchaeology provides is to salvage relevant information from forms of society which are fast disappearing. The colonial destruction of numerous peoples from Tasmania to North America was as horrifyingly efficient as it was speedy. The technique of flint-knapping used by the last Californian Indian, Ishi, was recorded by Nelson (1916), but such information was usually lost or badly recorded. What we have left now are the remnants of our slaughter. The traditional societies which did survive are fast becoming incorporated into world-wide economies. Wobst (1978) notes that most ethnoarchaeologists now mainly consider the local adaptive aspects of hunter-gatherer groups. Regional and inter-regional links are sifted out because they are 'modern', 'post-contact' and 'distorting'. If we do think it is important to examine traditional societies, ethnoarchaeology must not lose time in placing them in their modern world context.

The desire to study traditional, less industrialised societies is understandable for those archaeologists who wish to examine flint-knapping and other techniques which are no longer to be found in Western society. Yet there is a possibility that, after having overrun and pillaged Australian, African and American peoples militarily, economically and socially, we follow this up by an 'intellectual colonialism'. I have said that ethnoarchaeology is important in that it helps to break away from a Western ethnocentricism. But there is a terrible risk that in examining 'primitive' societies we are really just repeating that ethnocentricism in a new and more sinister form. We assume that our own 'developed' society is less relevant in finding analogies for Neolithic Europe in 6000 BC than are 'undeveloped' Africans or Australians. But 'primitive' Africans might not see it in the same light. They are not devolved, reverted or stagnant societies. There is a potential danger in 'dressing up' European Neolithic society like Kenyan tribesmen, in the same way that in the eighteenth century Ancient Britons were dressed like Virginians. This form of intellectual ethnocentricism is part of the evolutionary perspective which has gripped archaeology throughout this century. Breaking away from such biases leads to the third function of ethnoarchaeology today.

Ethnoarchaeological studies in Western industrialised societies are as equally valid as studies in the less industrialised world if the importance of a control over context is accepted. I have tried to show that the drawing of analogies for the prehistoric past must move away from formal cross-cultural studies, to a more careful consideration of the links between material patterning and its functional and ideational context. We need to understand *why* material is patterned in a particular way in each cultural milieu. This emphasis on the links themselves means that Western society is as good a source for analogies as are less industrialised peoples. If we can understand all the functional and ideological factors which cause variation in how we bury our dead in modern England, that is if we understand the links between burial and its context, then we can assess whether the modern information is relevant to a particular prehistoric situation. While technological studies of particular, fast dying-out, activities such as flint-knapping remain important, the more generally applicable 'contextual' studies do not depend on finding 'primitive' societies. Rather there is a need to consider all forms of society in their own terms.

The third function of ethnoarchaeology, and in my view the most important, is to develop ethnographic analogies which concern the principles which relate material patterning to adaptive and cultural contexts. But in saying this it also becomes apparent that a change is needed in ethnoarchaeological methodology. For the moment nearly all the ethnoarchaeological studies of which I know have been carried out by people trained as archaeologists and I have already suggested why this should be so. Ethnoarchaeology simply involves the archaeologist going off to do a bit of ethnoarchaeology, often as a sideline or second interest. The archaeologist treats the ethnographic data as if they were archaeological data and he uses archaeological methods (sampling, recording, etc.). As far as I am aware, there is no detailed account in the ethnoarchaeological literature of field methods, interview techniques, and the problems of sampling live populations. This remarkable lack results from what Gould (1978b) has called the 'materialist' emphasis of ethnoarchaeology. There is an assumption that the ethnoarchaeologist is concerned with the actual products of behaviour, with plotting material remains and with objective descriptions. But as soon as it is accepted that the context of material activities is the major concern, then anthropological field methods take on a real importance. It we are to find out the social and cultural framework which informs the making of a pot or the knapping of a flint blade, then we must understand the limitations, difficulties and problems of interviewing, observing and understanding members of other societies and their material products. We shall see that not only people but even pots can lie.

Ethnoarchaeological field methods

Various published sources of world ethnographic data are listed by Stiles (1977), but since I have defined ethnoarchaeology more narrowly than the general use of ethnographic analogy, as a field study, I will examine here only field methods. For more general accounts of anthropological methodology see, for example, Naroll and Cohen (1973) and Brim and Spain (1974).

Perhaps the major problem to confront any ethnoarchaeologist working in a contemporary society is that what people do may bear little relation to what they say. For example, in my initial work in the Baringo District in Kenya, I was told that many of the clay pots in use in houses and compounds were up to 80 years old. In fact in *Man* (1977) I published several maps containing such information. In subsequent years, after talking to anthropologists who had worked longer in the region than I had, and after talking to the potters and observing the frequency of pot breakage, I realised that it was extremely rare for any pot to last more than eight years. Similarly, I was told by a number of informants that a group of pots came from a particular source. After measuring the pots it became clear that the information was almost certainly incorrect.

In modern western society individuals often mislead when asked questions concerning various aspects of material culture. For example, many may be embarrassed or ashamed to answer correctly questions concerning the amount of different types of refuse that they produce. Work in Tucson, Arizona and in Milwaukee has demonstrated that estimates of garbage disposal rates based on verbal information were often severely misjudged (Rathje 1979).

Perhaps the most widely discussed instance of a lack of correspondence between verbal information and actual behaviour concerns the notion of the 'type'. Are the categories and types of artifacts identified by the archaeologist purely of his own making, or do they correspond to a 'native' classification? Ford (1954) saw types as archaeological and imposed, while Spaulding (1953) suggested that native categories could be inferred by using various statistical techniques. There are now a large number of examples such as those given by Gould (1974), Hardin (1979) and White & Thomas (1972) which show that archaeological and native categories do not coincide. White and Thomas, for example, note that the primary archaeological division of stone artifacts into cores and flakes is not made by native New Guinea highlanders. Clearly, in studying the cultural context and ideological basis of material culture patterning, we may be examining meaningful behaviour which is not expressed at a particular verbal level. What are the reasons for this?

There is a wide range of factors which may cause a disjunction between what people do and say. One reason is that there is a real difference between verbal and non-discursive knowledge. For example, we may know how to speak without being able to explain the grammatical rules of the language. So, in material culture, we may know what to do even if we cannot explain it verbally. This appears to be the case in modern western society where what people say about material culture is probably less thought out than their views on religion, sex, politics and the like. Material, everyday knowledge is not and need not be an area of discursive knowledge.

In some cases this undiscussed, hidden meaning of material things can be used strategically in social relations. For example, women may be able to make subtle and effective statements about their social position by using everyday artifacts which are not consciously discussed and regulated by dominant male members of society. But it is difficult to generalise. In other societies, true knowledge about the meaning of things and their spatial arrangements in settlements may be controlled by an elite minority. This dominant group may maintain its position partly by a withholding of knowledge about how the world is put together and the members of that group may intentionally mislead the uninitiated (cf. Barth 1975). How difficult it is going to be, in such a situation, for the ethnoarchaeologist to penetrate the relationship between what is said and what is done.

Much of the confusion may, however, result from simple and direct lying where the informant seeks immediate gain from the ethnoarchaeologist. For example, in my Baringo example, it is probable that the ages of pots were grossly exaggerated because it was thought that I might want to buy pots (in the footsteps of the anthropologists who had worked in the area before me). It became important to be known in the area as someone who did not have purchase in mind. Other reasons for intentional misleading are extremely numerous and include the possibility that the researcher is an inappropriate sex or age, that the area has had a history of maltreatment by white colonial powers, that missionaries have encouraged a feeling of guilt in relation to traditional activities, that the interpreter is not respected, or simply that the ethnoarchaeologist, wishing to measure pots and refuse, is perceived as a fool, unworthy of attention.

A further reason for a lack of correspondence between what is seen and heard may result from problems of comprehension. Whether the researcher is trying to learn the language or is using an interpreter, there may be many misunderstandings. In fact, the informant with the best will in the world may be unable to understand and comply with the questions asked. Binford (1978) records that, in retrospect, his initial questions of the Nunamiut Eskimos could not be answered in a straightforward way, however much this frustrated him at the time.

The very presence of the ethnoarchaeologist may mean that people behave in a different way so that what they say and do may be different from what is observed. The outsider always changes the situation that is being observed. Yellen (1977, 289) discusses how food is distributed within a society, but this includes food distributed to an anthropologist. The ambiguous position and standing of the outsider may cause entirely novel ways of distributing food and of acting within the home environment.

Given that the verbal and non-verbal often do not coincide, and that the degree of coincidence varies with culture and context, we need to examine models which link the ideal and the actual together. Yellen (1977) provides an example from his work amongst the !Kung Bushmen. In practice, !Kung individuals move widely and social ties are loosely organised, but the !Kung see themselves as a series of loosely defined territorial groups. Yellen (ibid., pp. 48–9) suggests a model according to which these two contradictory aspects are part of the same system. The formal band territorial model provides a mental framework for deciding on and justifying varying courses of individual action and for predicting in a loose way what others will do. But in the !Kung environment there is a need to be able to adapt rapidly and flexibly. So, over the long term, there is a practice of individual changes and movements in order to rearrange the demographic map.

During the chapters which follow, other examples will be given of the structured way in which idea and practice may not correspond. But, as Bloch (1971) demonstrates in his analysis of the ideal component of Madagascan burial which contrasts with the practice of daily life, it is incorrect to assume that the material world is more or less 'real' than the non-material. Both aspects are organised in relation to each other, as complementary components in a cultural unit.

Given the pervasive 'problem' that spoken and observed information may not coincide, for whatever reason, some archaeologists have suggested the particular 'solution' that was mentioned earlier (p.40). The 'problem' is 'solved' if we accept Gould's materialist position. Wobst (1978) notes that ethnography involves the study of recorded behaviour, while archaeologists study actual behaviour. In a more extreme view, Schiffer (1978, 235) suggests that ethnoarchaeologists should only observe actual behaviour, and not study word-of-mouth reports. Such an approach would first of all be impossible since, as has been suggested, the very presence of the ethnoarchaeologist in a living situation affects and changes behaviour. The more the ethnoarchaeologist remains a remote outsider the more he/she changes what he/she observes. Also such a materialistic approach limits scientific research because it is difficult to find out basic questions concerning the observed data, such as where and when and by whom a pot was made, or who is the brother of the potter. Equally, it is impossible to examine the all-important two-way relationship between discursive and non-discursive knowledge, and to examine material behaviour within a social, ideological and cultural context.

The ethnoarchaeologist' must not duck the issue and play at part-

43

time anthropology. While the ethnoarchaeologist does bring to anthropology the training to observe behaviour and its products, there will be few research problems for which such observation is sufficient. The ethnoarchaeologist must also face the issues of how to examine what is said, thought and explained by informants.

One procedure would be to arrive in the field with a questionnaire worked out in advance with advice from sociologists and others trained in interviewing techniques. Such an approach would frequently involve filling in forms with yes/no answers. While there may be some research questions and cultures in which this approach would be adequate, there are considerable dangers involved. For example, in many countries informants will answer yes or no depending on the tone of the question; the main concern of the informant may be to provide a pleasing answer rather than a correct one. Such problems could be countered by introducing cross-checks in the questionnaire. But it may be difficult to assess all the biases of age, sex, colour and so on mentioned above with such an inflexible technique.

In many cases the informant will find the questions ambiguous or unclear. This is especially the case in an alien culture where there may be many subtle differences in meaning which cannot be accounted for in a prepared checklist. Perhaps the most serious disadvantage of the questionnaire technique is that the researcher cannot be led down new avenues. By far the best way to find out about the unknown is to listen and learn.

One extreme, but highly effective, example of this was used by Guilbert Lewis (1980) in his work among the Gnau of New Guinea. Even though one might use a tape recorder, the anthropologist is usually present, intruding into the scene. Lewis placed his tape recorder by groups of people talking and left. The people being studied had, by then, got used to the technical device being around and carried on their conservations and rituals regardless. The ethnoarchaeologist will usually want to record visual information, and since it will be impractical to film continuously and remotely, greater intrusion must occur. Indeed, there are many advantages in participating and becoming accepted, in so far as it is possible, within the study group. Understanding may come with closer contact, there will be time to learn the language, initial distrust may be allayed. During a long stay in which some participation is achieved, it is possible to use a variety of recording procedures; tape recordings of undirected discussion, notes or tape recordings of partially directed discussion in which questions from the researcher focus the informants on a particular topic, direct observation and recording.

Clearly the degree to which participant observation is used depends to a considerable extent on the nature of the research problem. Those interested in regional settlement patterns in relation to environmental features may have less need to understand verbal information than those concerned with the meaning of ritual. However, I find it difficult to envisage topics that could successfully be completed without any reference to the explanations of the individuals themselves. It is sheer cultural and intellectual snobbery to allow no reality to informants' analyses of their own situation. It is important to examine the relationship between the spoken causes of events and the outsider's identification of correlations and interactions.

As much as the interview technique depends on the research questions being asked, so does the sampling design. How many villages, areas, houses, pots or people should be studied depends on the aspects of behaviour that the analyst is interested in and the degree of certainty that is required in the conclusions. If the questions are fairly straightforward, such as the relationship between size of settlement and duration of occupation, there are numerous equations in sampling theory (Mueller 1975 : Cherry, Gamble, Shennan 1978) which can be applied in order to determine an adequate random sample (for example, of settlements). Usually, however, there will be numerous questions and variables to be examined and a more subjective assessment of sample size will be required.

Major problems in the sampling design may concern the differences between an archaeological and a living settlement plan. In the living situation artifacts, and even houses, are constantly being moved and it may (although this depends on the particular culture) be impossible to produce a map of the settlement 'frozen' at one moment. The ethnoarchaeologist may be particularly interested in this mobility but his recording may be confounded not only by the speed and frequency of moves, but by changes in functions of artifacts, removals from the village, re-use of houses and so on. 'Tagging' of artifacts may often be impractical or prevented by informants. For the moment there are few guidelines available to the ethnoarchaeologists faced with such problems. The particular solution will depend on the questions being asked and the circumstances and ease of work.

In all societies there is likely to be great variation in activities and use of artifacts at different times of the day, season and year. There may also be variations at longer intervals related to environmental and climatic fluctuations and historical and external political events. The archaeologist may be particularly interested in recording these various ranges of behaviour so that the resulting palimpsest can be compared with an archaeological composite pattern. Long and repeated visits to the study area are, therefore, necessary and are in any case implied by the need to participate and learn languages for which no grammar or dictionary may have been published. In practical terms, the ethno-archaeologist may have arrived in a study area at a time when women are busy in the fields so that they cannot talk easily and domestic tools and crafts cannot be observed. It will be desirable for the ethno-archaeologist to spend a total of at least one year in the study area.

Various other practical aspects of conducting ethnoarchaeological fieldwork in a foreign country are so contingent on the laws of that country and its particular relations with the home country that little of a general nature can be prescribed. It is, of course, legally and ethically important to obtain the necessary research and travel permits, and embassies will often be a good starting point here. For many third world countries, applications may now take six months to a year to be processed, and the outcome may well be unsuccessful. Plans must, therefore, commence early and alternatives prepared. Many countries are now, understandably, highly sensitive to the attentions of anthropologists seeking a traditional 'primitiveness'. Success in applications is best assured through those already working in an area, and by a clear and honest statement of research aims.

In conclusion, in undertaking ethnoarchaeological fieldwork the archaeologist is aware of responsibilities to the country and people studied and to the anthropologists who, in the future, will wish to work in the same or similar areas. Their work depends on the good relations set up by earlier researchers.

Involvement in ethnoarchaeological fieldwork also requires recognition of the peculiarity of the task. One has to be more than an anthropologist and more than an archaeologist. The differences from archaeology are clear. There are also differences from anthropology. First, there is a particular concern with material culture. While the materially constructed world, including everything from fine painting to hearths, is a hopelessly broad category about which to generalise, there are certain aspects such as the ambiguity of material as opposed to verbal symbols, and the non-discursive nature of much material organisation, which do allow material culture to be defined as a distinct area of analysis (for further discussion of this point see Chapter 10). Second, ethnoarchaeology includes and focuses attention on everyday mundane behaviour, not just the rituals and myths of societies. Third, as has already been noted, the ethnoarchaeologist is trained to observe behaviour which he/she can then compare with written and spoken information. In all these, and probably many other ways, ethnoarchaeology is a distinctive area of field research with particular problems of its own. As well as being versed in anthropological field techniques, the ethnoarchaeologist must also be aware of additional problems, some of which I have tried to outline in this chapter. It is only as further ethnoarchaeology is completed that a full text of appropriate field techniques and biases can be written.

3 The formation of the archaeological record

Having seen some of the history of archaeological anthropology and of its practice as ethnoarchaeology, part of the range of results which have begun to emerge can be examined. It will be necessary to evaluate the analogies which have been suggested and to suggest the types of ethnoarchaeology which have been and will be most successful. In Chapter 1 various desirable aspects of analogies were identified, and will be sought for in discussing the formation of the archaeological record, the processes by which artifacts become deposited in the ground, and the post-depositional processes by which they are disturbed and survive.

It is often difficult, however, to draw a line between depositional and post-depositional processes. Is trampling of artifacts into the ground by human feet or domesticated animal hooves depositional or post-depositional, and, in Schiffer's (1976) terminology, is it a natural or a cultural transform? It is easier to provide adequate relational analogies when some natural link can be suggested between the various components of the model and so it may be appropriate to begin with post-depositional processes in which there is little human or cultural input.

Post-deposition

For example, once a house has been built, its decay and collapse may often be entirely natural processes. The houses in *fig. 7* are all collapsing in similar ways. Rather than simply falling over or inwards, the whole structure rotates and sinks to the ground. As the wall posts are twisted round they cause identifiable changes in the holes, trenches and moulds in which the posts are set. The ethnographic case suggests to the archaeologist that one might look for such patterning in post-hole shapes and angles while digging a prehistoric round house. Such information would suggest that the house had been left to fall down by natural processes as opposed to having been dug up intentionally as in the Zambian case in *fig. 8*. Here huts are dug up and pulled down when the senior male occupant dies. These post-depositional traces would be very different from those left by the Baringo huts. However, we cannot assume that rotational collapse always occurs with round houses. Such a process in the Kenyan case is encouraged by the shallowness of the post settings and by the method of lashing the roof to the wall posts. Nevertheless, it would be possible to examine the various ways in which round houses of different constructions collapse, with the

a

b

c

7 a, b, c, Hut collapse in the Baringo district, Kenya

8 Pulling out posts and digging a trench to reach the base of posts in a Mbunda village in western Zambia

analogies being based on widely found physical principles.

Where faced with a structure built from unfired courses of puddled mud (tauf or terre pisé) or mud bricks, the archaeologist needs special skills in identification and interpretation. Any help that ethnography can give will depend on having similar ecological and pedological conditions. McIntosh (1974) has provided much evidence from a study of the process of deterioration of mud walls in a contemporary West African village (Hani, in Western Ghana) which has proved of value in interpreting features on a nearby archaeological site at Begho. Some of his observations may, however, be of wider interest. Buildings made of terre pisé were estimated to last a maximum of 20 years without major repair and they could last over 70 years with constant attention. The most vulnerable part of the mud building is where it meets the ground. Water dripping from the roof, splashing during sweeping, and capillary water transporting soluble salts through the wall all result in undercutting (*fig. 9*). The wall usually includes sherds and other rubbish incorporated during building. As the wall decays, the lighter material and finer particles are carried further from the wall than the heavier debris and sherds. At the archaeological site at Begho, these various characteristics may sometimes be most visible in cross-section (*fig. 9*).

Of the many other types of features encountered by the archaeologist which have undergone natural decay after use, perhaps one of the most common is the pit. These, whatever their shape, size or function,

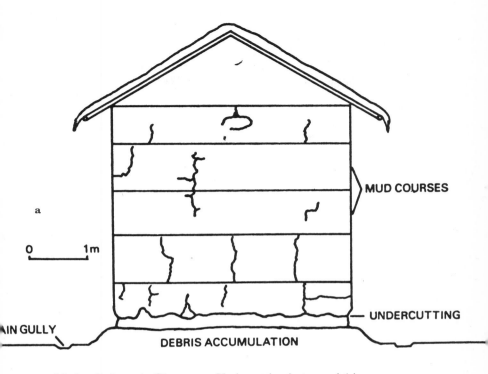

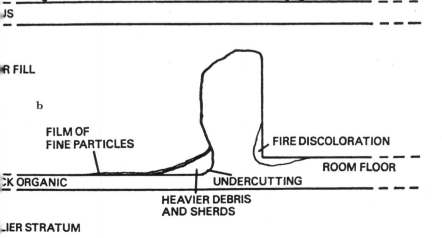

9 Mud wall decay in Ghana. **a** Undercutting in terre pisé in a contemporary village. **b** Mud wall stump in an archaeological section (not to scale) (McIntosh 1974)

may often be left open before they are completely filled. Rubbish pits in Western Zambia are frequently abandoned at this stage (*fig. 10*). The slight hollows which are all that remain of the pits act as a sort of rubbish trap. The wind tends to whirl in the small depressions, depositing a range of small fragments of organic and other refuse. At the top of the pit, then, a lense with a high density of small fragments is formed, and these fragments represent a general cross-section of the smaller material lying around the settlement. While excavating an Iron Age site in England (Hodder 1982a) dense lenses of small debris were found at the top of pits and there was a difference in the content of the material from the rest of the pit. It now seems likely that the upper Iron Age pit layers resulted from the same process as was witnessed in Zambia.

10 Pits in various stages of infill in villages in western
Zambia. **a** and **b** Pits being used to dump domestic refuse. The posts
are placed around the pits to warn people and animals. **c** An out-of-use
pit acting as a collector of wind-blown material

a

b

c

Although in the above cases care must be paid to the similarities in materials, climate and environment, the use of an analogy seems reasonable because the linking principles are at least partly concerned with widespread natural processes such as rain and wind action on particles of different size and density. Relational analogies, in which the reasons for the working of the analogy can be expressed, have also been applied to various non-human forces acting on bone residues.

The early ethnographic work in this branch of 'taphonomy' was carried out by Brain on Hottentot bone refuse and by Lee on abandoned Bushman camps. A particular example of such studies grew out of Isaac's (1967) interest in interpreting bone data from Olorgesailie, a series of Acheulian sites in East Africa. At the archaeological sites the amounts of bone associated with artifact concentrations varied greatly. At many sites only small splinters and a few teeth were preserved. Could this have been due to some natural agency? To answer this, in an area near Olorgesailie, 55 large bones and bone fragments (5–20cm in length) and more than 60 bone splinters were dumped. *Fig. 11* shows the situation after four months. Scavangers and various natural agencies had caused most of the refuse to be dispersed and most of the larger bones had been removed entirely. So, on the archaeological site, the small number of small bones did not necessarily indicate that large amounts of meat were not processed at the site.

Other aspects of bone assemblages affected by scavangers have been examined by looking in lairs (for example Crader 1974; Hill 1980; Binford 1981). Such work developed from a particular archaeological controversy between Dart, Washburn, Ardrey and Brain concerning bone assemblages at early man (australopothecine) sites. At these sites particular parts of carcases seemed to be over- or under-represented. Did this mean that the bones were being used as tools, or that the assemblages had been affected by scavanging animals? Isaac (1967) describes preliminary studies of bones in caves frequented by hyaenas. This and other work indicates that gnawing by dogs, jackals and hyaenas can lead to highly distinctive assemblages. The biases partly result from the different composition and density and maturing rates of different types of bone. Here again there are natural processes which allow generalisation to archaeological assemblages. Bone assemblages collected by scavengers often show distinctive characteristics, such as a particular ratio between ribs and limb bones. By comparison with ethnoarchaeological collections, it now appears that many of the Palaeolithic habitation assemblages from British caves may in fact be scavenger collections (K. Scott pers. comm.)

In the work of Isaac and Crader cited above, it was the small bones that survived. This may sometimes be the result of an additional natural process examined in great detail by Gifford and Behrensmeyer (1978). A camp site made during a foraging expedition by the

54

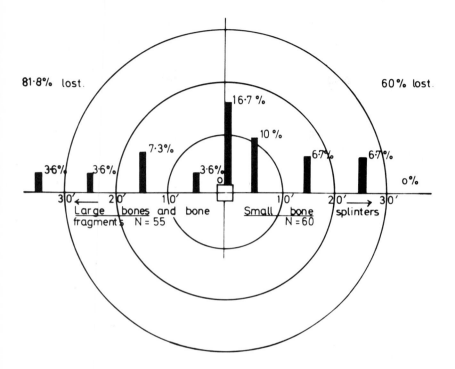

DISPERSAL OF BONES AS OBSERVED 14 SEPT. 1965.

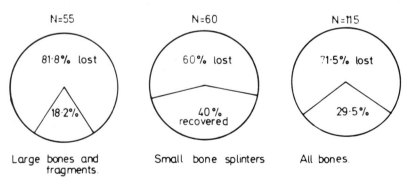

11 The dispersal of bones by scavengers and natural agencies. Top: Bar diagram from centre to left shows dispersal of large bones in the concentric divisions indicated. Bar diagram from centre to right shows data for small bones. Bottom: Graphic representation of bone loss. All loss percentages are minimum values (Isaac 1967)

Dassanetch in the Turkana region of Kenya had been occupied by eight men for four days. Gifford observed that while at the camp, the men hunted and ate 40 terrapins, 4 crocodiles, 14 catfish, 2 perch and scavenged 15kg of meat from 2 zebras killed by lions. When they left the site it was a 17 × 17m scatter of bone with the densest concentration 3 × 3m around the hearth. The scatter was plotted and then replotted the following year. The bones that remained on the site were the smaller parts of the skeleton and those that break up into small pieces. These survived largely because it is the smaller fragments that get trampled below the surface and are thus slightly protected from rain wash and scavenging.

In all the above examples the authors are at pains to emphasise that their ethnoarchaeological data should only be used as an analogy for the past when similar environmental conditions can be demonstrated. The relevant aspects of the environment (rain, wind, scavengers, etc.) can be identified because there are known links between the different aspects of the analogy. The model is based on known natural processes. There is no attempt here to include human and cultural factors. These are more important in the examination of depositional processes, and it is here that we shall begin to run into problems of application.

Deposition

An obvious initial point that has frequently been made is that in many societies few artifacts are left during the abandonment of a settlement. This is especially true of pastoralist groups (such as the Turkana studied by Robbins 1973), who move frequently and have little 'baggage'. The tribes that produced the residues in *figs 7* and *12* practise some agriculture but they are largely pastoralists. Little is left to be found on these abandoned homesteads except a few broken calabashes and bones, and what is left is not at all representative of the activities once carried out. However, the amount that is left on a site by the inhabitants is not directly related to the frequency of move and type of economy. Indeed, it could be argued that because pastoralists must 'travel light' they would leave more behind on settlements, not less. What is or is not left on a site is linked to a complex set of cultural values which have not been the subject of ethnoarchaeological publications.

It is at least clear that what is left behind on a site is a very distorted palimpsest of the activities which once took place. Artifacts and structures on a site often go through long sequences of use and re-use. In the Lozi area in western Zambia, broken pots and sherds are used for a large number of purposes from the feeding of domestic animals to the collection of water (*fig. 13*). This re-use sequence means that the final location of sherds may have little to do with the original location and function(s) of the pots. Ochsenschlager (1974) provides a more

56

12 The interior of an abandoned hut in the Baringo district of Kenya. The posts for beds and roof are visible

13 A broken painted pot which had been set in the ground and used to collect rainwater in a Lozi village in western Zambia

detailed example of pottery re-use from contemporary southern Iraq. Here the 'kuzi' pot form when reasonably intact is used for water or salt, but when badly cracked is used for grain. When broken, large sherds are used for feeding and watering chickens and turkeys in the courtyard, or for storing or organising small quantities of a wide variety of things in the house.

Re-use of houses and other buildings also occurs. Amongst the Fulani in Cameroun, buildings are continually re-used as living huts, sleeping huts, guest huts, men's huts, batchelor's huts, kitchen huts, storage huts and animal pens (David 1971). Continual re-arrangement of individuals in huts was also noted by Cranstone (1971) and Heider (1967) in New Guinea. Such re-use would clearly affect attempts to reconstruct the social organisation or range of functions on an archaeological site. Amongst the Dugum Dani in New Guinea (Heider 1967) the problems extend even further because once a compound site has been abandoned it may be turned into a garden and be dug over, so destroying all post-holes and traces of the once substantial buildings.

Given all these problems it is hardly surprising that archaeologists visiting recently abandoned camps have found difficulties in reconstructing the associated activities and social organisation. Informants who once lived at or knew the camp are not able to corroborate all the archaeologists' guesses (Bonnichsen 1973; Lange and Rydberg 1972). However, it is necessary to move away from these 'spoilers' (Yellen 1977) and from the negative listing of difficulties and complexities. Abandonment and re-use procedures certainly are complex and varied, but it is necessary to examine what causes the variability. One hypothesis might be that, the less the capital outlay or labour required in constructing a building, the greater the fit between it and its personnel. The argument behind this statement is that buildings into which little labour has been put can easily be rebuilt to meet changing needs. This is an energy-saving, efficiency viewpoint which fits well with our own western cultural context. But one could well argue the opposite: that the less the capital outlay the less the fit. The argument here would be that buildings into which little effort had been put were those that had no particular importance and could be used for a variety of different functions and numbers of people. Clearly it is fruitless to argue in this *a priori* way, imposing a pseudo-logic. There is a need to develop relational analogies which examine abandonment and re-use behaviour in determinant cultural contexts. Only when we have understood some of the cultural links involved in particular cases, can generalisation be attempted.

This need to examine cultural contexts is evident in a range of other studies of depositional processes. The debate between Yellen and Binford about whether the on-site activities of hunter-gatherers do or do not result in localised residues depends on a range of cultural and contextual factors which have hardly begun to be examined (Binford 1978). Similar arguments apply to the long series of discussions (summarised in Binford 1978) concerning why imbalances may occur in bone assemblages between proximal and distal ends of bones, or to Yellen's notion that the diversity of maintenance tools relates to the length of site occupation. In all these cases the cultural reasons for material cultural patterning and relationships remain to be probed.

For some relationships between depositional processes and social variables it could be argued that there is some natural or necessary causal connection. David (1972) makes the point that a pot type which is used often and breaks frequently will have a higher frequency in a site assemblage than a storage pot which is seldom used and seldom breaks. That 'use life' affects assemblage composition is a mathematical certainty. Human behaviour also has necessary constraints. Studies of discard on the Arizona University campus found that small items (less than 4in in dimension) were discarded almost independently of rubbish bins, but that large items were placed in the bins (Schiffer 1976, 188). Generally one could argue that small items, just because they are less easy to see and are less of a nuisance to passers-by, are less likely to be organised into special-purpose refuse areas. Small items are also less easy to hold and are more likely to be dropped. One could say the model depends on basic characteristics of human eyesight and finger agility. A related finding by White and Modjeska (1978) in New Guinea was that large axes lost in the forest zone were generally 'lost for good' while the probability that on-site losses would be found and recycled was high. Frequency of movement and greater visibility on sites mean that large axes would tend to be found in this zone.

But, of course, much depends on the value attached to an item and the nature of its use. Neither Schiffer nor White and Modjeska examine the total cultural context within which artifacts of different sizes are dropped and left. There is a need to explore the way in which artifacts of high value are curated; that is, how they are kept, cared for, re-used and remade until finally discarded.

Some clarification of the concept of curation has been provided by Binford (1976) although, as we shall see, the contribution is one of description and definition and not explanation. Binford found that many of the tools of the Nunamiut Eskimos were highly curated. The tools were transported around by the hunters. The artifacts returned to the home base or residential unit for repair and waste products resulted. But the tools themselves were carried around and often discarded or lost away from base camps. In such a situation there will be no association in site assemblages between the by-products of activities (for example, bone and food residues) and the tools used in those activities. In fact Binford makes a series of statements about societies without and with curation. For example, in situations without curation, 'other things being equal', the more tools there are in assemblages, the more tool-making debris. With curation, there is no relationship between the total numbers of tools found and the quantity of tool-making debris.

In these statements Binford has defined clearly and in great detail exactly what curation involves, and has provided the archaeologist with another way of classifying societies. But for this information to be used as an analogy with explanatory value, we would need to know something of the process which leads to curation; why some societies do or do not curate. Since it is probable that most societies curate some things but not others, a more realistic question might concern why some artifacts are curated and not others. The attempts which have been made to answer these questions have focused on energy and labour investment. It might be claimed that the greater the amount of energy invested in an artifact, the less likely it is to be discarded until its use-life has ended. While it may be the case that in western society today high-value curated artifacts are those on which greater energy has been expended, it would have to be demonstrated that the same was true of all societies. And even if the Nunamiut do maximise the use of their materials, we are not told enough of the cultural context to understand why this should be so.

As was shown in Chapters 1 and 2, one method of trying to support analogies is to show that the processes described occur across a wide range of cultures. Explanation and insight are sought not in the particular cultural context, but in the covariation of variables. So one way to examine why people deposit their refuse in varying ways is to carry out a cross-cultural survey. Murray (1980) has used this technique to examine Schiffer's generalisation that with increasing site population (or perhaps site size) and increasing intensity of occupation, there will be a decreasing correspondence between use and discard locations for all elements used in activities and discarded at the site.

The analysis was carried out on 79 cultural groups taken mainly from the Human Relations Area Files. Differences between the discard activities of migratory and sedentary groups were sought. Murray acknowledged that her survey suffered from difficulties of defining living spaces in the two types of society. What she found is that in migratory populations discard tends to be carried out in living spaces defined as open areas around hearths or in compounds. In sedentary populations the living spaces, now defined as the insides of huts, tend to be kept clean. Clearly there is some correlation between discard and inside and outside activity areas, but whether there is any significant difference between migratory and sedentary populations, and whether the findings 'test' Schiffer's generalisation is unclear.

Murray gives a fair account of these difficulties but there are other problems which are inherant in all cross-cultural surveys. For example, to what extent have the sedentary societies studied been more accessible to western missionaries and governmental control? The Lozi in Zambia are sedentary, they keep their houses clean and dig pits for refuse. But this is not the traditional practice. It was introduced by health inspectors of the colonial and present government. There is a more general lack of independence between ethnographic societies which will bias any correlations. What is known as Galton's problem (McNett 1979, 41) is that traits may not be independent but may be spatially distributed as a result of diffusion. This 'autocorrelation' effect means that high correlations may occur between traits which are not causally related, but happen, because of diffusion, to cover overlapping areas.

It is apparent, then, that for various reasons we may be able to identify a correlation without knowing its cause. Indeed it is a characteristic of cross-cultural surveys that the analyst may be given little idea of why a particular correlation occurs so that she/he has to provide one from her/his own cultural background. For example, Murray suggests that in long-term habitation areas discarded material would create 'discomforts (from odour, unsightliness, etc.), safety or health hazards, or limitations to activity space' (1980, p. 492). This is clearly an imposition of European and American standards of life onto the ethnographic data, and while Murray may well be correct in the cause that she gives, it is necessary to demonstrate the link by more detailed examination of cultural contexts. That is, there is a need to develop relational analogies.

A move towards a relational analogy for depositional processes comes from a historical context. Deetz (1977) notes that in seventeenth-century archaeological sites in North America refuse was just thrown out, 'broadcast' from the house, and often, to us, alarmingly near the door. Pigs and chickens near the house probably ate what was edible, leaving the rest to become slowly covered with soil. In addition, artifacts were trodden into small pieces and became mixed up. But soon after 1750, people dug square pits, often up to 7ft deep, for household refuse (artifacts and food remains). Preservation of remains is good and large pieces of material occur.

This change in discard habits could be linked behaviourally to an increase in population size and concentration. But Deetz shows that different sites of different densities, first dig pits in the same phase. Because the timing of the change corresponds to other changes in traditions, Deetz suggests that it is linked to an alteration in world view, or way of life, around 1750. The ordering of refuse in the later period is equivalent to the ordering and separation of types of food, the use of individual as opposed to communal eating plates, and other changes in attitudes which occurred. There is an overall trend from the communal to a concern with balance and order, centred on the individual. The material changes are related further to changes in the central place of religion, changes to a free-enterprise mercantile system, and the scientific revolution.

While the relationships between these changes remain to be clarified, and how the re-organisation of refuse affected individuals and their social strategies has yet to be fully examined, Deetz has made the extremely important point that discard behaviour and attitudes to dirt are parts of a wider set of cultural values and must be explained in those terms.

It is perhaps surprising that the present generation of younger archaeologists has not been more aware of the importance of the cultural and historical context of discard behaviour. Many of the generation were, in the sixties, hippies, or knew hippies. At least in England, many hippies used dirt, disorder, and a generally dishevelled aspect as part of a confrontation with a dominant adult world. Dirt and discard became a form of rejection. What the dominant groups in society saw as dirt was taken and used to confront and disturb them.

A different but related process has been observed carefully and with great insight by Judith Okely (1975). In this case the minority group is not middle-class youth but Gypsies. Okely examines the symbolism and pollution taboos in Gypsy society, and in particular she shows the important role played by women in such contexts. Her analysis is not concerned with a series of abstract norms. Unlike the example provided by Deetz, there is a full analysis of the use of dirt symbolism in a social and economic context.

Gypsies hold a special ecological niche in the larger society in which they live. They are directly dependent economically on a sedentary society around which they circulate supplying goods and services. By exploiting their mobility and by not restricting themselves to one occupation, they fill occasional and intermittent gaps in the system of supply and demand. Much of this work carries with it low-grade status and it is associated with the 'refuse' of the larger society – the sedentary non-Gypsy 'Gorgios'. The scrap and rag collector, picking through material which the Gorgio classifies as dirt, is prepared to adopt the posture expected of a despised scavenger. Gorgios and Gypsies have conflicts over land-usage and there is a policy of prosecution by Gorgios and evasion by Gypsies. But when confronted by Gorgio authorities, the Gypsy may adopt a subservient and humble posture.

Okely suggests that, because of their economic niche and the values given to that niche by the wider society, Gypsies carry the risk of self-degradation. There is a danger of a lack of self-respect and an increasing sense of unreality. The integrity of Gypsies as a group is continually threatened by their low-status position. To cope with this, Gypsies attempt to protect the inner self symbolically, by making a fundamental distinction between the inside of the body and the outside. The outer skin with its discarded scales, accumulated dirt, by-products such as hair, and waste such as faeces, are all potentially polluting. The outer body symbolises the outer public self as presented to Gorgios who are themselves classified as dirty. The inner body symbolises the secret, ethnic self.

This notion underlies much of the patterning of settlement refuse (and other aspects of material culture) which would be immediately identifiable archaeologically. Such attitudes form the archaeological record. The insides of Gypsy caravans are spotlessly clean, relating to the need to keep the inner body clean. All food that passes into the body must be carefully and ritually cleansed. The outsides, the camps as seen by Gorgios, are dirty, often covered by litter and faeces. This is the outside world as expected by Gorgios, but in a sense also, the dirt disturbs and threatens Gorgios and thus gives Gypsies an active and powerful role in Gorgio society.

In terms of the formation of the archaeological record, other aspects of material culture fit into the same scheme. Gypsies prepare food carefully and the residues might be expected to show the careful and multiple stages of preparation. Washing habits are crucial areas of concern. Eating utensils, and the tea-towel for drying them, must never be washed in a bowl used for washing the hands, body or clothing. A washing-up bowl used for other activities is permanently contaminated and can never be made clean. The personal washing and laundry bowls are potentially polluting and are usually placed outside the trailer. Personal washing bowls must be kept visibly different from washing-up bowls (e.g. one plastic, the other stainless steel), in case other Gypsies might accuse a woman of confusing the two bowls. Each person in the family may have his/her own cup. More

14 A Gypsy encampment in the east of England

generally one could describe the patterning as one in which utensils are distinct for each task, and activities of different types occur in distinct spatial locations. There is much classification and separation between categories. In contrast, Gorgios use kitchen sinks for multiple purposes. Gypsies either board up their sinks or commission caravans without them and instead use a variety of bowls.

So, there is a particular type of organisation of dirt, forming contrasts, and also categorisation and separation of space and artifacts. This evidence has been associated with a model in which a sub-ordinate, despised group gains self-respect through a symbolic concern with internal and ethnic purity. Yet the outer dirt, as with the hippies, is a useful strategy of social reaction and it allows a particular economic niche to be maintained. The Gypsy example is very relevant archaeologically. One thinks of minority dependent groups such as hunter-gatherers on the peripheries of agricultural societies. There is a need for more ethnographic studies examining such relationships.

But there is another model for the same pattern, related to the position of women in society. Okely shows how Gypsy women play a central role in the concept of purity and in relations with Gorgios. Gypsy women act as intermediaries between the pure Gypsy male and the impure, polluting Gorgio society. They bring in food from that society and prepare it for the men, and its purification is in their trust. The women go out 'calling' from house to house in Gorgio society, selling things. They thus come into close contact with Gorgio males and there is a danger that outside sexual contact will pollute the Gypsy ethnic group. There are thus strong controls by the Gypsy men over the purity and conduct of their women. Virginity, monogamy, abstinence and correct adherence to cleansing rituals are stressed. But, equally, women have a mute 'power' in the sense that the threat of impurity is in their hands and can be held over the men. More generally, Mary Douglas (1970) has suggested that, where absolute male rights over women are contradicted by women's abilities to be independent and to avoid punishment, there may be a strong sense of pollution and the patterning of dirt and containers noted above may result. In fact, the two models are not contradictory, and in the Gypsy case the status of women is linked to the ethnic border situation. Archaeologically one can monitor differences between women and men in burial contexts. More generally, it is necessary to specify structural models (relational analogies) of types of society in which women have potential power, and then look for varied categories of evidence for categorisation and contrast in settlement debris and in the use of domestic space.

The two reasons for the organisation of Gypsy discard behaviour also proved relevant in explaining the patterning of refuse of Nuba tribes in central Sudan. I have published a detailed account of these data elsewhere (Hodder 1982), and only a brief description will be provided here, mainly to emphasise the archaeological visibility and relevance of the way in which cultural values shape discard residues. Like the Gypsies, the Nuba are a minority group within a wider society. They exist, partly isolated on massifs in an extensive plain occupied by historically aggressive Arabs. There are close economic ties between the two groups. The Nuba are highly concerned with purity and with preventing symbolic pollution. The Nuba group studied which has the greatest emphasis on purity, the Mesakin, is so located as to have closer economic ties with the Arabs than another Nuba group, the Moro.

In addition, Mesakin women have considerable social influence and there is ambiguity and conflict over rights to children and resources. In the more rigid patrilineal system of the Moro, male rights over women are less able to be contradicted. So, again, it is of interest, in view of the models described above, that the Mesakin separate pure from impure with greater emphasis.

How are these different social and cultural attitudes manifested in material residues? For example, the Mesakin discard cattle bones, associated with men and seen as pure, separately from pig bones associated with women. Again the proliferation of separate categories suggested in the Gypsy example is found, forming the archaeological record. The Mesakin often allow their living compounds to become covered with dirt, partly because animals are allowed to wander into the living quarters (*fig. 15*). To us, the floors of the areas in which cooking and eating are carried out are excruciatingly unpleasant. The danger of imposing our own attitudes is clear. The Mesakin can live in the filth because they go to great lengths symbolically to protect their food and their bodies. The dirt acts in various ways; in reaction to the sense of cleanliness of the Arabs, so that the Mesakin themselves can cope with their hated minority position, and as an integral part of the tensions between men and women. The dirt threatens Arabs and, associated in the domestic sphere with women, it can be seen as having a double significance. For the men, the dirt helps to establish the subordinate position of women in the face of real female power in society. For the women, their outer association with dirt threatens the men and supports female strategies of contradiction and withdrawal. Some further aspects of the Nuba concern with purity will be examined in Chapter 8, but for the moment the archaeological importance of examining why people do different things with their refuse has been suggested.

Conclusion

The concern in this chapter has been to derive reliable and valid models for the depositional and post-depositional processes which result in the formation of the archaeological record. The discussion has

a

b

15 a and **b** The interior of two Mesakin Nuba compounds where the build-up of dirt and refuse is allowed despite the cooking, eating, sleeping and daily activities which are carried out in the compound. Some of the refuse is caused by the excretions of animals (such as the piglet in 15b)

centred on how things get into the ground. In the chapters which follow, more general aspects of the relationship between material culture and human behaviour and ideas will be examined.

In searching for relational analogies, which might be used reliably, both natural and cultural processes have been described. For post-depositional activities, reference can be made to natural laws concerning the habits of animals, the physical characteristics of bones, the movements of water and wind. For such processes we can be fairly sure that we can identify the conditions in the past which are relevant to the use of the analogy. We know why a particular natural process (such as water dripping from the roof of a house) leads to a particular set of archaeological remains (such as undercutting of mud walls) and we can support the analogy by identifying whether the relevant conditions existed (similar climate and environment, archaeological models of houses with roofs, nature of clay and matrix used in building).

But in moving to human processes such as the discard of refuse on a settlement, there seem to be few natural constraints. Humans walk with difficulty bare-footed on areas of freshly knapped flint, and they probably will not sit on the windward side of a smoking fire. But tolerance of dirt is socially and culturally relative and we need to begin contextual studies which examine why people organise their dirt, and their attitudes to dirt, in different ways as part of different social and economic strategies. It does not help to know cross-culturally that discard behaviour is correlated with other socio-economic variables. If we know why a particular social process (such as the coping by minority groups with their subordinate status in a wider dominant society) leads to a particular set of archaeological remains (such as categorisation of utensils, containers and activities, and separation of inner 'clean' from outer 'dirty' areas), we can support our use of an analogy by identifying whether the relevant conditions existed (economic interdependence, conflict, small egalitarian, subordinate groups, other evidence of ethnic boundary maintenance, concern with the body, etc.). There is a need for an expansion of the type of work carried out among the Gypsies which examines the various social and historical causes of discard behaviour.

Above all, it is necessary to use such contextual studies to break away from the tendency to impose modern western bourgeois values on ethnographic and archaeological data. Two widespread and central components of contemporary attitudes are the quantification of value in terms of efficiency and energy maximisation, and a developed Victorian notion that cleanliness is next to godliness. We have seen in this chapter how both these attitudes have been assumed by several ethnoarchaeologists to be universal. In fact, they are not and we need not only to be aware of that fact, but also to build models about what variation in such attitudes causes and is caused by.

4 Technology and production

Having examined analogies for the way in which artifacts get into the ground and are there disturbed and distorted, it is possible to begin discussion of the ways in which the materially constructed world is organised by people before it is broken up, discarded and deposited. In this Chapter questions such as 'how was this object made?', 'what was it used for?' and 'what was the organisation of the process of its production?' will be examined. The use of analogies to answer such questions have again ranged from the formal to the cross-cultural and relational.

Formal analogies

Direct comparisons of the forms of archaeological and ethnographic artifacts have frequently been made in the interpretation of tools. A large number of examples is provided by Grahame Clark (1952) who frequently set photographs or drawings of ancient and modern artifacts side by side in order to emphasise their formal similarity, and to support his interpretation of a similar function. Osier wheels used for salmon in modern Sweden were compared in this way to 'Stone Age' traps of a similar form from Denmark. Here the comparison was made to an adjacent region and environment. Sometimes the parallels were more far-ranging. In *fig. 16* blunt-ended wooden arrowheads from Mesolithic Maglemosian sites in Denmark are compared with similar modern artifacts (Burjat, Wogul, Eskimo) (ibid, p. 37). Clark suggests that the Maglemosian artifact is similar to a type found all over north Eurasia and north America which is used for shooting birds and small furred animals. The implication is that the Maglemosian objects had similar functions. As the variety of arrowheads from Zambia in *fig. 17* suggests, there is a need for a wider study of the relationship between arrowhead shape and function.

The objects depicted in *fig. 18* are characteristic of the Iron Age in England. Their function is unknown and has been the subject of a bewildering range of guesses, based on parallels with objects in contemporary and historical societies (Hodder and Hedges 1977). When Stukeley showed a drawing of two at the Society of Antiquaries in London, they were variously thought to have been for combing the manes of horses, for tattooing, or as 'amulets hung round the breasts of the Druid priests in sacrifice'. Other early suggestions included instruments of torture, 'flesh brushes', objects for decorating pottery, combing the hair, making sinew thread and skin dressing. Nowadays,

68

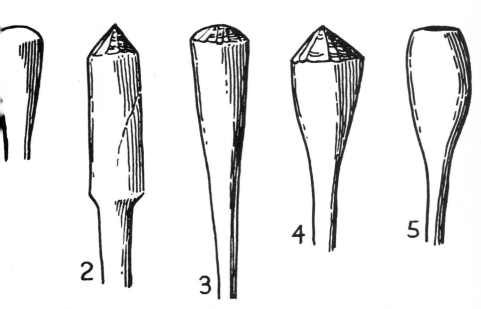

16 Clark's (1952) comparisons of wooden arrowheads for shooting birds and small game from Mesolithic sites in Denmark (1, 2) and from modern societies (3-5)

17 Different types of arrowheads, used for different functions by Lozi groups in western Zambia

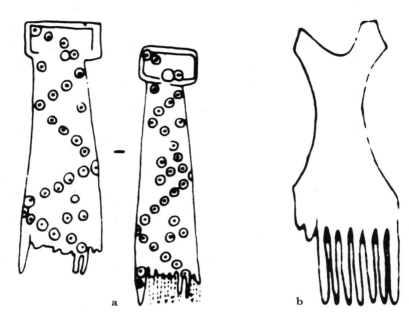

a   b

the artifacts are called weaving combs since it is suggested that they were instruments with which the weft was beaten in on the loom.

This idea comes from comparisons with known weavers' combs from Egypt, India, Persia, Syria and America (the Hopi). In fact, there is no good archaeological evidence to corroborate the weaving hypothesis, and the formal analogies are not, in any case, very close. Indeed closer analogies are to combs with one of the functions suggested in the nineteenth century. In *fig. 19* is shown a hair comb used widely in East Africa (and now in the western world). It has some remarkable formal similarities with some of the Iron Age objects, including the squared end, and dot-and-circle ornament on the face. Clearly it would be invalid on the basis of these similarities to assume a similar function for the Iron Age combs. The large number of different formal analogies must be differentiated between with a more careful examination of context. For example, inspection of the weaving analogies used shows that a weaving comb is never known to have formed part of the equipment connected with the warp-weighted loom which is the only type we have evidence for in prehistoric Britain. The analogy also seems inappropriate because there is no good evidence of a close association on Iron Age sites between the combs and other weaving equipment. Other avenues of enquiry in the search for an analogy that fits the Iron Age data include comparative studies of wear on the teeth of the combs, breakage patterns, and patterns of association with other artifact types.

70

18 (opposite) Iron Age artifacts from
a England and
b Scotland, termed 'weaving combs'

19 Hair comb from **a** modern Kenya and
b in use in Kenya

Relational analogies based on natural processes

In certain instances parallels of past and present technical processes have been made with an understanding of why a particular procedure should lead to a particular end result. Here the analogy is supported by reference to various natural and widely occurring events. When considering how a pot was made, for example, the properties of clay can be assumed to have been constant. The effects of turning pottery on a wheel leave identifiable traces the specificity of which can be examined by trial and error. Here ethnoarchaeology is an adjunct to experimental archaeology and it has a primary function to suggest ideas to the experimenter. For example, observation of modern traditional potters shows that the effect called by archaeologists 'stick polishing' can be well produced with a rounded stone; incising 'after firing' is frequently done on unfired polished pots; smudging to produce black wares and reduction firing to produce grey wares can be two very different processes.

Examination of processes such as that shown in *fig. 20* allows an understanding of how particular technical procedures can be identified from the distinctive traces that are left on the pot. Barrelet (1980) and Balfet (1980) discuss the ways in which one can distinguish cooking and oven traces in the firing of pottery. Jarrige and Audouze (1980) compare modern pottery making in Baluchistan with Chalcolithic evidence of the firing of pottery in the same area and infer a similar technical procedure. All such uses of analogy are pursuasive because there is a good understanding of the physical properties of clays, and a uniformity in the processes of expansion, contraction, heating, drying, rubbing, and their effects can be calibrated.

The same is true of the working of metal. A good example of the use of analogies concerning the technical process of iron production is provided by Schmidt (1980). Examination of material from iron furnaces of the Early Iron Age in West Lake, Tanzania, showed that very high temperatures had been reached during iron smelting. It was hypothesised that the high temperatures had been produced by placing the tuyères *inside* the furnaces so that air passing through the hot pipes was preheated.

It is interesting, in view of the comments in Chapter 2 on the relationships between experimental archaeology and ethnoarchaeology, that experimental tests of the above hypothesis carried out in North America by Schmidt were felt to be unreliable and it was thought that a more authentic context was needed. An ethnoarchaeological study was carried out of modern smiths in the same area as the archaeological data. These smiths placed the tuyères inside the furnaces. The smelting procedure was recorded and after a lapse of 9 months the remains of the furnace were excavated (*fig. 21a*). Formal comparisons showed that there were similarities between the remains of the past and present processes (*fig. 21b*).

20 Stages in the process of making clay pots by an Njemps woman, Baringo district, Kenya. **a** Crushing the clay which has been collected from the base of an anthill. **b** Sorting out the finer clay particles by shaking on a skin.

20 (cont'd) **c** Adding
water. No temper is
added. **d** Forming the base
of the pot. The pot is made
entirely on the potter's lap.
No support is used at any
stage. **e** Adding
coils. **f** Smoothing the
coils with the fingers and
thumb.

c

d

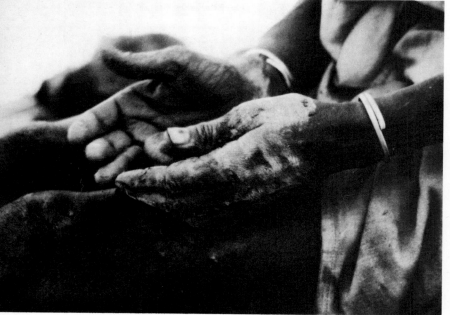

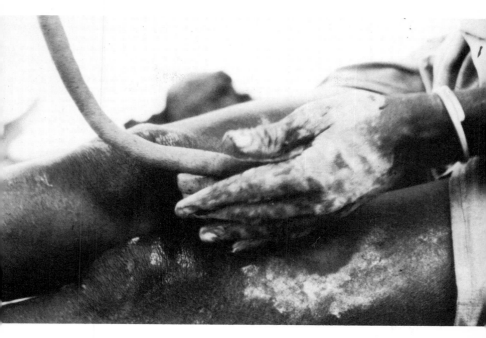

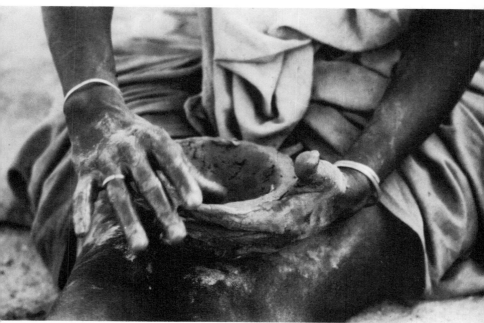

20 (cont'd) **g** Smoothing and thinning with a piece of calabash (gourd). **h** Further smoothing after the addition of further coils. **i** Beginning to bring the upper wall of the pot inwards. **j** The final pot shapes after firing in a bonfire

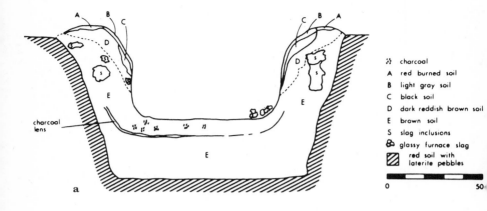

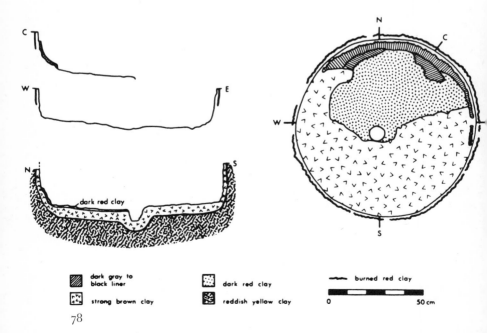

21 Ethnographic and archaeological evidence of iron
smelting. **a** Profile view of iron smelting furnace built in Nyungwe,
Kiziba, Tanzania in 1976. **b** Profile and plan views of an early Iron Age
smelting furnace pit (Schmidt 1980)

Much hinges on this particular analogy since the process examined was very advanced and the work resulted in the conclusion that iron producers 2000 years ago had the capacity to produce steel in furnaces in which temperatures exceeded 1800°c. These temperatures are higher than are thought to have occurred in Europe. The analogy, however, is carefully applied and is soundly based on knowledge of how furnaces of a particular shape, with tuyères in a certain position, are associated with preheating and therefore high temperatures.

As already suggested, ethnoarchaeology is here acting in a way similar to experimental archaeology, although Schmidt obtained more satisfactory results in the former instance because traditional knowledge and expertise could be tapped. Other aspects of iron-working which it may be impractical to examine experimentally are the side effects such as the amount of wood that has to be collected for charcoal. The use of 200kg of charcoal in one smelt in Tanzania meant the harvesting of more than 2000kg of wood. Haaland (1980) has also provided evidence of the massive deforestation that may occur in conjunction with iron smelting. Here again, the use of an analogy is based on universal relationships between wood, charcoal and heat production. Although there remains much quantification to be carried out, the archaeologist can have relative confidence in such models.

There are a large number of other technical processes for which ethnographic parallels have been sought and I only wish to describe a few more here. Those archaeologists interested in the methods and amount of energy required to clear woodland have turned to ethnographic accounts to fill in the detail of the considerable amount of experimental work on tree felling (for references, see Steensberg 1980). Carneiro (1979) records the efforts of a contemporary Venezuelan Yanomamö to cut down a tree with a stone axe. Unfortunately the informant and practitioner had only ever used a steel axe and he had considerable difficulty in coping with the 'new' technique. However, some of the results do correspond with the conclusions of axe experiments. For example, the tree was chopped down with relatively short, quick strokes, without putting one's whole might or strength to each blow. Also, it was possible to use a cleft-stick technique of hafting, and Steensberg (1980) provides evidence of a variety of hafting methods used in New Guinea.

Carneiro's actor cut all the way round the tree instead of notching it on one side only. In Steensberg's search for ethnographic parallels in New Guinea, the different methods of cutting the trees down, and the different types of tools used were related to the wood chips produced, and to the marks on the tree stumps and log ends. With this type of information it would be possible on an archaeological waterlogged site at which wood was preserved, to make suggestions about the techniques of felling that had been used.

Similarly information can be provided on the tools used in the task.

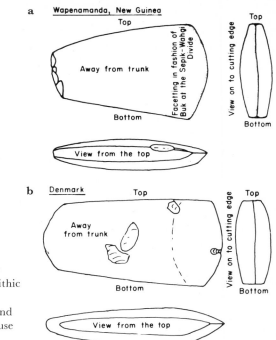

22 Stone axes from **a** contemporary New Guinea and **b** Neolithic Denmark showing similarities in shape and presumed method of use (Steensberg 1980)

In particular, resharpening of tools may lead to distinctive axe shapes. Carneiro was informed that in the recent past axes were sharpened every day. Resharpening of New Guinea blades noted by Steensberg produced a distinct facet on the cutting edge, which was applied to the side of the axe away from the tree trunk. Such information allowed Steensberg to explain similar facets on Neolithic axes from Denmark and to suggest which side of the axe had faced away from the trunk (*fig. 22*). It seems likely, however, that a range of different processes might be responsible for these rather simple characteristics of stone axes, and alternative analogies might be sought.

Another area in which experimental archaeology has played a primary role but where ethnographic data may offer some insights is in the construction of houses. As noted in Chapter 1, the archaeologist may wish to assess the type of building that once stood in a particular pattern of post-holes. There may be interest in the techniques used, in the height of the building and the number of rooms it contained, and the type of roof the walls could support. Experiments are necessarily hampered by the limited range of experience of the archaeologists and by his or her unfamiliarity with equivalent work. In *fig. 23* are shown some sequences of hut construction from Kenya. Some characteristics of these sequences which are of interest to archaeologists, especially those working in the same Kenyan locality, are that no hole is left in the

a

b

23 House construction in the Baringo district, Kenya. **a** to **c** (overleaf) Early stages of hut construction in the Mukutan area

23 (cont'd) **d** to **g** Hut construction near Lake Baringo. **d** Posts are simply rammed into the ground. **e** A shelf at the base of the roof holds up the thatch. **f** Roof interior showing details of binding.

e

f

23 (cont'd) **g** Mud has been placed on the walls and thatching is in progress

roof for the smoke from the hearth to escape, that there may be a 'second storey' or 'first floor' (more clearly seen in *fig. 7a*) in which individuals may sleep or store materials, and that the ceilings are extremely low so that all people except children may have to crouch and bend. There is also great variety in roofing system, including flat roofs (*fig. 24*). Excavation at the location of decayed huts of this type in the Baringo district, Kenya, showed that no traces survived except the hearth. This evidence is a reminder, if any be needed, that lack of evidence of constructions on archaeological sites does not preclude the possibility of substantial buildings involving considerable technical skill.

Other techniques which have been or might be studied ethnographically include the construction of monuments such as the statues on Easter Island (Heyerdahl and Ferdon 1961) and the hillforts of the Maori in New Zealand. Warfare methods may also be of interest, whether it is the daily raiding and skirmishing endemic to pastoralist groups in East Africa, or the planned campaigns of military states. Here, however, we are moving away from universal physical laws, to human choice and strategy for which no easy 'fingerprint' may be found. But, whenever the archaeologist asks not what particular technical process was used, but why, then he must enter the social and cultural arena where links between process and form are varied and complex. It is to the relationships between techniques and their social and economic context that we must now turn.

84

Cross-cultural relationships

There have been many suggestions that widespread relationships exist between methods of production and socio-economic variables. For example Phillips (1971, p. 341) noted that in 75 per cent of ethnographic examples women make the pots and in 98 per cent men do the hunting. So, in the particular prehistoric society being studied by Phillips, women probably made the pots and men probably made the chipped stone tools. The difficulties with these types of cross-cultural survey have been described in previous chapters. In this case we are not told why women make pots as opposed to men and we know nothing of the causal links which relate females and ceramic production. In other words, we have no idea of the relevance of the ethnographic data to the archaeological case. In addition, because the relevant causal ties are not explored, the statistical correlation has little explanatory value.

Other cross-cultural observations include the effects of the existence of trade in a society. Increased trade may lead to increased production and may affect the type of pottery produced. For example, Nicklin (1971) shows that the need to transport pottery safely in bulk may lead

24 An Njemps house with a flat roof in the Baringo district, Kenya

to pots of uniform-size gradations being produced so that they can be stacked in carts or boats. There may also be a link between the organisation of production and the settlement pattern. Rowlands (1971) suggests that dispersed settlement is likely to be associated with dispersed metal production, while nucleated settlement might encourage more centralised production.

Cross-cultural relationships may also be suggested between the patterns of subsistence organisation and production. Arnold (1978) notes that groups living in areas with scarce or depleted resources may become involved in pottery production. Pots can be exchanged for subsistence goods from adjacent regions with good arable soils. Marked seasonality in an economic cycle (for example where there is a distinct rainy season) may result in high demand for tools, and therefore bursts of craft production, at certain times of the year. Rowlands (1971) suggests that seasonality might result in the return of a large amount of scrap metal to a smith in a period of intense production, so resulting in the production of hoards – the 'founders hoards' of broken and worn-out implements found in prehistoric Europe. However, there is limited evidence of hoards in the ethnographic literature.

A series of generalisations have been put forward concerning the scale and specilisation of pottery production. In some cases, potters (such as the individual in *fig. 20*) participate in normal subsistence activities and they could be called part-time or casual. Others spend more of their time at and obtain more of their resources from potting and could be termed specialists. In her examination of contemporary Berber pottery production in the Maghreb in North Africa, Balfet (1966) found that pottery was produced at three scales: (a) non-specialist production by women in their own home for their own use; (b) in certain cases women and men earn some money from pottery manufacture and these may be termed semi-specialists; (c) there is also a sphere of large scale highly specialised production corporations involving only men.

In the Maghreb these differences in scale of production appear to have many other consequences. For example, in household production women are not concerned with being near large deposits of clay. But the large-scale specialised centres are generally in the neighbourhood of a major deposit. The non-specialised women tend to pot by hand, while at the specialist level it is done with the wheel. In other parts of the world this relationship between specialists and the use of the wheel may be less strong (Nicklin 1971). In the Maghreb the non-specialists use open firing techniques while specialists use kilns. The pottery produced by the non-specialists rarely shows major change. Such stagnation over long periods of time is not characteristic of the specialists.

In none of these cases are the reasons for the particular relationships clearly examined or specified. Thus it is difficult to know to what extent one can generalise to other societies in the present and the past. The problems can be identified by considering a further relationship suggested by Balfet. She noted that non-specialists produced a great variety of pottery styles and that there was freedom in decoration. The more specialist the potter the more standardised and monotonous the shapes and decoration of the wares. This notion has been used by archaeologists such as Prudence Rice (1981) in developing cross-cultural evolutionary models – Nicklin (1971, p.17) has provided a further link. Trade and export may encourage specialisation and standardisation in one product.

While it is certainly the case that greater centralisation may lead to standardisation within a series of distinct types, the assumption that this should always be so is clearly derived from our own cultural context in which maximisation of effort and profit are the prime concerns of production. It makes no sense to us to centralise without increasing efficiency and thus producing more standardised wares. The Woolworth mentality is strongly engrained. But ethnographically, different relationships may be found. The spear and stools shown in *fig. 25* are produced by particular individuals in localised areas

a

b

25 Contemporary artifacts from the Baringo district, Kenya.
a Socketed spear-head. **b** Wooden stools

87

within the Baringo district of Kenya. While the spears and stools produced by each group of craftsmen are broadly the same, there is considerable detailed local variation in their shapes and sizes. This variability occurs because, despite the partly specialised production, the craftsmen are sensitive to local preferences and demands. More generally, specialised production may often occur in a context where varied consumer demands, and an absence of emphasis on highly efficient production, allow variability in the styles that are produced. Conversely, the baskets and wooden eating bowls shown in *fig. 26* are locally made by individuals in each household, but the styles are highly uniform and monotonous over wide areas. In this case, these particular artifacts are given particular social significance and there is a strong feeling of conformity in relation to them.

Results which corroborate those from Baringo have been obtained from the Lozi in Zambia (Hodder 1982c). It is clear that we cannot read off a scale of production or specialisation from the degree of uniformity in the products. In understanding the link between production and style we need to know more of the social and economic context. We need to build relational models which explain why, in particular circumstances, people should want to make standardised or non-standardised pots, why they should want to produce efficiently on a large scale, and so on.

This point is of even greater importance when one considers the way in which specialisation of craft production has been linked into general evolutionary models. The Prudence Rice example has already been mentioned, and one might also refer to Renfrew (1973a) and Peebles and Kus (1977). It is often assumed that craft specialisation and control over production is linked to ranked societies, chiefdoms and states. It is easy to see how an archaeologist might proceed from stylistic uniformity in pottery to the reconstruction of chiefdoms with the aid of other pieces of evidence like a settlement heirarchy, rich burials and long distance trade. We have already seen that the link between standardisation and specialisation is weakly defined. Equally the link between craft specialisation and ranked societies is far from universal. Such relationships will be examined further in Chapter 6, but for the moment we can note the evidence of the Lozi in Zambia. The Lozi were and are ruled by royal personages, and a complex bureaucracy. By any standards this a highly ranked society. Yet most of the craft production is, and always has been, carried out at the household level or by local specialists not linked to the royal establishments. Pottery production was carried out by women, largely for their own use. Although there were potters who were closely linked to the royal centres, their work was mainly for those centres themselves. There was no market at the capitals and exchange of craft products was by person-to-person reciprocity. The only craft product controlled by the Lozi elite was iron although the centres of the royal elite were not located at the iron sources or production zones.

There is a need for a careful and sensitive examination of the various cross-cultural relationships that have been suggested in respect of craft production. The organisation of production and the styles of the output must be related within a total social and cultural context. While there has as yet been little work of this type carried out, some initial examples are provided below.

Relational analogies and cultural context

There has been considerable discussion in archaeology of the status of smiths, potters or knappers. Rowlands (1971) refers to Gordon Childe's and David Clarke's belief that smiths often formed a separate 'detribalised' class or caste of specialist craftsmen. Ethnographically,

26 Pots, baskets, wooden eating bowls and a stool of the Tugen in the Baringo area, Kenya

however, smiths tend to be well integrated into a local social context with local dues, obligations and rights in the community. Also, they or their wives and children may participate fully in subsistence activities. Some smiths have high status, but others may be despised or have low status. Some are associated with elites, while others are not. There is thus much variability in the social status of smiths, as there is for potters, knappers and other crafts people. We can ask why there is such variation and what causes the crafts person to have high or low status in any particular situation.

One study which attempted to examine the context within which crafts people work and their status is Gallagher's (1972; 1977; see also Haaland 1981) examination of knappers in central Ethiopia. Twelve informants who make and use stone tools today provided data on the quarrying of obsidian for stone tools, the use of the tools for hide-scraping, the reworking of tools and their disposal. Of the detailed and valuable analysis provided by Gallagher, it is perhaps relevant to draw out the fact that production is on an individual basis and is not centralised. Yet only one tool type is made – the hide-scrapers – and each indivdual makes identical tools and 'debitage'. Once again the cross-cultural expectation that uniform production of a standardised type indicates centralised production proves inadequate.

Current users of the stone tools belong to ethnic groups known as Gurage, Arussi-Galla and Sidamo. The hide-scrapers and tool-makers are called *faki* and they form an heriditary caste, the craft being handed down from father to son. The caste is endogamous (marriage partners are found within the caste) and it is despised within Ethiopian society, being thought to have the 'evil eye'. There are a number of such castes in Ethiopia which have their own codes and are not well integrated into the wider society within which they live. The artisan caste is considered polluting and huts of members are often located on the peripheries of villages. The *faki* are dispersed among other territorially ethnic groups. Within such a context, rather like the Gypsies described in Chapter 3, there are mechanisms for maintaining self-respect and support from one's group. It may be the case that the widespread uniformity in the artifacts produced enhances social ties and the sense of conformity within the group. That the caste is despised and thought polluting may also play an important social role. In a very different context in Kenya, I suggested (Hodder 1982) that the smiths, who had a 'witch' aspect, were prevented in this way from gaining social power. As producers of essential tools and of artifacts with symbolic significance, the smiths have the potential to reap economic benefit and obtain a degree of social control. Yet the power cannot be attained because the smith is placed in a separate category. Similarly, it would be of interest to examine whether the polluting aspect of the *faki* prevents their gaining social position. On the other hand, by being polluting yet providing the wider society with an essential service, the *faki* have a power of a certain type and which may be considerable in certain circumstances. Certainly the despised aspect may prevent others from learning the craft of the *faki* livelihood; their economic position is assured.

Potters do not form a separate caste amongst the Nuba in Sudan, but concepts of pollution are again here relevant to the differences in the organisation of production of the Moro and Mesakin, the two tribes studied (Hodder 1982). The Moro make pots in special workshop areas away from the villages. Production is thus separated and to a certain degree centralised. The adjacent Mesakin, on the other hand, make pottery in amongst the houses and compounds of the villages. Production is dispersed and not separated from other activities. In both tribes women make the pots.

No evidence could be found of any differences in the degree of stylistic variability amongst the pots of the two tribes. In Moro and Mesakin societies, the centralisation of pottery production is not seen as a chance to streamline production and produce batches of similar pots. In Nuba society the centralisation and decentralisation have quite a different meaning. For the Nuba the organisation of pottery production may relate to the strong sex pollution taboos noted in Chapter 3.

In many walks of life the Moro and Mesakin use the symbolic separation between pure and impure in different ways, and the results of this difference are seen in the pottery production. The Moro take steps to keep pure and impure, male and female, separate. The compounds are kept clean, pigs (associated with women and dirt) are kept in special pens, male and female activities are separated. Thus it is of interest that the pottery production, carried out by women and potentially polluting, is removed physically from the village into separate pottery-making areas. Pottery manufacture is organised separately and is carried out at certain times of the year.

The Mesakin, on the other hand, mark the boundary between pollution and cleanliness by complex decoration and ritual. Their compounds are often dirty (*fig. 15*) and, unlike the Moro, the compound floor is surrounded in rich decoration. The Mesakin more often decorate calabashes and pots. Dirt is not separated, it is brought near, but the boundary between clean and unclean is marked clearly. Similarly, the pottery is made at all times and places amongst the dirt and bustle of the villages. But the pots and their use in the compounds are surrounded in ritual and protective designs.

This example demonstrates the futility of cross-cultural generalisations which do not examine craft production as part of a total cultural context. The archaeologist could only interpret the Nuba situation by comparing the organisation of production (derived from direct evidence of work areas and not from arguments concerning stylistic uniformity) with a wide range of other material culture evidence from the same context, such as the organisation of refuse, animal bones, decoration and, as we shall see, burial, settlement pattern and the like.

Variability in the organisation of production has also been examined by Spriggs and Miller (1979) in Ambon-Lease, a series of islands in Maluku, Eastern Indonesia. The most remarkable aspects of the pottery production were that it was restricted to certain villages and that each pottery-producing village retained distinctive and different techniques. For example, differences occurred as to whether the pot was hand-formed, whether a paddle and anvil was used, the proportion of temper mixed with the clay, how the surface was treated. What caused this technical variety, even in the production of similar shapes? One answer might be in terms of technological constraints. For example, minor differences in the nature of the clay and available tempers may have necessitated different techniques, as may the use of fresh as opposed to salt water. Spriggs and Miller indicate that an additional interpretation in their case might be that whether one makes pottery or any other speciality, and the method used, are part of the general emphasis in this area on identity maintenance and differentiation. In addition, one technical dichotomy reflects exactly a religious dichotomy. The archaeologist must consider the possibility that variability in production is part of socially maintained cultural variety rather than being due to localised variation in technological constraints. As in the Nuba case, the way to support such an analogy would be to examine other aspects of the material culture evidence in order to determine the degree of cultural variety and the social and economic reasons for its maintenance.

Conclusion

This chapter has developed very much like the last. As with depositional and post-depositional processes, certain aspects of technological and productive processes can be explained by reference simply to physical constraints, the universal characteristics of clay, metal and stone. In answering the question 'how was that artifact made?' the archaeologist can go a long way, by comparing tell-tale marks on objects with those studied experimentally and ethnographically. But if the archaeologist wishes to ask more ambitious questions about why the artifact was made in that way he/she may turn to cross-cultural statements about the relationships between the organisation of production and other socio-cultural variables. However, most such generalisations to date have had little success and little explanatory power because they were insufficiently interested in why a particular relationship was found. Ethnoarchaeological studies need to examine more carefully the total cultural context and the values given to production within that context if they are to provide adequate analogies for the past.

5 Subsistence strategies

In the preceding chapter one type of production about which the archaeologist may be able to provide most information and which has traditionally been seen as being most important was not examined; that is the production of food. In this chapter I will scratch the surface of the massive amount of ethnoarchaeological and anthropological information on how people get their food. Perhaps the major service done to archaeology by anthropological accounts of subsistence strategies, especially hunting and gathering, has been to make archaeologists aware that many of their basic assumptions about non-western economies were false.

Hunters and gatherers

There now exists much information available to archaeologists concerning societies which live only by hunting and gathering in various parts of the world (for a recent review see Smiley *et al* 1980). To take one example, more or less at random, de Montmollin (1980) examines nineteenth-century ethnographic data on the Point Barrow Eskimo, Alaska. He shows that the various subsistence activities of these Eskimo at different times of the year (such as whaling, sealing, polar-bear hunting) would leave distinctive archaeological residues but with different degrees of archaeological visibility. Settlement systems, site size and so on are discussed as being 'fingerprints' of this particular way of life. While there is little attempt here at generalisation, such studies do have the value of throwing doubt on assumptions about the simplicity of 'band level' societies such as hunters and gatherers in limiting environments like North Alaska. Barrow society had an elaborate storage and transportation technology, social complexity, economic exchange with other societies and relative nucleation and sedentariness.

These complex aspects of what were assumed to be simple societies are in fact characteristic of many hunting and gathering societies, and they will be examined in some detail below. Examples such as the Barrow Eskimo may furnish the archaeologist with more realistic models. But there is a danger that the archaeologist uses such evidence to build a limited and somewhat romantic view of an 'aboriginal' way of life. In changing one set of assumptions for another the archaeologist may be no nearer, because of inadequate care in the analysis of ethnographic data, an understanding of Pleistocene hunters and gatherers. This will become clearer if we consider some of the generalisations which have recently been based on ethnographic data.

In 1968 a book appeared which had a great impact in archaeological studies of hunter-gatherers. It did what studies such as that of the Barrow Eskimos have continued to do. It upturned prevalent archaeological assumptions about the poverty of a hunting and gathering subsistence. The book was Lee and de Vore's *Man the Hunter*. In his own article in this edited volume Lee was able to challenge two accepted views of hunter-gatherers, largely as a result of his own work amongst the !Kung Bushmen of the Kalahari, Botswana: (a) hunter-gatherers are primarily dependent on the hunting of game animals; (b) the hunter-gatherer way of life is arduous and precarious.

As far as the first viewpoint is concerned, many hunter-gatherer societies are largely dependent on gathered resources. Amongst the !Kung vegetable foods comprise 60–80 per cent of the total diet by weight. The gathered food is more reliable because it is abundant, sedentary and predictable, but hunted food is preferred. Fifty-eight hunter-gatherer societies were drawn from Murdock's *Ethnographic Atlas*. Only one sixth of these societies emphasised the less reliable source - hunting. But the relative frequency of gathering societies is not uniform across the world. It decreases with distance away from the tropics. This effect occurs because the abundance and variety of edible plants decrease away from the equator. (For a critical discussion of this viewpoint see Hawker *et al.* 1982.)

The second viewpoint is denied by the fact that for most of the year food is locally abundant and easily collected by the !Kung. It is easy to understand why the !Kung do not wish to change their subsistence to arable farming. For them a diet based on mongongo nuts is more reliable than one based on cultivated foods. In one camp Lee found that adults worked only 12–19 hours a week obtaining food, but that this work provided an adequate diet. Woodburn, in the same book, noted that the Hadza hunter-gatherers probably spend less energy and time obtaining their subsistence than do neighbouring agricultural tribes and that much of adult male life is spent, for example, gambling.

These notions concerning the overall ease of hunter-gatherer subsistence have been further developed by Sahlins (1972) and many others, but it is another aspect of the rich and provocative !Kung and Hadza data that leads the discussion on. We have seen that ethnographic work suggests that certain resources are emphasised in particular environments because they are secure, stable, easy to collect and so on. From such information we might be able to build analogue models which will predict where settlements ought to be located to maximise the use of the resources in a reconstructed prehistoric environment. Such an approach has been followed by Jochim (1976) who collects ethnographic data to show that plants and fish are generally seen as more secure, low-risk resources while hunting is a high-risk resource with low return. Also, hunter-gatherers prefer food that is easy to collect, tastey and varied. However, hunting is frequently seen as having higher prestige.

From the ethnographic data Jochim suggests that the attributes of resources which are most often taken into consideration by hunter-gatherers are: weight, density, aggregation size, mobility, fat content, and non-food yields. These aspects can be assessed for any animal, fish or plant species and be used to provide a combined 'score' for each resource – the most productive, easiest to obtain, etc. resource having the 'best' score. Jochim shows that this method can predict proportions of animals hunted, and the location of settlements in an application to ethnographic data from the Ojibwa. Similarly, Hawker *et al.* (1982) show that the Aché of Paraguay follow the cost/benefit considerations of optimal foraging theory.

Such work, involves grappling with a series of difficult assumptions. For example, it is assumed that use of the environment is maximised for least effort and that different societies rate different aspects of resources in similar ways. Maximisation is a common assumption in archaeological work on subsistence strategies, but it needs to be measured by independent means. In his work on the Nunamiut Eskimos, Binford (1978) has shown how archaeologists could identify whether groups in the past had maximised their use of meat resources from a study of animal bones. It could be said that site catchment analysis (see below), when used to compare on-site evidence of how the environment was used with evidence for the potential resources in that environment, provides a measure of maximisation. But, however valuable the detail of Binford's and the site catchment work, no insight is provided into the contexts within which maximisation might be found. Since Binford in his book called 'Nunamiut ethnoarchaeology' does not provide information on the Nunamiut as a whole, it is difficult to assess why they might maximise their use of resources and which sections of society received most benefit. Again, the social and cultural context needs to be examined.

Notions of maximisation and optimisation can be examined in another aspect of subsistence strategies, human and settlement mobility, by a return to Botswana Bushmen. While archaeologists often discuss mobility as if it were a unitary phenomenon, ethno-graphically individuals within the same society move around for different purposes, for varying lengths of time and in different combinations. Ebert (1979) suggests, as a result of work amongst the Bushmen, that links can be made between mobility and stone tool assemblages which would allow the amount and nature of mobility to be assessed. For example, it is hypothesised that tools manufactured to be carried about are smaller than those used in one place. Also, tools intended for multiple episodes of use are expected to be the result of greater input of energy during manufacture and maintenance than tools only used once. This hypothesis is clearly fraught with western assumptions of efficiency, energy saving and optimisation. Tools and the economy are seen as being subject to criteria of effort minimisation. While this may be true in some societies, other cultural values may be present. In any case, we need to know why maximisation and minimisation should be present in these spheres, and we need to examine whether particular strategies are 'optimal' for all sections of society (male, female, old, young etc.).

In the ethnoarchaeological work described so far, there has been little concern with placing subsistence strategies in a wider social and cultural framework and there has been a repeated danger of imposing western assumptions despite the insights offered by the *Man the Hunter* and later volumes (Lee and de Vore 1976). Ethnographic work on hunter-gatherer subsistence in relation to territorality (Campbell 1968), settlement pattern (Peterson 1968; 1971) and more generally (Yellen 1977; Schire 1972; Harpending 1977; Williams 1974) is impressive, but rarely has the place of hunter-gatherers, in a wider context, been adequately assessed (Wobst 1978). For example, to what extent are maximisation, low workloads and mobility affected today by the position of hunter-gatherers on the edges of, and incorporated within, very different societies? We tend to assume that the minutely studied !Kung are in some sense 'original', comparable to Pleistocene hunter-gatherers. Are they?

Wilmsen (1979; 1980) has provided ethnographic and historical documentation of long-established close contact between Herero pastoralists and Bushmen hunter-gatherers (Zu/oasi), and between these groups and Europeans. In all areas, Herero and Zu/oasi have interacted, both cooperatively and competitively, since approximately AD 1000. Herding and foraging go on side by side. There is multi-tiered ownership of places and things in the form of use rights and mutual obligations rather than incontestable control. Space associated with one social group is layered upon that of others, thereby reducing the need to partition land into exclusive parcels. All previous workers have looked at the subject Bushman group in isolation, adopting a parochial stance, viewing the patterns of movement from particular waterholes. Wilmsen has shown that, on the contrary, the Bushmen are part of a wider system.

Bushmen hunter-gatherers are by no means unique in this respect. Around the edges of pastoralists and agriculturalists in parts of Kenya are groups called Okiek or Dorobo, and I have published (1982) an ethnoarchaeological study of one of these hunter-gatherer units. In fact these Dorobo turned out not to be Dorobo; also they were neither hunters nor gatherers. They largely consisted of refugee Maasai pastoralists who had, for varied reasons, lost their cattle and had become Dorobo hunter-gatherers whilst building up new herds, meanwhile escaping persecution. To be a hunter-gatherer in this context thus often involves a 'temporary' (sometimes lasting several generations) change of lifestyle in the hills and woodlands collecting honey and hunting, whilst being involved in a close relationship with adjacent pastoralists and agriculturalists.

To what extent one could use any ethnographic data from such societies to interpret Pleistocene hunters and gatherers is questionable. However, the problem is only an example of an aspect of all use of analogy from the present to the past. As was suggested in Chapter 1, analogies should never be transported wholesale. Similarities *and* differences should be assessed. Then, in determining whether the similarities allow the analogy to be applied we refer to an understanding of the cultural links between the different aspects of the model. Are the similarities observed relevant to, because linked with, the unknowns which are being interpreted? Also, can the differences be accounted for? For all this we need to know why a particular ethnographic society works in the way it does and this is where the existing studies have been lacking. In examining hunting and gathering subsistence, the wider context has been avoided. There has been a romantic desire to see the Bushmen and other modern hunter-gatherers as representative in some way of the Pleistocene. But we need to place them in their modern context. It is only when we have done that, and assessed how their subsistence strategies are linked into a wider world arena; also when we have understood why the subsistence works in the way it does, that we can assess the similarities and differences between Bushmen and Palaeolithic societies and evaluate the relevance of the analogy. We will be able to reconstruct a different past when we understand modern hunter-gatherers in their own particular and peculiar context.

While there have been few attempts to situate modern hunter-gatherers in a wider context, divisions of hunter-gatherers into different types, each with its own isolated economic and social context, have been discussed. While my description is here overlapping with the account of bands and tribes in Chapter 6, it is important to note that subsistence itself has often been seen as the basis on which other aspects of society might be built. We can follow the development of subsistence-based models for hunter-gatherers by leaving the Kalahari and turning to the other favoured hunting ground for ethnographic analogies, namely Australia. Here, a particular group, the Wikmunkan of Cape York Peninsula have been the subject of several studies.

An early analysis was of the 'spoiler' sort (Yellen 1977). Thomson (1939) aimed to demonstrate, by a judicious choice of ethnographic data, the limitations of the archaeological record. His point was that, if one looked at a nomadic hunting group such as the Wikmunkan in different seasons of the year, it might appear as different groups because the seasonal adaptations differ so greatly. In some parts of the year a people may spend their time as nomadic hunters, in pursuit of bush game, wild honey, small mammals and vegetable foods. A few

27 Typical camps and house types, each related to seasonal life and occupation, among the Wikmunkan tribe, Australia (Thomson 1939). **1** Sleeping platform used immediately after the rains. **2** Large wet season house. **2a** The same; bark removed to show structure of

framework. **3** Wet season shelter. **4** Wet season communal
house. **5** A modification of type 4. **6** Breakwind used in camps on
exposed beaches and sandbanks. **7** Fork for hanging food and artifacts,
either erected alone or with the breakwind. **8** Shade used in hot weather

months later the same people may be found established on the sea coast in camps that appear permanent or semi-permanent, having apparently abandoned their nomadic habits. In each part of the year different house types are built (*fig. 27*). This type of negative tale convinced many archaeologists that any attempt to reconstruct or consider cultures was fruitless. If the Wikmunkan could produce different cultures at different times of the year, the archaeologist should concentrate only on subsistence adaptations.

Rather than take a negative tone, Thomson could have asked why there is so much variation in this case and moved towards a positive statement of value to archaeologists. An attempt at explanation is made more recently by Wills (1980), who notes that the Wikmunkan inhabit an environment characterised by the alternations of wet and dry seasons, corresponding to NW and SE monsoons. Like many hunter-gatherers the social structure and subsistence strategy are extremely flexible in the face of this variation and in the face of longer-term climatic fluctuations. In each part of the year (see *fig. 28*) different parts of the environment are used, resulting in a confused palimpsest (*fig. 28e*) of settlement which the archaeologist would have pains to make out in detail. Certainly reconstruction would be difficult if just one site was examined, but if the region was studied as a whole the variable and complex palimpsest would be noted and could be interpreted as a flexible adaptation to the particular environment. (For a similar regional model see Foley 1981.)

The Wikmunkan can be used as an example of a more general model about the use of the environment, derived from Eskimo and other ethnographic data. Binford (1980) divides hunter-gatherers into two broad categories – Foragers and Collectors. A Forager system is characterised by 'high residential mobility, low-bulk inputs and regular daily food procurement strategies' (ibid, p. 9). Foragers are more sensitive to local resource availability and they do not store food. In the settlement system there are two types of site – the residential base where most activities take place, and the 'location' where only extractive tasks are carried out. This adaptation is in response to variability within the environment and it is parallel to Gould's (1977) 'opportunistic strategy'. A Collector system, on the other hand, is characterised by what Binford calls 'logistic organisation' in which subsistence strategies are organised to procure specific resources in specific contexts. Such systems have a wider range of site types with specific functions and there may also be food storage. When food resources are limited to dispersed patches, both Foragers and Collectors may find themselves tied to specific geographical locations.

The Wikmunkan actually follow a mixture of the two strategies. During the wet season and late dry season they occupy semi-permanent base camps from which task groups go out each day collecting and hunting, in the Collector category. In contrast, in most of the dry season the Wikmunkan are in the Forager category. They do not conform to one type, but result from a flexible strategy in a particular environmental context. Binford allows for such 'mixed' categories in his typological scheme, but his explanation for the occurrence of different types is weakly developed beyond a reference to the physical environment. Binford correlates the Forager and Collector strategies with aspects of the environment such as its richness, variability and security, and he claims to have identified explanatory, causal processes. But the validity of these causal relationships must be doubted since they are narrowly subsistence orientated. In his article, Binford pours scorn on social and cultural factors. But many characteristics of Wikmunkan culture, for example, are not linked immediately to or 'caused by' subsistence. For example, Wills notes that the Wikmunkan, like other Australian aboriginal groups, often form aggregations for strictly social purposes such as marriages and initiations. These aggregations were only possible where there was local resource abundance, but they did not occur because of those abundances. Needham (1962) sees the internal arrangement of every Wikmunkan camp as a symbolic representation of the social organisation. More generally, it should be recognised that the whole adaptation may have social and ideological causes or constraints and that the archaeological patterning may not simply be the result of ecological adaptation. At least we must examine social and cultural factors before we can validly claim that they are irrelevant to adaptive behaviour.

Rather than concentrating on the immediately visible technical aspects of obtaining food, as in Binford's classification, we can attempt to identify underlying implications of the different systems and move towards a fuller explanatory processual model. Understanding the underlying processes will lead to a placing of subsistence within a wider social context, and will involve a search for causes beyond the visible data which is the hallmark of scientific procedure. Instead of distinguishing between hunter-gatherers in terms of food procurement systems, Woodburn (1980) has examined the underlying nature of those systems. In particular, do they involve a delay between the input of labour and the return for that labour, or is there immediate return?

Woodburn's immediate-return system, similar to Binford's Forager strategy, is seen as being characterised by the !Kung of Botswana and the Hadza of Tanzania. The societies are highly flexible and individuals do not have long-term commitments to each other. Food is acquired with tools in which there is minimal investment, and is immediately shared. It is obtained fairly easily without much co-operation or competition over resources. The giving of food does not lead to long-term obligations and status. Territories are not major constraints on individual movement, and there is little concern with ancestors and the past or with future planning. Delayed-return

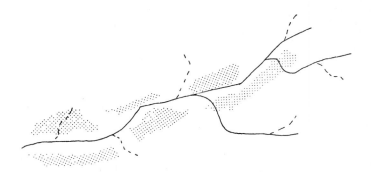

a

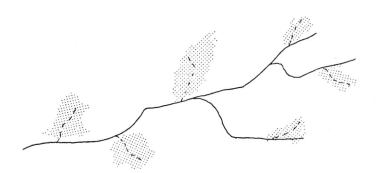

b

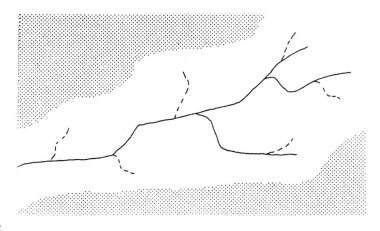

c

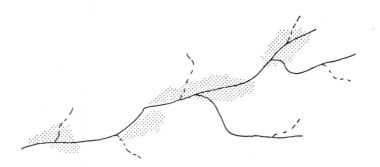

d

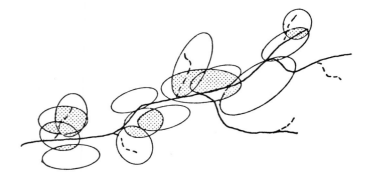

e

28 Wikmunkan postulated seasonal use of the environment (Wills 1980). **a** Wet season camps. **b** Early dry season camps.
c Mid dry season camps. **d** Late dry season camps.
e Schematic representation of spatial overlap in Wikmunkan season camp locations, based on **a** to **d**

systems, similar to Binford's Collector strategy, include sedentary or semi-sedentary hunter-gatherers with storage and property accumulation, and fishermen who invest in boats, dams, large fish traps, etc. As with farmers, the system of production involves intrinsic delay, and so institutions are needed to hold the group together and to organise the distribution of products. The ancestors and the past are important ideologies in these respects.

It should be mentioned that Woodburn's distinction is very similar to that made by Meillassoux (1973), although Meillassoux equates the difference with that between hunter-gatherers and farmers. Woodburn, on the other hand, allows for both hunter-gatherers and farmers in the category of delayed-return system. Woodburn's work does involve classification, but because it seeks to identify aspects of societies at a deeper level than Binford's, it has much greater explanatory power. The immediate and delayed return systems can be used analogically with great effect in archaeology. They allow a wide range of different aspects of the evidence, from subsistence to society and ideology to be linked into the one model. But there is a danger that Woodburn's work be used to produce a highly deterministic and behavioural hypothesis. With knowledge of the technology, economy and environment, the whole society can be built. Subsistence could be taken as determining all other aspects of life. But we need to consider the contrary hypothesis that, for example, a delayed-return subsistence system could have a social basis, allowing for forms of social control through the redistribution of products. There may also be cultural values which must be integrated into a processual explanation.

In general there seem to be few ethnoarchaeological and anthropological studies which place the subsistence strategies of hunter-gatherers in an adequate context. The archaeologist must search hard for data which can be used to build sound relational analogies. Work such as that by Wilmsen and Woodburn has begun to show the way and some insight into the types of study which might be undertaken will be provided in an account of a mixed hunting and farming society at the end of this chapter. For the moment, other types of subsistence strategy will be examined, although, as Woodburn's study implies, the divisions between hunter-gatherer, pastoralist and agriculturalist are somewhat arbitrary and others may have more explanatory interest.

Pastoralists

Despite all the published anthropological studies of pastoralists (for example, Barth 1956; Gellner 1973; Dyson-Hudson 1972; Johnson 1969; Bates 1973; Ingold 1980; Hole 1978; 1979), archaeologists have remained fuzzy about the nature of this subsistence strategy and its archaeological reference. This is partly because most modern pastoralists are closely linked to farming groups and it is unclear how far independent pastoralist systems might have been viable in the past. But it is also because the studies which have been published have frequently paid little attention to archaeological indicators. So I wish here to concentrate on two studies which have examined what pastoralists might look like 'in the ground'.

Audouze and Jarrige (1980) compare sedentary agriculturalists and three nomadic ethnic groups in the Kachi plain, Baluchistan. Good quantitative detail is often provided for the similarities and differences in house types, their frequency, construction and placing within settlements and their length of use. Relationships of settlements to soils are also examined, as is the question of whether house differentiation relates to wealth differences in sedentary and nomadic settlements. It was found to be easier to identify hierarchy in the sedentary villages. Other points, concerning lack of pottery amongst nomadic groups and the general paucity of durable material culture, have been made by, for example, Robbins (1973) (see above, p. 56).

Indeed, it is generally accepted that nomads and herders are difficult to find archaeologically, but Hole (1980) wished to assess whether, in his particular study area of Khuzistan and the Zagros Mts, there would be any way of identifying them, and by what characteristics. Modern nomads in the area were examined with the assumption made that even if social and technological aspects of herding had changed between the seventh millenium BC and the present, the basic characteristics of the environment (climate, seasonality, topography, needs of animals) would have remained the same. Modern transhumant pastoralists in the area are probably more specialised than prehistoric counterparts, but Hole suggests the following archaeological indicators.

Table 1   *Transhumant pastoralists*

Characteristic	*Archaeological indicator*
1 Seasonal pattern of movement from pasture to pasture with herds	Sites located near seasonal pastures and routes of migration rather than near arable land or water
2 Tendency to follow the same annual pattern	Sites should show repetitive occupation at the same season
3 A style of dwelling that can be discarded or carried	Impermanent shelters or tents and discontinuous occupation

(continued overleaf)

4 Subsistence based on meat and milk from wild/domestic stock, wild or domestic cereals, acorns, or other storable plant food	Faunal remains with high percentages of the predominant domesticates (sheep/goats) and perhaps some wild. Tools for processing plants (mortars, pestles, sickles) may be present. Storage facilities and ovens
5 Social organisation which allows for changing composition of co-operative work groups and for corporate or individual ownership of herds	Sites should show evidence of groups of shelters or tents. 4–6 family shelters arranged formally or informally but the distance between shelters is unlikely to exceed 10 metres
6 A sense of territory with resources held in common	Difficult to identify territories except in subtle differences in the physical arrangement of the tribal groups
7 A systematic effort to increase the number of livestock by means other than improvement of territory	Few improvements (terraces, dams, etc.) in territories around sites though there may be corrals and other facilities

Of particular interest to archaeology more generally is that the term pastoralism is often used to mean groups without farming, yet in Hole's case there are many aspects of an agricultural way of life. There are even pots, despite their fragility. So the definition of pastoralist needs to be extended. Many of the so-called pastoralist groups in East Africa also farm, hunt and fish, in varying and ever-changing combinations (Hivernel 1978). The distinctive characteristics of Hole's pastoralists are their mobility and repetitive transhumant cycles. But it is in these respects that the present may differ from the past. The modern specialisation of transhumant groups in Baluchistan, as much as in the Mediterranean, may not have extended back prior to the development of a market economy and production for sale. Although certain aspects of a transhumant mode of life may well have existed in the remote past, it may have taken a more partial and less distinctive form.

It follows, then, that we should not expect any absolute list of archaeological indicators of pastoralism. Hole's account is of great value in that it provides a set of characteristics to look for, but we need not expect any complete 'fit'.

Agriculturalists

It also follows that the definition of an agricultural as opposed to pastoral way of life may be difficult. However, it is more my concern here to examine ways of identifying the nature of the farming strategy itself rather than to provide overall categories and definitions.

For example, an early use of ethnographic analogy to interpret farming techniques concerned the spread of farming into central Europe, associated with a cultural group termed Linearbandkeramik (LBK). By 1950, Childe (p. 97) had used ethnographic data to support the notion that the LBK was produced by shifting short-term settlement. People at a site used up the land around it and then moved on. Childe talked about 'their crude agricultural technique, one still illustrated by some hoe-cultivators in Africa today'. Grahame Clark (1952, p. 92) compared the spread of Neolithic farmers to the pioneers of Ontario or New England and to recent historical periods in Scandinavia. This information, together with pollen evidence showing phases of burning and clearance, were said (p. 95) to indicate 'extensive, shifting agriculture of Neolithic times' on the loess soils of Europe. The ethnographic data also provided Clark, and more recently Steensberg (1980), using New Guinea data, with the details of when in the seasonal cycle trees were cut and burnt, of whether stumps were left in the field, and of the need to leave the forest to regenerate.

Many of the analogies for shifting agriculture come from areas where soils are thin and acidic and deteriorate quickly, such as tropical Africa or parts of Scandinavia. Recent work on the European Neolithic has pointed to the extreme richness of the loess soils on which the LBK spread. New archaeological data suggest long-term occupation on single sites with highly developed regional farming economies. It seems that analogies had been used which were inappropriate simply because the environmental contexts in the past and present were different.

It is also necessary to locate the adoption and spread of farming in a social context and analogies have been described (e.g. Meillassoux 1973 – see above) and ideas applied (e.g. Bender 1978). More generally it can be claimed that who eats what, where, when and how, and who produces, are all social phenomena. There have been many attempts to link subsistence and social characteristics into overall models, and some of these will be described in the chapter on social organisation which follows. As with the models for hunter-gatherer society, many of these generalisations give a primacy to the subsistence base. For example, the need to irrigate is seen as leading to greater complexity in social organisation. Differences in the form of state societies can be related to differences in whether hoe or plough agriculture predominates (Goody 1971).

Despite, for example, Boserup's (1975) overturning of the food-population link, locating the prime generative processes in population increase rather than in subsistence innovation, archaeologists have often continued to prefer social models which have subsistence as their base. For instance, Sherratt (1981, p. 297) uses ethnographic data to suggest that in simple hoe agriculture the major subsistence contribution comes from the female in sowing, weeding and harvesting, and there are suggestions of a world-wide association between simple hoe-based agricultural economies and matrilineal inheritance. Plough agriculture and pastoralism, on the other hand, are seen as being associated with male dominance in subsistence, virilocal residence and patrilineal descent. In a world sample, two-thirds of plough agriculturalists and two-thirds of pastoralists have purely patrilineal inheritance. In societies with shifting cultivation, most agricultural work except clearing and breaking of the ground is done by women (Friedl 1975). The production of hand-made pottery and the making of grinding stones are also female tasks (Haaland 1981; Murdock and Provost 1973). Fishing, except for the collection of molluscs, is done by men, as is herding and the production of flaked lithic tools. In hunter-gatherer societies, women gather plants and men hunt.

The difficulties with these types of cross-cultural generalisation have been discussed above (p. 85). Here again there is often little understanding of why the links occur, and in what contexts. In particular, we are left to wonder whether hoeing leads to female labour and then to matrilineal inheritance, or the other way round! Nevertheless, returning to the problem of the spread or adoption of agriculture, it may be possible to see the process not simply or primarily as the spread of an economy, but also as a set of changes in the social relations between men and women. 'The Neolithic revolution would thus most probably be a revolution brought about through the activities of women' (Haaland 1981) and in which an increased female importance in subsistence production could have led to a greater potential for female participation in the social sphere.

The same need to consider social strategies is perhaps more elegantly shown by a consideration of one of the most important techniques for reconstructing farming economies; site-catchment analysis (Vita-Finzi and Higgs 1970). The technique is also applicable to hunter-gatherers and here the Lee and de Vore volume in 1968 again provided the relevant analogy. Based on the !Kung data, the area habitually used for resources by hunter-gatherers was set at a circle with a radius of two hours walking distance around the site. The range for agriculturalists came from Chisholm's (1962) work on modern farmers in South Italy, and was set at one hour's walking distance from the site.

A greater amount of ethnographic data on the site territories of hunter-gatherers, and of a new category, swidden cultivators, has been collated by Bakels (1978) (see table 2). Bakels also asks some additional questions about the relationship between the size of site territory and the walking distances. Clearly what the site territory looks like on the ground will depend on whether travel is by foot, cart, boat, etc. In providing such information Bakels is providing one aspect of context that Vita-Finzi and Higgs did not concern themselves with.

Table 2 The size of the area, which is visited daily from a settlement: some data from the literature on hunters/gatherers and swidden cultivators* (Bakels 1978)

HUMAN GROUP	TYPE OF ECONOMY	RADIUS OF ACTION OR 'TERRITORY'	WAY OF TRAVELLING
Anbara Australia	hunters/ gatherers	50km²	on foot
Australian aborigines	hunters/ gatherers	10–13km	on foot
Women from Arnhemland Australia	gatherers	6–8km	on foot
Pitjandara women Australia	gatherers	5km	on foot
Kung Bushmen Botswana	hunters/ gatherers	10km	on foot
G/wi Bushmen			
men	hunters	24km	on foot
women Botswana	gatherers	8km	
Hadza women Tanzania	gatherers	hour's walk	on foot
Birhors India	hunters/ gatherers	4–8km	on foot
Copper Eskimo Canada	hunters	8km	on foot
Memba Zambia	swidden cultivators	for cultivation a few km for fishing up to 16km for visiting up to 25km	on foot
Yako Nigeria	swidden cultivators	120km²	on foot
Kapauka New Guinea	swidden cultivators	45min = 1.8km	on foot
Tsembaga New Guinea	swidden cultivators	orthographically 8.2km² to gardens: 20min walk down hill and 30min walk up slope	on foot
Iban Borneo	swidden cultivators	up to 1.5km slightly further than 1.5km	on foot by boat

(continued overleaf)

SUBSISTENCE STRATEGIES

HUMAN GROUP	TYPE OF ECONOMY	RADIUS OF ACTION OR 'TERRITORY'	WAY OF TRAVELLING
Hanunoo Philippines	swidden cultivators	6km² one hour's walk to garden = 1km with heavy load 2 hours' walk for a coil of rattan	on foot
Lamet Indochina	swidden cultivators	2.48km walking speed 3km/h	on foot
Maroni River Carib women Surinam	swidden cultivators	45 min 2 hours or more	on foot by boat
Kuikuru Brazil	swidden cultivators	6–8km	on foot
Average Amazonian cultivators Brazil	swidden cultivators	5km	on foot

*In a large number of cases the radius of action is given in real distances and not in hours' walking distance. For a correct judgement of the data, the passableness of the terrain should be mentioned. It was impossible, however, to compare the geographical descriptions from the literature studied. It is assumed that in one hour's walking distance, a distance of 5km or less is covered.

Evidence from Africa (Jackson 1972) indicates another contextual aspect that needs to be taken into account. In areas where soils are easily over-used and eroded, the zones nearest a settlement may be the least used, not the most used as predicted by site catchment analysis. This is because the nearby soils are quickly eroded. The degree to which such a pattern occurs may also depend on the extent to which the subsistence strategy is linked into a wider cash economy. This is a general problem with much of the ethnographic data used by site catchment analysts. In particular, the recent farmers of S. Italy, on whose unknowing activities so much prehistory has been based, are keyed into a market economy which is a wholly inappropriate context for, for example, prehistoric Europe.

However, there is more than one type of farmer in S. Italy. As well as those producing for the market, there are also those farming only for subsistence. Ammerman (pers. comm.) has examined the land use patterns of these two groups. How any parcel of land in S. Italy is used depends on who owns it, the size, history and social position of the family, and whether production is for the market or for subsistence. What is grown on a particular piece of land does not depend on soil type. For example, areas of dune sand are used for arable farming by subsistence farmers, but this land is not classified as arable by the market producers. The main point here is that classification of land depends on the social context. In site catchment analysis, on the other hand, no reference is made to this social aspect. Soils are classified as arable or not arable, and from the percentages of each soil type in the site territory or catchment, the economy of the site is discussed. Ammerman's ethnographic observations highlight the enormous dangers of such procedures. We might, *a priori*, say that a catchment area with much dune sand was largely non-arable. But, without considering the social and wider economic context, we might be entirely wrong. The dune sands and other 'poor' soils may well have been used as arable. The models provided for site catchment analysis need to be broadened and the implicit assumptions concerning maximisation of production assessed.

Bones and seeds

In considering site-catchment analysis, the account has already moved away from a consideration of categories such as hunter-gatherer, pastoralist, agriculturalist, to a review of some of the models which have been applied to all forms of subsistence strategy. Since two of the types of archaeological data which have been most frequently used to reconstruct past economies are bones and seeds, I will concentrate on these here. There are also many parallels between the analogies used in reference to both types of information. Both allow analogies to be partly based on universal processes occurring in the natural world, but both also commonly provide an important arena for the play of human symbolic behaviour.

In reconstructing past relationships between man and animals, analogical references can be made to the changes that occur in animal bones at different ages, such as fusion of epiphyses, or in different conditions. For example, modern and medieval data on tooth-eruption stages can be used to infer the ages of cattle and sheep mandibles in archaeological deposits (Halstead 1982). These sequences may have changed slightly since prehistoric times, but the archaeologists can be relatively confident of their modern gauge. It is possible to assess in similar ways whether parts of carcasses were utilised to maximise the meat or bone-marrow resources of animals (Binford 1978).

But beyond these observations the archaeologist may wish to consider why a particular pattern of animal and bone use is found on a site. Here, partly because bone reports have traditionally been separated off from the main text of site reports, scarcely integrated into the overall interpretation, bones have been seen as subject to a scientific 'culture-free' area of analysis left to specialists. In addition, accounts of herd management and carcass usage have been couched largely in terms of resource control, although Yellen (1977) and Gifford (1977) have emphasised that the distribution of parts of carcasses may be socially controlled. But neither in the link between bone residues and stock management nor in the explanation of that management itself, has the cultural and symbolic sphere been examined. This is remarkable, given the almost universal ethnographic observation, including western contemporary society, that animals and parts of animals are as good to think as they are to eat. The organisation of the animal world and the parts of carcasses offer a wealth of natural patterning than can be used as hooks on which to hang the logic of the cultural and social world of man. It has already been suggested in Chapter 3 that, amongst the Nuba, the pig/cattle dichotomy reflected that between women and men and would have influenced the formation of the archaeological record. All use of animals, however maximising, is infused with cultural meaning, and the bone residues are as much indicators of that context as they are of herd control; indeed the two aspects are inseparable. The symbolic dimension of animal slaughter and carcass treatment is described by Deetz (1977) for eighteenth century America, and an ethnographic example will be referred to below.

In regard to archaeological assemblages of seeds, ethnography can contribute both (A) to the non-cultural processes which in the processing of grain lead to particular residues, and (B) to the cultural factors by which these processes are organised and their residues converted into archaeological samples. For the 'A' category, work by Halstead and Jones (pers. comm.) on the island of Carpathos in the Aegean has examined the formation of seed residues in a context where the inhabitants still reap with sickles and thresh with animals or flails. Many of the deposits are heavily affected by non-cultural, mechanical processes. For example, one could suggest what particles and weeds might fall to the ground during winnowing if the seed densities and wind velocity were known; knowledge of the size of sieves would lead to understanding of why only certain sizes of seeds were found in residues. The ethnography can push the archaeologist to think more carefully about some of these processes. For example, it had been supposed that many weed seeds would be blown away during winnowing. The ethnography showed, however, that the spikelet bases were retained and were not blown away, and small weed seeds were not removed because they stayed in 'heads' or bunches rather than being broken up to be lost individually.

For the 'B' category of processes, it is probable that the extent to which different stages and types of plant processing are separated relates primarily to overall cultural concerns with eating and the entry of food into the body. In the Nuba case, in which there is considerable symbolic emphasis on categorising separately different stages of food preparation, the flour is piled in a separate area surrounded in 'purifying' decoration. More generally, as with animals, the plant world is a universal source of oppositions and patterns to be given symbolic meaning. In the particular case these will be used within a historical context as part of social ends, but the archaeologist cannot assume that his seeds are culture-free.

Messer (1979) has examined the use of wild plants and weeds by present-day Zapoteck Indian cultivators in the Valley of Oaxaca in the southern highlands of Mexico. For example, information on which parts of plants are considered 'edible' by the Indians helps to explain why such plant parts occur on archaeological sites. This work is partly aimed at providing information of relevance to archaeologists working in the same area. There is a need to extend such studies to the broader questions of why particular plants were preferred, their historical and cultural meaning, and why they were used in a particular way.

It might be objected that, since archaeologists can never hope to recover the symbolic significance of bone and plant use, they should concentrate on subsistence information such as compositions of herds or crops, and their adaptive advantages. In my view refuge in this objection makes explanation of the past little more than a tautologous descriptive account. The objection is possible because of a viewpoint that the cultural and the functional can be separated and discussed in isolation. In reality it is not possible adequately to examine bones and seed assemblages without considering the cultural factors affecting the formation of the residues. Equally, it is not possible to explain subsistence patterns without reference to the cultural context. Archaeologists through ehnography, must grapple with the cultural and symbolic in their 'economic' data, however difficult this might be.

One aspect of bone and seed symbolism which is relatively easy to distinguish is the degree of categorisation involved in the practice of processing resources. Are the parts of the carcass butchered in a repetitive, organised way? Are seeds and weeds kept separate? Are bones from different stages in the butchering and food preparation sequence kept separate? In general, what is the degree of order and opposition? Where there is much organisation, what other contextual information exists, such as the occurrence of particular bones and seeds in graves of particular age and sex groups, or in particular parts of settlements? The Gypsy example in Chapter 3 shows how such cultural concern with food preparation and separation may be used within social strategies to give meaning. With the aid of wider studies of this sort, the archaeologist may be able to approach a fuller understanding of bone and seed data.

Conclusion

Subsistence strategies have been a major concern of archaeologists searching ethnographic data for analogies. But throughout there has been a tendency to pick on particular modern societies. The !Kung Bushmen and the S. Italian farmers spring to mind. Detailed studies of particular cultural groups have been emphasised as important throughout this book, in order to understand the total cultural context. But the social groups which have been subjected to most ethnoarchaeology, have been so because they were convenient to study, because relevant anthropological studies already existed, because few other comparable societies could be found, or because of some romantic view that the groups were in some sense 'less spoilt' by modern contacts. They were not studied intensively by ethnoarchaeologists in order to understand the subsistence strategies in a total context. Indeed the most valuable studies for examining the 'whys' of subsistence strategies are ambitious cross-cultural discussions by, for example, Woodburn.

Some insight into how contextual studies including subsistence strategies might be carried out is provided by Hugh-Jones' (1979) account of Pirá-paraná Indians in South America. Her study area included sections of widely dispersed and non-corporate (i.e. unbounded) groups which are exogamous, patrilineal and patrilocal. The whole of Pirá-paraná culture is informed with a dichotomy between continuity through descent in the male line, and the breaking of that continuity by the bringing in of outside women to procreate. This dichotomy is patterned through time. For example, children are associated with the family unit which includes external women, but initiation transfers growing boys into a unified society of descent group youths. After men are married and have children they are fathers of families again. The opposition between descent and marriage relations is thus a cyclical process. It can also be seen spatially in the house (*fig. 29*). Childhood is spent in the family in the peripheral spatial compartments, initiated youths sleep in the central communal part of the house, and married men with children return to the peripheral compartments.

The plant foods of the Pirá-paraná are linked into these same opposititions, and Hugh-Jones gives a detailed account of how the various processing activities are symbolically meaningful and linked into the major social dichotomy described above. For example, male is associated with cocoa and tobacco, and female with cassava and pepper. When an abandoned and burnt house is planted, it is planted with pepper in the compartments around the side and at the women's end, and tobacco in the centre and at the male end. Similarly, the 'mundane' world of animal foods is the basis of a highly complex symbolism. Male is associated with unreliable food sources such as hunting for meat, whereas female is associated with manioc. Male relates to wild food and female to cultivated food. The processes of killing, washing, butchering, cooking and eating meat are described as metaphors for the obtaining of foreign women in marriage and raiding, for the husband's control of the wife's reproductive power, pregnancy, birth and socialisation.

HOUSE

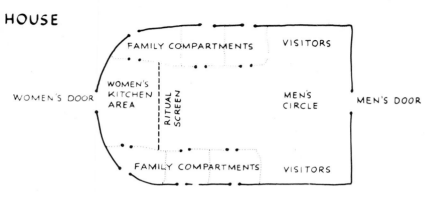

HOUSE AS BODY

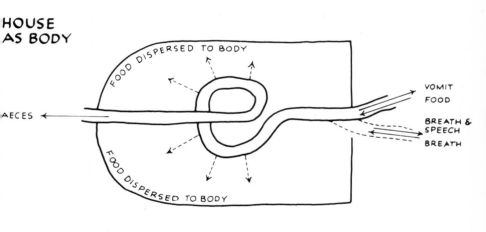

29   a The internal arrangement of Pirá-paraná long houses and   **b** the model of the house as a body (Hugh-Jones 1979)

Such contextual studies play havoc with the organisation of this book since they cut across categories of subsistence, settlement, ritual, etc. in the way that relational analogies concerned with cultural processes should. Since in a previous chapter the symbolic organisation of refuse was discussed (p. 62) it may be of value to refer to the disposal of materials amongst the Pirá-paraná. The area around and in front of the male end of the house is kept clean, but the area outside the woman's door is littered with debris and is the area for woman's crafts. As is shown in *fig. 29b* the process of food being brought in, used and discarded links refuse to faeces, and the position of women in this scheme is significant.

Whatever the details of this scheme it is clear that the organisation of subsistence activities must be understood by comparing with other types of information within the same cultural context. From the various associations and contrasts it is possible to build up towards an overall picture to which more general explanatory models can be applied. While Hugh-Jones does not provide broad generalisations about the relationships between society, symbolism and subsistence that she has so elegantly described, her work provides an indication of the type of ethnoarchaeology that could be tackled and used as the basis for general explanatory models.

6 Social organisation

The point has been made throughout the preceding chapters that the links between discard, production, subsistence and the organisation of social relations are strong, and that relational analogies must incorporate the social context. Indeed, discard, production and subsistence could be described as being part of the social sphere so that in reconstructing them one is also reconstructing social organisation. Traditionally, however, archaeologists have used the term social organisation to mean a restricted range of characteristics of human groups, in particular their size, kinship and exchange patterns, and degree of interpersonal ranking. The main types of data used as indicators of these characteristics are settlement patterns, cemetery organisation and regional distributions of exchanged items. We shall see, however, that the notion that settlement and burial patterns are 'indicators' of some aspect of society beyond themselves may itself be mistaken.

Settlement

When excavating a site on which individuals are thought to have had their settlement, the immediate problem is how to convert the plan of post-holes, beam-trenches, floors and pits into a picture of what went on at the settlement. What do the various features represent? What does this pattern of post-holes mean? Assuming that the archaeologist has been able to distinguish features (post-holes, floors, etc.) of different dates, ethnographic models are used to aid the reconstruction. In Chapter 1, the interpretation of circular post-hole patterns as round huts was described, and in Chapter 3 the various depositional and post-depositional biases which might affect settlement evidence were discussed. The various problems with relating features to single functions make consideration in this chapter of the interpretation of particular features on sites difficult; they may have had multiple uses.

The analogies which are sought for different interpretations of the functions of settlement features will depend entirely on the archaeological case being studied, and here I will only refer to ethnographic data used for one period and area in the past – the Iron Age of southern Britain. One common feature on settlement sites in this period is the pit. Bersu (1940), in his excavation of the Little Woodbury settlement, had used ethnographic parallels to argue against the traditional interpretation of their use as pit-dwellings and suggested that they were for the storage of food. He referred to similar

30 Arrangements of posts in a square can be used for different above-ground structures. **a** Granaries in western Zambia. **b** Drying racks in Kenya. **c** Scaffold burials among the Yankton (Ellison and Drewett 1971)

b

c

features in the Middle Ages of Hungary and in modern Rumania and to the 'caches' of Ohama Indians in North America. Even though the Iron Age pits probably had a variety of functions, those with constricted necks are, according to Ellison and Drewett (1971), very similar to pits of the New Zealand Maori who have damp and infestation problems equivalent to those encountered by Iron Age farmers in England. Because of this similarity in environmental context, and because of general parallels in social organisation and scale of the two societies, the Iron Age pits could have secured the same function as the Maori pits. The Maori use them for storing staple food crops and as containers for water. They say storage is necessary to preserve crops against attack by insects and mould.

Bersu followed Pitt-Rivers in seeing the four-post structures illustrated in Chapter 1 (*fig. 3*) as raised granaries, and supported the argument by parallels with modern Holland and elsewhere. But there are a number of other possible functions for such simple arrangements of post-holes (see *fig. 30*). Information other than the post-holes themselves allows a certain amount of differentiation between the different functions. For example, the Iron Age British four-post arrangements are frequently placed near the edges of settlements, and this is also the case for the granaries in certain Lozi settlements in Zambia (*fig. 31*). So far so good. But, in a context of tribal warring, the Maoris do not put storehouses near the edges of settlements because of the danger of attack (Ellison and Drewett 1971). They do, however, build wooden fighting platforms on four, five or six posts in such a location. The Iron Age in Britain certainly saw much warfare and it is possible that four-post structures placed near the edges of hillforts could have been linked to defence. The context would support such a use, but it would also support alternatives. For example, the North American Indians of the Mississippi area (i.e. the Yankton, *fig. 30c*) expose their corpses on scaffolds 7–8ft high, 10ft long and 4–5ft wide. In many places in the British Iron Age there is minimal burial evidence but, as Ellison and Drewett point out, fragments of human skeletons are often found mixed with settlement debris, scattered across sites or in pits. It may be the case that bodies were exposed or left to decompose on scaffolds and then the bones removed, sometimes becoming incorporated in settlement residues.

The four-post example, perhaps better than any other in this book, shows that the archaeologist may not be able to distinguish between different hypotheses and that searching for relevant data in the context itself may not solve the problem. In this case to know that, cross-culturally, 'x' per cent of societies with four-post structures used them for granaries, would hardly be helpful. In deciding between the different analogies, other aspects of the data could be considered (see Chapter 1), such as the detailed depths and dimensions of the post-holes and their distance apart, the presence of grain assemblages of a

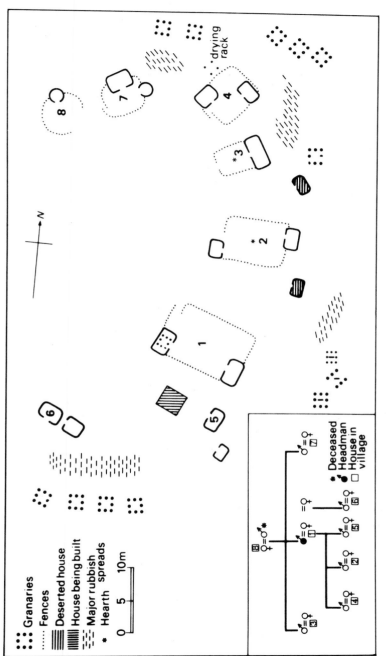

Granaries ⋮⋮⋮

Fences ⋯⋯

Deserted house ▥

House being built ▦

Major rubbish

Hearth ⁚⁚ spreads

*

0   5   10m

* Deceased
● Headman
□ House in village

N

drying rack

8
7
4
3
2
1
5
6

31   The location of granaries around the edge of a Lozi village in western Zambia distinctive type in the post-holes and surrounding area, and the spatial association on settlements with pits used for grain storage. The archaeologist in this way tries to work towards an explanation, building a shaky edifice of hypothesis upon hypothesis in which the joints and mortar must continually be re-examined and re-assessed. But at any stage, however much of the context is compared, no single solution may emerge.

It has been assumed that in building up their hypotheses, archaeologists can at least identify what *is* a settlement. Unfortunately even this assumption may repay scrutiny. In many cultures most activities which we might *a priori* associate with settlements actually take place off sites (Foley 1981). Indeed the settlement site may be the whole region in which human activities of various sorts have taken place. Even palimpsests such as that in *fig. 28e* provide a partial picture since many activities take place outside the camps. So, while in certain contexts it may be possible to identify different types of sites (base camp, kill site, etc.) each with distinct boundaries around it, in other cases, either because of an original lack of repetition in the spatial location of activities or because of depositional and post-depositional distortion, the boundaries of sites may be difficult to define.

It is at this initial level of the recognition of activities, structures and sites that various telling games have been played (Bonnichsen 1973; Lange and Rydberg 1972). The trick here is to find a recently abandoned camp or settlement, interpret it 'blind' as an archaeologist, then find a willing previous inhabitant and see how one has scored. When Bonnichsen did this on an Indian camp site in Alberta, the four general mistakes made were: (1) items were misidentified and assigned to the wrong functional categories; (2) false associations were made between items; (3) activity areas were wrongly interpreted; (4) relationships between activity areas were wrongly interpreted.

While Bonnichsen, Lange and Rydberg were not entirely wrong in their reconstructions, it is necessary to provide more positive indications of what archaeologists should do if they are to improve the reliability of their interpretations. Their work does illustrate the need for the careful development of analogue models for the primary level of identification and interpretation of function. But discussions such as that of four-post structures in the British Iron Age must go hand in hand with explanations of why the structures are there at all and how the sites as a whole were organised. It is to this higher level that I now wish to turn.

Once it is possible to identify sites and inhabited areas, it may also be possible to assess their size. And it is from the size of houses and settlements that archaeologists have attempted to wrest that most important aspect of social organisation, population size. In the Lee and de Vore (1968) volume, 'magic numbers' such as 25 as the population of hunter-gatherer domestic units were identified. Such ethnographic information encouraged the archaeologist to identify methods of estimating population size. Naroll (1962) had already suggested that settlement size was a good estimator of population and had provided a figure of 10 sq. m. dwelling space per person. So one had 'simply' (although some of the difficulties involved have already become apparent) to assess the square metres of dwelling space on a site and divide by 10 to produce the population size.

In S.W. Asia archaeologists have long been using general figures such as those supplied by Naroll and the figures of 100 or 200 inhabitants per hectare of settlement area. Ethnoarchaeological work by Kramer (1979; 1980) and Sumner (1979) has begun to lay bare the advantages and difficulties inherent in such approaches. In traditional villages in the Zagros Mts in Iran, Kramer found that architectural features and size were indeed the best measures of population. Some relationships occurred between population and compound area, roofed area and dwelling area, kitchens and living rooms. Other measures used by archaeologists such as mortuary data, nature of regional food resources, and numbers of grinding stones, storage vessels or pits, would all be unreliable estimators in the Zagros. On the other hand, a series of factors other than population was found to affect settlement size. For example, Kramer noted that the number of people per hectare of inhabited area varied regionally within S.W. Asia, and that it is inaccurate to use general figures for the whole area. Kramer had felt that data from modern S.W. Asia would be the best indicator of how to estimate population in the same area in the past since climate and way of life have remained generally comparable. However, there is considerable variation within the area, and it is not at all evident that climate and economy are relevant to the size-population relationship. They may not be the most relevant parts of context.

In searching for more relevant variables, Kramer found that people-area estimates probably vary with size or class of site. Sites at a higher hierarchical level, say with greater administrative functions, may have different numbers of people per square metre than sites at a lower hierarchical level. More generally, densities of individuals may vary according to site size. Sumner found that in modern village populations in the Fars Province of southwest Iran big villages were more densely crowded than small villages. In a huge world sample, Fletcher (1981) has demonstrated that for different general classes of settlement, including cities, low densities do not occur in the larger examples. Wiessner (1974) has put this point in a mathematical way. Using regression analysis she shows that, according to formulae such as those suggested by Naroll, population size is a function of settlement size and a constant. But data from Bushman camps indicates that another parameter should be added to the equation so that, for example, as the settlement size increases the constant itself changes. As settlement size increases one uses the constant (e.g. 10 sq. m.) multiplied by some other parameter. However, Wiessner notes that this 'other' parameter might itself vary with a range of other social and cultural factors. In other words, the effect of settlement size on the area-population relationship may depend on other variables.

One of these other variables may be the wealth of the inhabitants, as Kramer noted in the Zagros Mts. Another may be function. In Baluchistan the size of the courtyard may indicate whether and which types of domestic animals are kept rather than wealth or population size (Audouze and Jarrige 1980). Kramer also found that the best measure of population varied with the type of population. In the Zagros Mts if one is interested in determining the number of co-residing couples, the number of dwelling rooms may be the best measure. But if one wants to estimate number of people, metric area of dwelling space (i.e. living rooms and kitchens) is more reliable. But dwelling area is not as good as total metric area of the compounds in determining wealth of compounds.

Given all the factors which may affect the population estimates, it is not surprising that in certain cases no relationtionship can be found between settlement and population size. The only way to break through the complexity is to understand more of the processes involved in the organisation and control of settlement and population densities. So far a series of correlations have been identified but understanding of the causal links is weakly developed. For example, why do population densities increase in large settlements? Why does wealth affect densities? Until the reasons for the correlations have been examined, it is difficult to see how archaeologists can arrive at reliable measures of past population sizes. This is because the archaeologist will be unable to decide which of the complex of possible factors affecting the people-area relationship is relevant in a particular case. The archaeologist can only do this when he knows what aspects of a past context are relevant to the problem. For example, I suggested that the economy at a site may not be relevant. Wiessener (1974) suggests the opposite. She may be right, but I would first want to be shown why the economy was relevant and in what contexts. Similarly, if we could understand why settlement size affects the people-area link then we could say whether, in a particular past context, this variable was an important one.

There are few ethnoarchaeological studies which ask these 'why' questions in relation to population size and density although there are numerous psychological studies of density tolerances. Fletcher (1981) indicates that a critical factor in limiting densities may be the finite ability of the human mind to process information. As densities increase, the frequency of interpersonal interaction may also increase until at some point the brain can no longer process the new impulses it receives. But below this limit there is considerable variation in the densities at which people are willing to live. And here there are cultural influences. Interaction can be limited by building an environment which channels flows of people, limiting contact to certain individuals. Thus the layout of a village will affect population-area relationships, as noted by Sumner in Iran. Other symbolic and social strategies may so reduce interpersonal relationships to repetitive predictable behaviour and sign-making that a high frequency of interaction can be supported. (Forge 1972 suggests that ritual and social hierarchy develop in such contexts.)

Thus one class of reasons for explaining the relationship between population and area concerns the channelling of information flows. It may be for this type of reason that higher densities are supported in larger nodes where there is more centralised organisation of inter-action and information flow. On the other hand, people may put up with higher densities in bigger centres because other advantages of living there (e.g. more service functions, political connections) out-weigh the discomforts caused by high densities, and the attraction of people to the centres may increase the densities. So, in examining the population-area link, in an archaeological case, one has not only to consider whether settlements of different sizes are similar in plan and social structure, but also whether the bigger centres offer a wider range of functions. This is a good example of the value of knowing why a correlation occurs when using an analogy. If it does prove to be the case that information flow is the main reason for the relationship between settlement size and population-area estimates, then settle-ment size would only be relevant in the explanation of a past settlement pattern if the layout and channelling of informaiton differed in the bigger centres. If bigger centres were only bigger and did not differ in internal structure from smaller centres then straightforward population-area estimates could be used, without the settlement size parameter.

Beyond these reasons concerned with information flow, it is also the case that space, and amounts of space, are important symbolic media that can be manipulated socially. This may be one of the reasons for the affect of wealth on population-area relationships. For example, individuals of higher status may use expanses of space to indicate prestige and largesse. Such effects will depend on cultural context and it is a general observation that attitudes to interpersonal distance and crowding are culturally variant. Ethnoarchaeologists have yet to incorporate explanations for such differences into their studies of settlement size.

As with size, so with sedentism, there have been few studies which relate characteristics of settlement organisation to a total cultural context. While we now have various correlates for sedentism, under-standing of the relationships is limited. In Chapter 5 settlement mobility was discussed in relation to subsistence strategies. In this chapter the social correlates of settlement mobility and sedentism are also examined. But the addition of 'the social' does not imply the existence of fully contextual studies.

Sedentism has been related by several researchers to increases in birth rate and to general population increase (Lee 1972; Binford and Chasko 1976) although there is some debate about the link (Harpending 1976). Sedentism may be caused by localised resources, attraction of individuals to trading posts, or by the prevention of movement by neighbouring social groups. Hitchcock's (1980) work amongst the eastern Botswana Bushmen has identified five further correlates which are summarised here. (1) In mobile hunter-gatherer situations, camps tend to be small and roughly circular with the huts facing inwards towards a generalised work space. There is little functional differentiation of areas within camps. In sedentary cases houses are more randomly distributed and there are dividing fences and specialised work areas. Differences in the 'wealth' of houses emerge. (2) Activities become more differentiated on age and sex lines in sedentary situations. (3) As a group becomes more sedentary, a greater number of activities will be carried out at the settlement, there will be more food refuse produced and more clearing away of refuse. There will be more chance of relating activities to residues on hunter-gatherers sites, although there is considerable debate about this correlation (see Chapter 3 and Binford 1978; Yellen 1977). (4) There are more specialised tools and a greater number of processing constructions in sedentary sites. (5) Changes in the nature of hunting strategies occur in conjunction with sedentism. For example, hunting trips can be longer and can cover wider areas; more traps are used. Hitchcock specifically restricted his study to the characteristics listed and it was not possible to obtain an understanding of why, for example, huts were re-arranged in the way described. Certainly there is no universal link between circular settings of huts and hunter-gatherer or non-sedentary populations. The explanation of why dirt was reorganised is likely to be complex, as was shown in Chapter 3.

There are many other cross-cultural correlates for the internal arrangements of settlements, and the same problems can be identified. For example, a random sample of societies from the Ethnographic Atlas showed that a significant association existed between circular ground plans of huts and relatively impermanent or mobile settlement patterns, and between rectangular house ground plans and more permanent sedentary communities (Robbins 1966). Whiting and Ayres (1968) identified the same correlation and found that societies with curvilinear house plans tended to be polygamous and those with rectilinear houses tended to be monogamous. It might be thought that one could establish the reason for a correlation of this sort simply by assessing the strength of the correlation itself or by searching for other correlates. We may notice today a close correlation between the numbers of storks in a town, and the numbers of babies. And we might want to believe that storks cause babies. But the real reason might be that storks nest in chimneys and that there is some relationship between numbers of babies and numbers of chimneys. It would be difficult, if not impossible, to understand this link by searching endlessly through all the things that correlate with numbers of babies and storks. The only way to decide between the alternative hypotheses is to examine, in a case study, whether babies are produced by storks, and to observe the habits of storks.

This little parable will become relevant if examples of cross-cultural studies of the social dimensions of settlement patterns are considered which do attempt to provide reasons for the correlations identified. Ember (1973) has developed an archaeological indicator of post-marital residence showing that, in a randomly drawn sample of ethnographically described societies, matrilocal residence (the man moves to reside in or near the woman's family after marriage) as opposed to patrilocal esidence (the woman moves to the man's area of residence) can be simply and accurately predicted from the living-floor area of the average house in the society. In the first of two random samples sufficient data on house size could be collected for 18 prevailingly patrilocal societies and four prevailingly matrilocal societies. Societies not prevailingly one way or the other were discounted. The mean living floor area proved to be 326 sq. ft (standard deviation 547) and 868 sq. ft (standard deviation 179) respectively. The floor area measure used was average floor area. In human groups with seasonal homes, the season of the year with largest house dimensions was used. Where more than one room was lived in, the room area was summed, and storage and special cooking areas were discounted. In the second sample, data were collected in the same way and ten patrilocal societies had a mean floor area of 232 sq. ft (standard deviation 140) and five matrilocal cases 1236 sq. ft (standard deviation 814).

Other variables such as recent depopulation of an area or presence of commercial exchange were found to distort the relationship between post-marital residence and house size. The archaeologist, if he uses such figures, must be able to identify non-storage and cooking areas, and the functions of houses and rooms. When this is possible, Ember suggests that if living floor area of the average house is greater than 550–600 sq. ft, residence is likely to have been matrilocal, and, if the average living-floor area is less than 550–600 sq. ft, residence is likely to have been patrilocal.

The reason given by Ember for this correlation is that in matrilocal societies the women are brought up together and are socialised for living together, for example as the wives of one husband living in one large house. In patrilocal societies the women tend to live in separate houses. Divale (1977) has replicated Ember's results but disagrees with the reasons for it. Divale notes that matrilocal societies are those which tend to have frequent external warfare, high solidarity and absence of local community feuding. They also tend to have men's houses and local exogamy for males. Solidarity is increased because the male interest group is broken up and the males in a local community are strangers. The larger houses, presumably, reflect this community solidarity and lack of local disputes.

There is clearly a danger in both these explanations that post-marital residence rules are accepted as 'givens' that 'cause' other attributes. In fact matrilocality and patrilocality, and house size and compartmentalisation may be the surface effects of other underlying processes in the relationships between men and women. It seems unlikely that we could understand the reasons for the cross-cultural links by just amassing other correlates and providing *a priori* judgements. Both Ember and Divale may be right or both may be wrong. There may be one overall reason for the correlation, or there may be numerous reasons depending on context. Once more the ethno-archaeologist needs carefully to examine settlement space, like storks, in a cultural context before she/he can have much confidence in the application of the results of cross-cultural surveys.

While other studies by Ember (e.g. 1967; 1971; 1972) have examined the determinants of post-marital residence in greater detail, many archaeologists have followed a rather different procedure. According to Binford (1972, p. 61) a Soviet archaeologist (Tretyakov 1934, p. 141) was the first to suggest that post-marital residence might be reconstructed from the distribution of ceramic designs in a settlement. If fingerprints on the insides of vessels indicate that it was females who manufactured pottery then, in societies where matrilocal residence was the rule, there would be less formal variability in the executionof ceramic designs than under conditions where patrilocality was the rule, since patrilocality brings about a mixed population of female potters who have presumably learnt their craft in scattered parts of the countryside. If, within a village, a number of family units co-existed, each family living in a different section of the village, then under matrilocal conditions, in which mother taught potting techniques to daughter, each section of the village would be characterised through time by different styles and designs. In a patrilocal situation, each woman might make styles similar to those she had learnt 'back home' before marriage, but over several generations this variability would not have any stable association with particular segments of the village. Thus, given female potters, matrilocality is expected to be associated with design homogeneity within and differences between family units. Patrilocality is expected to be associated with hetero-genity of designs. These models have been refined and developed by Deetz (1965), Hill (1965; 1970), Longacre (1964) and Whallon (1965).

Such 'sociological' interpretations of pottery designs are based on the assumption that the homogeneity of cultural expression within a group varies directly with the homogeneity of the group's composition

(Binford 1972, p. 62). Much ethnographic information now suggests that it may be difficult to make any such assumption. For example, the Stanislawskis' (1978) study of the Hopi-Tewa shows that female potters may copy styles from individuals other than their mother. Indeed they may adopt styles from potters outside their own family. If a woman marries into a village (patrilocality) she may make designs similar to those she made in the village of her birth, or she may make a point of adopting the designs in her new village as part of a desire to be accepted and welcomed. Equally, an individual woman brought up and married within one village (matrilocality) might make pots very different from her neighbours or from her mother if she needs to set up social barriers, to set herself off, and to reject others. The composition of a group is not directly and passively reflected in pottery designs. Rather, the designs are used actively as part of social strategies.

This last point can made clearer by examining one village of the Lozi in Zambia (Hodder 1981b). The pots in *fig. 32* were made by three women living in the same village. The woman who made the 'A' group of pots was the wife of the headman of the village and she had been

32 Pots produced by women in a Lozi village, western Zambia. **a** View of the village.

c

32 (cont'd) **b** From left to right, the C, B and A groups of pots made in three separate compounds in the village.   **c** Detail of C group of unpainted pots (left) and B group of pots (right).   **d** Detail of A group of pots

d

taught potting by her mother before coming to the village. She painted her pots often with distinctive isolated red triangles. Her daughter-in-law who made the 'B' group of pots (*fig. 32c*, right) employed closely similar designs and her pots had similar dimensions. However, she had not learnt potting from her mother-in-law. She had learnt to pot before coming to the village, but had obviously copied, or been copied by, her mother-in-law. A reverse pattern was found for the woman who made the 'C' group of pots (*fig. 32c*, left). Married to the brother of the headman, she *had* learnt to make pots in the village by watching the other two. Yet her pots were different – unpainted and with different dimensions.

So in this Lozi case the composition of the pottery assemblage does not vary directly with the composition (in terms of origin or social unit at birth) of the population of a village. In this example, post-marital residence is patrilocal. But since potters are able to pick and choose the designs they use, there is no direct link between residence patterns and pottery assemblages. If we want to understand why the potters in the Lozi village make the designs they do, we need to examine in detail the daily social processes and the active use of pottery designs within the village. In the village there was a noticeable degree of antagonism between the oldest man – the headman – and his brother (the husband of the woman who made the unpainted 'C' group of pots). This antagonism was reflected in bad relations between his wife and the two other women. The 'A' pots were made by the headman's wife and the similar 'B' pots by the wife of the headman's favourite son. The friendship and common feeling between these two women was reflected in the pots they made even though the potters had learnt their craft in widely separate villages. The different pots made by the wife of the headman's brother reflected the antagonism between two parts of the village and between the headman and his brother. However, the pot designs do not simply 'reflect' common feeling or social division. They also contribute. Thus, the fact that the headman's brother's wife will not conform and make similar pots aggravates the tensions within the village.

So, once again, it is inadequate to look for simple correlates between social organisation and the patterning of artifacts within settlements. Even if cross-cultural associations can be identified we need to know why they might occur and this involves examining the mechanics of social process and material symboling in detail. We can understand and explain the past better once we have watched carefully the storks and the babies in particular cases.

The main reason why attempts at determining cross-cultural correlates for material patterning have failed is that material culture is not a passive 'reflection' of group composition and human behaviour. There are no simple relationships between settlement space and population size, round houses and polygamy, the distribution of

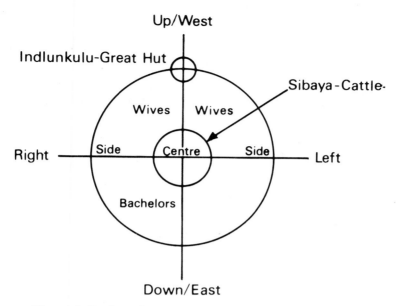

33 The symbolic dimensions of the Swazi homestead (Kuper 1980)

designs and post-marital residence, because settlement space, house shape and pottery designs are used actively to represent but also to affect the lived world. Thus, in any particular social context, new rules are sought to achieve familiar ends; the material world is manipulated to have symbolic and emotive effect.

Settlement patterns, as all material culture, do not directly reflect social organisation but may be organised in relation to it. The dispersed settlement pattern of the Tallensi in W. Africa is complementary to a tightly knit social structure. The constructed material world may often provide an alternative to other spheres of human experience; a release, an escape, a contrast. It seems reasonable to suppose that ethnographic cases will be found in which an egalitarian society is associated with a settlement pattern in which clear differences in wealth would be observed archaeologically. For example, certain houses in settlements may be larger or richer. The appearance of wealth could be part of an ideology encouraging personal endeavours but which is not associated with real rights, privileges or status. Indeed, a hierarchy in the settlement domain may be one way of coping with constraints on hierarchisation in other spheres.

The organisation of settlement space and of the movements of people through that space is used actively as part of social relations. The effects are symbolic and ideological and it is to this *representational* aspect of settlement patterns that we can now turn. Of the large amount of anthropological literature on the symbolism of settlement space I wish to consider only a few examples. The archaeological importance of these studies, as in the case of Hugh-Jones' work described at the end of Chapter 5, is that settlement space is related symbolically and ideologically to other aspects of life within a cultural context. In some cases, attempts are made to examine how settlement organisation 'works'.

Fig. 33 shows how the Swazi homestead of the southern Bantu, with cattle byre in centre and major hut at the west, is organised along a number of basic dimensions; for example (up/west) to (down/east) and (centre) to (side/periphery). A similar scheme organises the insides of each hut. According to this arrangement, women and men eat and work in different parts of the huts, visitors are placed in particular areas and certain sacred zones are associated with ancestors. Careful repetitive ordering of settlement space is frequently observed ethnographically (for a vivid and excellent example see Humphrey 1974) and can be identified archaeologically (Clarke 1972; Hodder 1982c). In the southern Bantu case, Kuper (1980) does not provide details of the social significance of the observed patterning but he does show how the same scheme orders many aspects of life within the same cultural context. It is these transformations (*fig. 34*) which the archaeologist can hope to identify (for an example see Hodder 1982c) and use as a basis for a reconstruction of the symbolism of settlement space. Swazi burial ritual and marriage ceremonies are organised in comparable ways; as are the storing, threshing and cooking of grain, and the eating of meat.

Other ethnographic studies have incorporated an assessment of how such symbolic representations and complementary arrangements play a part in social relations. The settlement and house form is a choice between alternatives reflecting an image of an ideal life expressed through socio-cultural forces. While the climate, site, materials and technology may constrain built forms, they do not determine them. Rapoport (1969) has shown the importance of the symbolic as opposed to the material conditions of settlement construction by considering two groups with contrasting house forms in a uniform arid environment in the south-western United States of America. The two social units are the Pueblo Indians and the Navajo.

The Pueblo build communal dwellings with communally used roof-space and a lack of differentiation (*fig. 35*). The whole building looks inwards to the kiva, a central sacred and ceremonial space which is itself an early house form. The Pueblos and especially the kivas are orientated to the sun movements and the solstices and are in turn related to ceremonial cycles. The religious and ceremonial knowledge centred on the kivas is in the hands of the men and is the basis of their power. Here Rapoport indicates how control of the symbolism of settlement space, and the correspondences set up within that space

34 A schematic summary of Swazi symbolic dimensions (Kuper 1980)

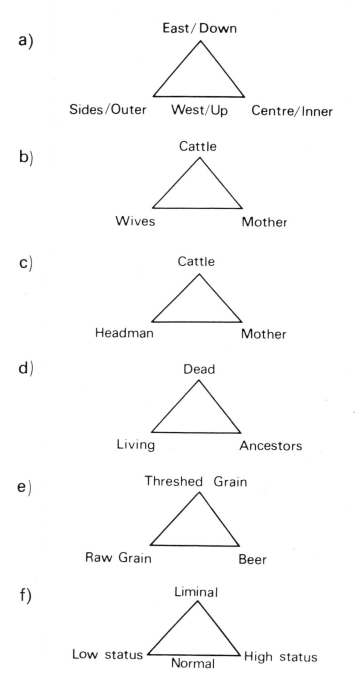

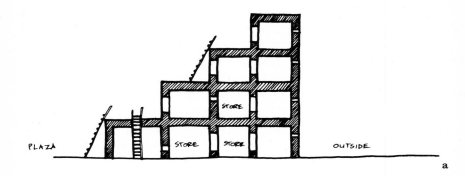

IDEAL SECTION THROUGH PUEBLO TERRACE (NOT TO SCALE)

35 The Pueblo. **a** Ideal section through Pueblo terrace.
b Diagrammatic plan of Emerson Ruin, Colorado, showing orientation
(Rapoport 1969)

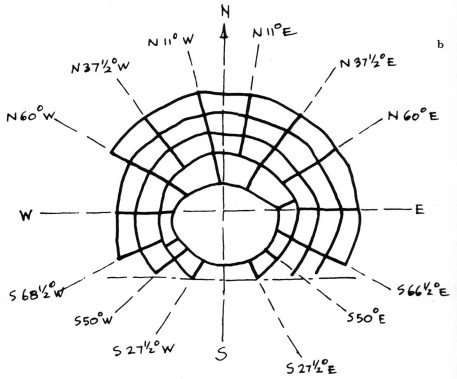

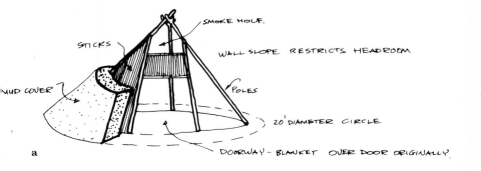

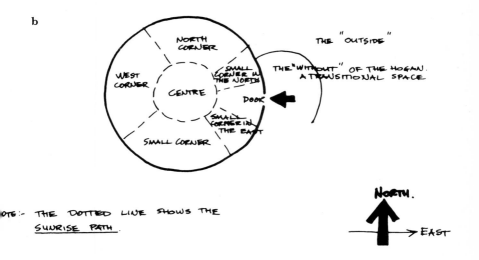

36 The Hogan. **a** Construction of forked stick Hogan. **b** Diagram of internal layout of all Hogans (Rapoport 1969)

between secular and non-secular domains, may be used to social advantage. But according to Rapoport there is complementary power in the female-centred kinship system. The mother's house remains a man's real home even after his marriage.

The Navajo Hogan, on the other hand, is not communally organised and does not face inwards, but is a separate family unit facing outwards. The Hogan is again ordered by a religious and mythological scheme related to movements of the sun. Within this arrangement, male and female are separated with women located on the south side, men on the north (*fig. 36*).

Both the Hogan and the Pueblo occupy the same physical environment, they are built by people with a similar economic and technological base, who have been in contact for hundreds of years, who have profoundly influenced each other in many ways, and who have both been affected by Spanish and American contact. Yet they are structurally different in settlement form (*fig. 37*). Rapoport's example allows us to distinguish what variables are relevant in explaining house form. Clearly the material background is inadequate to explain why the settlement patterns are different. It is necessary to look beyond the material world to other characteristics of the two cultural contexts. The structural models summarised in *fig. 37* depict the Hogan as emphasising an individualistic outward-looking concept. The Pueblo, on the other hand, projects a communal harmony. This basic difference can be related to other spheres. Navajo language leads to sharply defined categories, the Navajo abhor death and the dead, they have accepted outside innovations more readily, in their art they work from the centre outwards, they plant corn in spirals starting in the centre, and they are very sensitive to personal body exposure so that excretion takes place in hiding outside. Pueblo Indians, on the other hand, stress continuity between life and death, their art works inwards from the periphery and in the past sanitation was generally poor.

Many of these characteristics of the two cultures, such as burial, art and the organisation of ritual, would affect the archaeological record. The settlement patterns of the Navajo and Pueblo could thus be situated by the archaeologist in a cultural context, and the similarities and differences between the various spheres of activity could be noted.

37 Schematic depiction of structural differences between Hogan and Pueblo (Rapoport 1969)

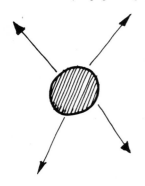

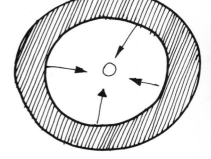

HOGAN

PUEBLO

The different types of evidence in each context are linked together by structural models, as I have shown elsewhere for the Nuba (Hodder 1982c). In the Navajo and Pueblo cases, underlying schemes (*fig. 37*) play an active part in representing and reproducing a set of social relations such as the male area of dominance in the kiva at the communal centre of the Pueblo.

The analogies which archaeologists seek for past settlement patterns must not expect that a shape or size of hut or building will have some universal meaning. One cannot 'read off' the nature of a society by looking at its settlement pattern. The fallacy of such a viewpoint has become clear in the above examples. Settlement space is a symbolic construction which must be understood as a unique creation. Yet the underlying principles run through many spheres of activity and the archaeologist has the data and ability to recognise these underlying regularities. Once they have been recognised their social significance can be assessed by the application of more general analogies. For example, it may often be the case that male dominance is maintained through the control of knowledge about the way the community and settlement are organised. In Chapter 7 general models will be described which link settlement structures to similarities or differences in ritual behaviour within a cultural context.

There is plenty of ethnographic data which might encourage the archaeologist to accept that it is feasible to identify oppositions such as male/female, inner/outer, sacred/profane, high/low status in the patterning of settlement remains (see especially Bourdieu 1977; Donley 1982; Moore 1982; Isbell 1976; Humphrey 1974). There is also a great potential for examining the way in which settlement patterns capture regularities in the natural world. Settlements are often layed out in accordance with movements of the sun, moon and stars and distinctive alignments and arrangements frequently result. How such organisation of daily space may act as a mnemonic, or may legitimate the social world has been described in ethnographic situations by, for example, Kus (1982). Generally, the built environment is part of a framework of meaning which is constructed as part of social strategies. Thus if settlement space is structurally congruent with the natural world the actions of individuals may be legitimised and given meaning. The relevant variables for the archaeological explanation of settlement patterns are primarily social and symbolic and it is to these spheres that archaeological anthropology should pay special attention.

Burial

If settlement patterns are ideological representations playing an active part in the social world, much the same can be said of burial patterns. We shall find that patterns in death are complementary to, but are not mirror images of, patterns in life. The generalisations which are used concerning the relevant links between burial and other aspects of life must be concerned with meaning and ideology, not only with adaptive functional utility.

The only aspect of burial about which cross-cultural regularities can be made without referring to the social and cultural context are those which are based on natural physical processes. For example, modern studies of rates of decomposition of human bone may aid the archaeologist who finds that certain bones are missing from burials. Are the bones that are underrepresented those that decay quickest? Data on differential decay rates have been provided by Pastron and Clewlow (1974) in a study of 18 burial caves in the Sierra Madre Occidental of Northern Mexico, among the Tarahumara Indians. After the bodies have been laid out in the caves, some bones, particularly the femur which is the heaviest and densest bone, survive longer than others. The figures for the bones represented in the caves were as follows:

Femur	35	Humerus	17
Tibia	27	Ulna	13
Fibula	12	Radius	7

On the whole limbs from the upper part of the body survived less well than lower limbs. Among the long bones, distal ends lasted longer than proximal ends.

	DISTAL	PROXIMAL
Femur	35	31
Tibia	27	21
Humerus	17	14
Ulna	13	10

These figures of bone decay from Mexico may not be generalisable to other regions since they are the products of distinct climatic conditions. There are marked alternations of wet and dry seasons in the Sierra Madre. Nevertheless, the relative decay rate of different bones is largely a function of bone density. Since certain bones, such as the femur, are universally denser than others, similar relative rates of decay might be found in other parts of the world.

Many archaeologists are primarily concerned with deriving information about the organisation of society from burial traces, and here there is little possibility of dependence on natural laws. Nevertheless, attempts have been made to derive laws concerning the relationship between burial and society which do not take ideology and cultural codes into account. For example, Binford (1971) suggested that there should be a strong relationship between the complexity of the status structure in a socio-cultural system and the complexity of differential treatment of persons in mortuary ceremonialism. In an ethnographic sample of 40 non-state organised societies, Binford claimed some support for his hypothesis, although his claim will have to be criticised below. Tainter (1978, p. 107) has asserted that Binford's ethnographic survey of mortuary practices confirms 'beyond serious contention the argument (still rated sceptically by some) that variability in mortuary practices must be understood in terms of variability in the form and organisation of social systems, not in terms of normative modes of behaviour'. Yet, as with settlement patterns, burial ritual is not a passive reflection of other aspects of life. It is meaningfully constructed and our cross-cultural generalisations must take the ideational and ideological into account.

Other 'laws' concerning the social dimensions of burial patterns do take ideology and legitimation into account. For example, Saxe (1970, p. 119) developed the hypothesis, further refined and tested ethnographically by Goldstein (1976) that 'to the degree that corporate group rights to use and/or control crucial but restricted resources are attained and/or legitimised by means of lineal descent from the dead (i.e. lineal ties to ancestors), such groups will maintain formal disposal areas for the exclusive disposal of their dead, and conversely'. Thus the presence of formal, including bounded, cemeteries is consistently associated with corporate groups practising lineal descent. Such a group's communal rights to restricted resources, usually land, are justified by links with the common ancestors who worked the land – that is with the dead. Why this link between society and burial should occur is not part of the hypothesis. What is the link between legitimation through ancestors and formal disposal areas for the dead? What is the link between competition over resources and legitimation through the ancestors? In such links there is a series of cultural norms, beliefs and attitudes which are assumed but which are not examined.

The importance of considering burial norms and attitudes to death can be emphasised by reference to Nuba interment. Various aspects of the Nuba in Sudan were described in Chapters 3 and 4, but here some general aspects of Mesakin and Moro burial will be recounted. Nuba burial involves inhumation, usually in single graves which are dug into the ground in the shape of inverted funnels. Very narrow entrances (0.3–0.55m across) lead into a chamber that widens towards the bottom where it is wide enough to lay an extended corpse. The chamber entrance is sealed with stones and then covered with a small mound. Artifacts may be placed in and/or on top of the grave. Graves occur in cemeteries which, amongst the Mesakin, are placed around and within the hill communities, sometimes immediately adjacent to the houses. Funerals are the main occasions at which large numbers of cattle are killed. Relatives and friends may sacrifice up to 20 head of cattle, each depending on the closeness of his/her relationship with the deceased. In addition to these common features of burial, there is a wealth of local detail which can be exemplified by the Mesakin Tosari community. Here men are generally buried on their left sides, women on their right, extended and looking east. The body lies on its side with one hand under the head. The orifices of the face are sealed with wax and the body laid out in a shroud, with body ornaments, in the grave chamber. Sorghum flour and seeds, sesame seeds, alcohol, water and meat may be placed in the grave. The objects used during life (spears, walking, dancing and fighting sticks, pots, calabashes, shields, head rings for carrying pots) are placed, often broken, on the grave. The number of these items depends on the age and status of the deceased. The mounds are up to 0.8m high, often covered with thorn bushes.

To what extent are the cross-cultural generalisations which have been suggested for burial practices relevant for the Nuba? The Nuba cemeteries do not have ditches nor walls round them, but they do often have paths which mark out the perimeters. So is Saxe's social model correct? Do the Mesakin Nuba stress common rights to the land which are justified by descent from dead ancestors?

At first sight, the answer to these questions would seem to be affirmative. The earlier ethnographic accounts (Nadel 1947) record that most land is passed down in matrilineal lines. The community at any one time depends on the communal labour invested by the ancestors, labour invested in terracing, well-digging, clearing fields of stones, manuring, building threshing floors and so on. The bounded cemeteries near the settlements could be taken as stressing the links through time in the common ownership and labour placed in the land.

Yet these earlier ethnographic accounts are only partially relevant today. At present, as Roden (1972) has shown, a new social and economic situation has developed. There has been considerable migration down from the traditional hilltop Nuba communities and the young in particular have become incorporated into a wider and more complex Sudanese economy. In spite, or perhaps because of, these changes involving different social relations and different patterns of land ownership, the burial pattern remains as an expression of stability, cooperation and continuity in labour and settlement. Burial customs act as an ideal and are not a full nor accurate reflection of what actually happens today in social and economic life. This disjunction between burial pattern and social pattern will become clearer as more of the Nuba data are considered.

A further characteristic of patterning at the within-cemetery scale is the distinct clustering of graves. Each cluster tends to have a major chief's grave and those buried in the cluster are usually related in some way. Each cluster in a Mesakin cemetery correlates with a named community section. Settlements are fairly dispersed but are divided into named sections and it is each of these sections that is buried in one of the cemetery clusters.

So the social model often used by archaeologists that cemetery clusters may relate to 'family' or clan groupings appears to fit the Nuba data. But again, when looked at in detail, the correspondence breaks down. In the first place, the distribution of Mesakin compounds is fairly dispersed, not highly clustered, in contrast to the graves in cemeteries. Secondly, the individuals in a cemetery cluster may have lived in completely different off-shoot communities many miles from the community by which the cemetery is located. Many offshoot groups still think of themselves as belonging to their area of origin and wish to be buried in the original cemetery.

Thirdly, the females buried in a cemetery group have usually spent their lives in quite other communities. Amongst the Mesakin, patrilocal residence means that a wife moves to live with her husband in her husband's community. But there is matrilineal succession which means that the children are tied to and live with the mother's brother and the mother's family back in her home area. So, many parents and children live separated. But the mother is usually buried back in her own home area where her family and children live, not in her husband's area where she lived most of her life, nor in the same cemetery cluster as her husband. So who gets buried where is complex and certainly reflects directly neither the composition nor the nature of the living social and settlement pattern. The artifacts in the graves in any one cemetery cluster were, in life, used in a variety of different settlement areas, social groups and community sections.

What the cemetery clusters do express is not the totality of what actually happens in social relations, but one aspect of it which is seen as an ideal – the ideal of matrilineal groups. In practice in daily life, the matrilineal line is continually frustrated by male dominance and competing paternal rights. But in death the matrilineal group is assembled 'pure', without the husband presence. As in the Madagascan example to be considered below, the pattern of death reinforces a societal ideal which is only part of what exists in practice and about which there is concern. Once again there is a distortion and structured disjunction between patterns in death and patterns in the living society.

The hypothesis that complexity of artifact associations in graves reflects, mirrors, social complexity in life can also be examined for the Nuba. More generally, what goes in the grave, the form of the grave and burial ritual can be considered in terms of their relationship to social organisation.

There is a clear relationship between death and grain in Nuba burials. Sorghum, sesame seeds, and flour or gruel are often placed in the graves. There is also a clear and explicit similarity between the form of the graves and granaries – they have equally small round entrances and deep dark chambers within. Pots, originally used for storing grain and grain produce as well as water, cover the entrance to the grave in the same way that they cover the small entrances at the top of grain silos. Amongst certain Nuba the dead are thought to be present at harvests. The association of death with fertility is also seen in the covering of mourners with ash and in the frequent use of ash in the burial ceremony. Ash is intimately associated with fertility and strength, and it is as a symbol of strength and continuity that it is placed alongside death at burial. These various emphases on fertility suggest a fear that misfortune in death may adversely affect the fertility and continuity of the crops and of the family and society. The frequent breaking on the grave of personal items – the items which 'are' the deceased – also removes the impurity and ill-effects of the dead.

The Nuba have a strong sense of impurity and purity. For example, there is a concern with symbolically protecting clean from dirt, while men regard women as impure and polluting – they eat separately and there are strong menstruation taboos. To this strong sense of purity, death is considered an impure threat. This general attitude to death results in the great amount of effort and ritual which surrounds the boundary between life and death. Because death is impure it is surrounded with ritual. But the attitude also results in a particular structure to the death ritual itself. Death is confronted with symbols of purity and strength – fertility, grain and ash. It is thus from the basic attitude that many of the features of burial can be understood – the shape of the grave, the breaking of artefacts and vessels, and the number and types of artifact placed in and on top of the grave. The threat of impurity is related to the social position and role of the deceased. In addition, the items owned by the deceased in life must be disposed of. Through these factors, status, age and sex are evident, reflected, in Nuba burial. These aspects of social organisation (but not as we have seen many other aspects) are 'reflected' in death ritual, but only because of and through the particular attitude to death found in the Nuba.

If, in the archaeological record, the Nuba case was followed by one without all this ritual, where death was less feared as impure, where little effort was expended in surrounding death and the dead with ritual, and where age, sex and hierarchical divisions were not expressed in graves, it could not be assumed that the society had become less complex. A change to a less complex or less differentiated burial rite does not necessarily entail a change to a less complex society. If age, sex and status are not differentiated in grave content, this does not mean they were not differentiated in life. Rather, the change to less differentiation in burial may relate to changes in attitudes to death, themselves related to changes in the ideological representation of social strategies. Because of the dominant role of cultural codes and ideologies, the aspects of social organisation which are represented in burial may be ideals picked out from practical social relations or even in contrast to them, reverting and distorting. These characteristics of burial can be seen in two further examples.

As in the case of the Nuba, the British Gypsies studied by Okely (1979) have a strong sense of group purity (see Chapter 3) which is seen as being threatened at death – a polluting event (*Ibid*, 87). All through life, Gypsy is contrasted with non-Gypsy (Gorgio). Gypsies associate Gorgios with dirt and pollution, and it is partly because of this that in the impurity of death a Gypsy can become Gorgio in that he dies in a non-Gypsy hospital and is buried in a non-Gypsy church graveyard. The society and attitudes of the living are inverted or disguised in death. Everything is turned inside out at death, and in the Gypsy burial, when the body is in the coffin, it is dressed in new clothing put on inside out.

The Gypsy fear of impurity in death also leads to many other characteristics of the death ritual. Before burial the corpse is kept outside the camp; replicas of things liked by the dead person are given as wreaths; actual personal possessions (clothing, bedding, personal crockery, tools) are broken up and burned on the perimeters of the camp, or buried a distance away or dropped in deep water. All this is to ward off the pollution resting with the dead person's objects. The deceased's animals, horses and dogs are killed or got rid of, and his/her hearse trailer is burned. All members then leave the camp in which death occured, at least for a while.

The Gypsy example shows again how the study of burial must be primarily concerned with attitudes to death and life, and that as part of these attitudes we must expect distortions, partial expressions and even inversions of what happens in social life. The same point is made most forcefully in the data collected by Bloch (1971) on Merina burial in Madagascar. In his study area Bloch found collective and repeated burial in ancestral tombs often located in the ancestral heartland well away from where the deceased had lived. In day-to-day life, villages move and split, and there is a complex and widespread network of interpersonal relationships. In the sphere of everyday behaviour, the Merina peasant is part of a practical organisation adapted to the economy and ecology of his region and involving flux. But he identifies through the tomb and in sacred behaviour with a quite different ideal organisation of ancestors and stability. The tombs and death ritual support an ideological and social framework (local stable groups) which does not exist in the practice of dispersed networks and overlapping, ungrouped, social relations. The tombs are a denial of the fluidity of the Merina society.

Studies of burial must not expect simple correlations between social organisation and burial. Rather they must identify the way in which prevailing attitudes to death can be derived from different conceptions of the living practical world. For example, the examples have shown how societies which emphasise group purity in their relations to others and in relation to dirt and uncleanliness often view death in a distinctive way. It can only be through such attitudes that mortuary ceremonialism can be interpreted.

Cross-cultural studies were earlier mentioned which purported to demonstrate that the links between society and burial are real and straightforward. Why is it that the complexity of the situation has been overlooked? How have archaeologists been able to derive such simplistic correlations from ethnographic surveys? In Binford's (1971) cross-cultural survey, 40 non-state organised societies were examined. It is not clear how this sample was derived, but in any case Binford was unable to test for correlations between death and societal organisation because of lack of data on the latter variable. The link had to be examined indirectly by correlating death practice with means of subsistence. It is not surprising, then, that any real relations were masked and that causal processes were obscured.

There is a need, then, for a careful, detailed and critical examination of ethnographic data on the relationship between social and burial organisations. In contrast to the existing surveys, this new work must attempt not only to catalogue and correlate, but also to explain. It is suggested as a result of the initial work reported here that such explanation must be in terms of attitudes to death and the way in which those attitudes are integrated within practical living systems and the associated beliefs. In death people often become what they have not been in life. When, why and how this should be so have yet to be fully understood, but we cannot assume simplistic and direct links.

Exchange

The distribution of artifacts which have been obtained, directly or indirectly, from a single origin provide important information for the archaeologist concerned with the reconstruction of past social organisation. When artifacts such as coins, pottery, stone axes or metal spears have passed from person to person, archaeologists talk of 'exchange' which they may sometimes distinguish from more institutionalised large-scale economic transactions termed 'trade'. Distributions of objects which have been exchanged or traded in the past may be clustered around major centres, implying 'redistribution' from those centres. Or there may be a gradual fall-off in frequences from the source of the exchanged item. Here down-the-line 'reciprocal' transactions between equals may be inferred. But from where do these terms 'redistribution' and 'reciprocal' derive and how does the archaeologist relate artifacts on maps to exchange processes?

In some cases the archaeologist may have historical information which aids the interpretation of artifact distribution patterns. For example, for the Medieval period in England it is known that transport of pottery by water resulted in less breakage and lower costs. The result of this difference in price can be seen archaeologically in distributions of pots extending farther along waterways than across land. Where such historical information is not available, there has been a tendency to assume that modern exchange processes also existed in the past. For example, in discussions of the exchange of Neolithic axes in Britain there has been talk of 'bulk-trade' of axes from source to secondary markets. Notions of bulk-trade and economic profit may well be wholly inappropriate for prehistoric exchange.

Realisation that prehistoric exchange may have been very different from what we are used to in the western world came from ethnographic data. Clark (1965) suggested after a visit to Australasia, where he became acquainted with traditional axe exchange systems, that Neolithic axes in Britain were passed from person to person by ceremonial gift exchange. What was of interest in the Australasian model was that it allowed axes to move from person to person over long distances without the people themselves moving very far at all. This notion seemed to fit the small-scale societies of the British Neolithic period. Australasia, and particularly New Guinea have been an important source of analogies for prehistoric exchange, and particularly for British Neolithic axes (Strathern 1969; White and Modjeska 1978). In 1966 Chappell published quantitative information (*fig. 38*) for the distribution of axe blades from axe quarries in East New Guinea. A general east/west division was noted on the map which related to a major linguistic boundary and which could also be identified in differences in the shapes of the axe blades. The Kafetu quarry produced blades of a lenticular section whereas the other sources produced planilateral blades. Similar evidence for the effects of cultural and linguistic boundaries on exchange patterns have been identified in Australia by McBryde (1978). Such effects can be located archaeologically by searching for 'kinks' in fall-off patterns of exchanged items and by comparing the patterns with other cultural material.

Beyond these specific analogies the archaeologist also requires a more general understanding of the social context of exchange. An appropriate framework which has been extensively used by archaeologists is the substantivist school of economic anthropologists (Polanyi 1957; Dalton 1969). For this school the economy is embedded in social relations. The focus is on relationships between people and on the different types of exchange such as reciprocity, redistribution and market. These different types of exchange act as integrating principles for society as a whole. Other anthropologists (e.g. Sahlins 1965; 1968) have linked the various types of traditional exchange to an evolutionary framework with, for example, reciprocity being tied to segmentary societies, and redistribution to chiefdoms and states. This evolutionary scheme has been grasped by many archaeologists (e.g. Pires-Ferreira and Flannery 1976; Renfrew 1973a; 1973b; 1977; Hodder 1978a) as a convenient way of relating exchange to social relations through time. Other substantivist concepts such as 'port of trade' and the substantivist definition of money have been used in the interpretation of archaeological material (Hodder 1979a). More

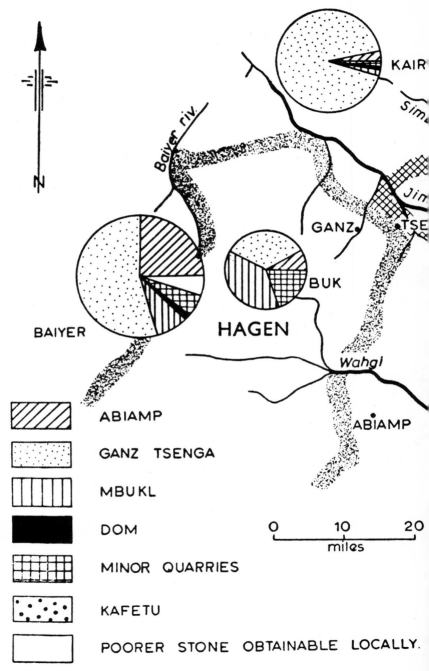

KAIR

Baiyer riv.

Sim

Jim

GANZ•   •TSE

BUK

BAIYER

HAGEN

Wahgi

•ABIAMP

ABIAMP

GANZ TSENGA

MBUKL

DOM

MINOR QUARRIES

KAFETU

POORER STONE OBTAINABLE LOCALLY.

0   10   20
            miles

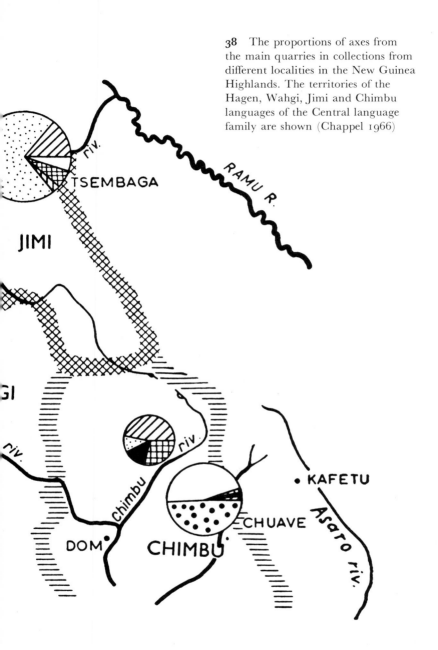

38 The proportions of axes from the main quarries in collections from different localities in the New Guinea Highlands. The territories of the Hagen, Wahgi, Jimi and Chimbu languages of the Central language family are shown (Chappel 1966)

generally, the widespread use of ethnographic models for the study of prehistoric exchange processes (e.g. Rowlands 1971; Clark 1965; Hughes 1977; White and Modjeska 1978; McBryde 1978) are concerned to understand exchange mechanisms as part of social processes, functioning to provide essential resources, maintain alliances or to establish prestige and status.

One ethnographic case study which provides information concerning a general relationship between exchange and social organisation is Sharp's (1952) analysis of the Yir Yoront in Australia. Amongst this group the status of older men is related to their control of the exchange of stone axes. These axes are loaned out to women and younger men, and it is through their control of the axes that the men achieve control of labour, prestige and position. The subordinate-superordinate relationship based on the control and loaning of axes is disrupted when steel axes become more widely available and can circulate outside the control of the older men. In prehistoric archaeology it may often be possible to suggest similar sets of relationships. For example, in the Nitra Neolithic cemetery in eastern Europe widely traded axes and shells are found only in the graves of men over 30–40 years of age. It seems reasonable to suggest that the status of these older men depended on the transactions they were able to control. Many other archaeological studies (e.g. Bender 1978; Frankenstein and Rowlands 1978) have suggested that hierarchical status can be obtained through privileged access to valued exchange items and their disposal within society.

A further general hypothesis concerns the relationship between the distribution of valuables and foods. Sherratt (1976; see also Wright and Zeder 1977) has used a notion derived from Rappaport that the exchange of valuables may act as a 'fly-wheel' for the exchange of subsistence goods between areas of variable productivity. Halstead (1981) has suggested that exchange may function as a form of social storage, ironing out local variations and uncertainties in subsistence production, and he has indicated that the use of valued, durable tokens may provide a mechanism for vital exchanges of food between a far wider network of communities than can be maintained by direct, reciprocal relationships alone. Individuals make social transactions which involve obligations to provide food in areas and times of uncertain productivity. The exchange network of food and prestige goods maximises productive utility. Unfortunately, in Pryor's (1977) cross-cultural analysis of types of exchange, no close nor necessary relationship could be identified between reciprocal exchange of food and non-food reciprocal exchange or ceremonial exchange. Rowlands (1980, 46) notes that in a hierarchical society the exchange of weapons, ornaments and livestock, for example, may form one system of circulation which is kept separated from the exchange of foods. For political reasons wealth from one sphere cannot easily be converted into prestige in the other. While the exchange of valuables may act as a pump to stimulate food production, the relationship between the two types of exchange may not result in immediate convertability.

Pryor's (1977) cross-cultural survey of the various correlates of different types of exchange both provided support for, and, as has already been found, rejected hypotheses for, the evolutionary and social emphasis in archaeological exchange studies. He found that reciprocal exchange and non-centric transfers are characteristic of societies at low levels of economic development. At high levels, market and centric exchange are common (ibid., 4). Reciprocal exchange of goods is more likely to be found, other things being equal, in hunting, fishing and farming societies than in gathering and herding societies because of the relative uncertainty of the food supply in the former cases. However, other correlates were not supported by the data. Wittfogel's thesis that economies relying on irrigation agriculture require stronger government and centric transfers (in money, goods and labour) in order to function efficiently had to be rejected. Similarly the notion that centric transfers are likely to increase in areas of climatic risk (arctic, subarctic, desert), as used by, for example, Chapman (1981), was also not supported by modern data. Hughes' (1977) study of New Guinea exchange systems emphasises that reciprocity and redistribution may operate as complementary structures within one social context. Polanyi, Dalton and Sahlins were concerned with overall distinctions between general modes of exchange and it may not be helpful to cite detailed instances where the correlation, between social form and exchange mechanism breaks down. However, it is clear that one-to-one relationships do not exist and that studies of the functioning of exchange within social contexts must involve careful and sensitive studies of how exchange is generated as part of the social strategies of individuals (see, for example, Rowlands 1980). For example, in some contexts status may depend on access to material wealth and material symbols may be restricted to the elite. In other contexts, emulation and downward movement of material symbols may form the principles of social stratification. It has yet to be shown that such differences are related mechanistically to different kinship systems. Rather the two exchange strategies represent different types of legitimation of power, and it is possible for the prehistoric archaeologist to distinguish between them. The process of emulation, for example, involves the rapid appearance and turnover of new valued goods to reinstate the status lost by the downward movement of earlier high status artifacts. New status goods must be found to replace the devalued artifacts (Miller 1982).

But if archaeologists are to reconstruct the ways in which exchange transactions are involved in social relations, they must acknowledge that the artifact itself has a cultural value on whih the social effect of the transaction will depend. The exchange artifacts plotted by archaeologists are not simply 'things'; they also carry meaning and have an emotive and ideological power. The artifacts exchanged are not arbitrary. They are appropriate within a cultural, ideological and historical context. Any adequate analysis of exchange systems must consider the way in which the symbolism of the artifact legitimates, supports and provides the basis of power of interest groups. It is necessary to develop ethnographic models of exchange in which the transfer of goods, whether prestige items of foods, has a relative cultural value. The involvement of exchange in the active construction of social strategies depends on the manipulation of the symbolism and contextual significance of artifacts.

Levels of societal complexity

In the discussion of exchange processes and their relationship to types of social organisation the notion of evolutionary relationships between different aspects of society was introduced. It is not my intention here to discuss all aspects of evolutionary theory in social anthropology and archaeology. However, certain aspects of the work of Sahlins, Service and Fried will be discussed and the application of their ideas in archaeology will be briefly described. The intention is more to use evolutionary theories as examples of the general themes concerning the use of analogy which are emphasised in this book.

Service (1962) identified two types of society termed egalitarian and hierarchical. The simpler, acephalous, egalitarian communities could be subdivided into bands and tribes, while hierarchical societies could be subdivided into chiefdoms and states. Band societies are largely equated with hunter-gatherers (see Chapter 5) and conventional views concerning this economic category were based primarily on the Australian Aborigines. Hunter-gatherers were all seen as being exogamous, patrilineal (or at least patrilocal) hordes or bands in clearly defined territories. Evidence from many other parts of the world has shown that these traits are by no means universal (see Chapter 5) for hunter-gatherers. Bands, however, remain as a class of small autonomous local societies.

Tribes usually practise agriculture and in comparison with bands they are larger in size and higher in density. Sodalities such as theoretical descent groups, age-sets and voluntary associations tie the separate communities of the tribe together. Fried, and Service in his later writing, suggested that tribes were the product of external pressures and competition. In particular, colonial influence resulted in the cooperation of distinct units against the common foe, and colonial administration encouraged the formation of larger well-defined and manageable blocks of society. However, similar pressures may have existed in the past outside colonial influence so that the 'tribe' may have a real ancestry.

In both bands and tribes, political leadership is founded on pursuasion rather than coercion, and status differentiation is based on personal achievement within the limits of age and sex constraints. There is equal access to basic economic resources. In chiefdoms, on the other hand, there is a hierarchy which cross-cuts age and sex divisions in society. Lineages are graded on a ladder of prestige on which the top lineage provides the chief. According to Service there is a ranking of all individuals on the basis of primogeniture in relation to one ancestor, with the chief as the closest living relative to that ancestor. Each person is located at a particular distance, and is graded outwards and downwards, from the chief. There is only a gradation of seniority rather than distinct classes or strata of people of equal rank. Society is based on kinship. The chief is surrounded by wives, retainers and assistants, and there are elaborate rituals and sumptuary rules (ceremonial practices linked to the chief). Service's model for chiefdoms was Polynesian. In Africa, chiefdoms may not be characterised by an overall ranking system for all individuals and lineages although the chiefs lineage remains supreme.

The stratified society as described by Fried (1967) can be seen as a short stage between chiefdom and state. There is differential access to basic resources such as land and water and this differential access implies differences in wealth. Differences in the control of wealth lead to patron-client relationships, but the complex political institutions characteristic of states do not exist.

States tend to have large, dense populations with well-defined territories (although many states in W. Africa have lower densities than adjoining non-state societies). They have highly centralised organisational foci, and specialised and centralised political institutions with several hierarchical levels. There is economic specialisation (for both subsistence and non-subsistence goods) and complex mechanisms of exchange. A centralised monopoly of coercive force is coupled with the ranking of whole groups into a class structure.

These various types of social organisation have been used in the characterisation of archaeological evidence. For example, Renfrew (1973a) has taken the various attributes of chiefdoms as defined by Fried, Service and Sahlins (1968), such as ranking, redistribution of produce by the chief and greater population density, and found that many of the attributes of chiefdoms were present in the late Neolithic and Early Bronze Age in Britain. Here one is clearly involved in a classificatory exercise; is this past society a chiefdom or not? But there may also be a sense in which the evolutionary typology is used as an analogy for explaining the past. If a past society can be identified as having certain characteristics of a chiefdom, then we might suppose that it had all the others for which there is no direct archaeological evidence. So, as in all use of analogy, we infer from similarities we can observe to similarities about which we are uncertain.

If such reasoning is to be at all plausible, it must be based on a demonstration that reliable links exist between the various characteristics of bands, tribes, chiefdoms, stratified societies or states. Unfortunately, ethnographic evidence has gradually been collected which demonstrates great variety between different types of society and a lack of determinacy in associations between the various traits which have been described above. One such searching ethnographic account is Earle's (1978) of social change in Hawaii. Here the conical clan (based on lineage ties to first born sons – the classic Service chiefdom) had begun to develop into a stratified society of chiefs and commoners in which there was also a separate class of managers of local production and an incipient bureaucracy.

In considering why this development away from the conical clan had occurred in Hawaii, Earle assessed the relevance of Wittfogel's irrigation hypothesis. But in Hawaii, irrigation was small in scale and would not have required management by a regional bureaucratic structure as Wittfogel's hypothesis suggested.

Another relationship which could not be identified in Hawaii was between chiefdoms and redistribution. Service had noted that chiefs provided redistribution for the exchange of foodstuffs and craft products between economically specialised communitites. But Hawaii communities were generalised (in that they had access to and used a variety of resources) and were self-sufficient. What little exchange of subsistence goods did take place between communities was not handled by the redistributive hierarchy. The Hawaiian redistribution system did not organise subsistence exchange.

Carneiro's (1970) population and warfare theories suggested that state formation occurred in physically circumscribed areas where emigration is not feasible. In Hawaii population did increase contemporary with stratification, but it is difficult to say that this increase caused competition over resources since agricultural resources were severely under utilised. Warfare did exist but it was not between local communities in competition over land. It was between regional chiefdoms for control over local communities.

The Hawaiian evidence throws doubt on many of the cross-cultural relationships which have been proposed within evolutionary anthropology. Similar lack of correlation has been found in other studies, particularly in relation to the association between chiefdoms and subsistence redistribution and ecological specialisation. Indeed, this evidence has led to a new description of traits characteristic of chiefdoms (Peebles and Kus 1977). It is suggested that chiefdoms can be recognised archaeologically in the following five ways:

(1) Ascribed ranking exists in that a higher level in society cuts across age and sex divisions and is ascribed at birth. Archaeologically one might expect ascribed ranking to be identifiable in cemetery studies. Wealthy young individuals in graves classified in a high status

category might indicate ascribed status. However, in view of the discussion of burial ritual earlier in this Chapter, it cannot be expected that wealthy child burials indicate ascribed status. Even where status is achieved, high status adults may furnish their dead children with tokens and rituals appropriate to their own (adult) position.

(2) There should be a hierarchy of settlement types and sizes and their arrangement should indicate the organisation of society. But, as was discussed earlier in this Chapter, there are dangers in assuming that settlement organisation is a passive reflection of social organisation or that there is a direct relationship between site size and status.

(3) Settlements should be located in areas of high subsistence sufficiency such that each settlement has access to a range of different resources. Local autonomy in everyday affairs is seen as encouraging adaptive flexibility and a reduction of the costs of information processing.

(4) There should be organised or specialist craft production. For example, there may be construction of monuments needing planning and a large labour force. There is also expected to be specialist, non-household production of pottery and a limited amount of pottery production centres. We have seen, however, that specialist pottery and other craft production can occur in egalitarian segmentary societies and that decentralised non-specialist production is characteristic of several ranked societies (see Chapter 4).

(5) If there is an unpredictable factor in the environment of a society (such as an unpredictable climate, warfare or unstable intersocietal trade), then special mechanisms such as storage occur to buffer these fluctuations.

Peebles and Kus have applied their classification to Moundville sites of the Mississippian culture, and the same model has been applied in European prehistory by, for example, Chapman (1981) and Ellison (1981). For the model to have more than typological value, it is necessary to explain why the various correlates occur. In the above list, an ecological or functionalist explanation is given; the correlates occur to allow better adaptation of a society to its social and physical environment.

There are many limitations of such a viewpoint (Hodder 1982b). In particular, there is no internal pressure for change, which always has to derive from outside the society. The model concerns the appearances of societies rather than the underlying tensions. The individual social actor is merely a pawn in some grand design. To see what an alternative model might involve we can return to Earle's discussion of Hawaiian society. Earle argues that the various functionalist correlates do not adequately explain why stratification developed in Hawaii. Instead he uses Goldman's model for Polynesian chiefdoms according to which the conical clan chiefdom based on birth and lineage (ascribed rank) was broken down by status rivalry and competition. A move began towards an 'open society' in which political office was achieved through largess and the elimination of rivals. As soon as the lineage structuring principle broke down in Hawaii, competition for office often occurred involving fighting and warfare which was financed by economic intensification. The general aim of the elite was to increase population in various ways (e.g. intensification and expansion through warfare), so that high status individuals could support their competitive claims to high office. The support for these claims was cemented through redistribution which, therefore, had a political force, and was not organised to help subsistence exchange. Redistribution was also linked to specialist craft production and the production of high status symbols. The whole competitive system based on intensification could only develop away from the conical clan when and where the environment allowed it; that is where islands were large and productive. In Hawaii the conditions were right and the internal process of change could move a long way towards stratification.

Earle's interpretation provides an excellent example of the type of relational analogy to which archaeologists should pay special attention. Here the various components of the model are linked, not by statistical co-occurrence, but by underlying principles which explain why the various attributes in the model are interlinked. The Hawaiian model 'makes sense of' a range of apparently disparate information available at the 'surface' level. It provides an underlying principle which accounts for population increase, redistribution of valuables rather than subsistence goods, intensification and warfare, environmental factors, and specialist craft production. In using the model analogically to explain the past, we can assess whether similarities to and differences from the Hawaiian evidence are revelant to our particular archaeological case because we have an hypothesis linking the various parts together — other related models are provided by Friedman (1975). In such models we do not have to assume universal reflections of social organisation in material culture (settlement and burial patterns) since individuals and sub-groups within society may manipulate and negotiate symbols, within a particular historical context, as part of ideologies. Social actions may be naturalised and legitimated through material culture in many different ways, and while we may generalise about the underlying principles, the surface appearance in material distributions and patterns will depend on the local historical sequence.

It appears, then, that there is little archaeological theory that can be described as fully evolutionary. Many of the models which have been applied are simply typological schemes (for example, bands, tribes, chiefdoms and states) and the reasons for correlations between variables and the reasons for change from one evolutionary type to another are inadequately specified. However, some models do exist which assume underlying social processes which, in certain conditions, lead to change in society and culture. It is the latter type of structural analogy which would appear to have most potential in archaeology and in studies of material culture.

Conclusion

This has been a long Chapter and reasons for its length are not hard to find. In particular, archaeologists have become more and more convinced that the key to explanation of the past lies in the social relations between human beings. Technological and environmental determination on the one hand, and cognitive universals on the other, have few modern adherents. Rather, material culture, economy, ritual and change are seen as products of social relations. But in searching for an understanding of social processes the archaeologist cannot rely on experiments. As was shown in Chapter 2, experimental archaeology is of little value in the reconstruction of the social context of material production. The source of ideas for simulating the social past on a computer is social anthropology, as it is for all hypothesis formation in relation to past social organisation. There can be little reference here to natural processes and physical laws. It is in the reconstruction of past societies that ethnoarchaeology meets its most important challenge.

But what type of ethnographic data needs to be collected in order to provide the archaeologist with productive analogies? In this Chapter the need to develop relational analogies in which 'why' questions have been answered as opposed to the collection of cross-cultural correlates has been further demonstrated. For example, a correlation between population density and site size has been noted. It was by suggesting reasons for this relationship (internal settlement layout and information flow) that it became possible to indicate whether one variable (settlement size) was relevant to the use of an analogy to estimate population size. In other words, if the layout was the same in both small and big settlements we would not have to adjust the people/area estimate according to settlement size. But if the settlements were different in layout we would, according to our theory, have to adjust the population estimates. In such instances a relational analogy is being used. If we know why a correlation occurs, we can determine which variables are relevant in fitting an analogy, and we can decide whether the similarities and differences observed between past and present will affect the validity of the analogical reasoning.

There is a similar insufficient concern with answering 'why' questions in other settlement, burial, exchange and social change modelling. A large number of cross-cultural associations have been noted in this Chapter, but co-occurrence does not necessarily lead to an understanding of the links. As the 'stork and babies' example showed, we may want to believe in a hypothesis (that babies are brought by storks) but the hypothesis is not adequately confirmed by noting recurrent associations between variables. Rather, detailed examinations of particular cases are needed in which observation of processes can take place (for example that babies are not brought by storks). The need for such studies was noted in the debates concerning the relationship between settlement size and post-marital residence and the relationship between social and burial complexity.

However, in many cases the reasons for a cross-cultural correlation between social organisation and material culture will not be immediately observable in an ethnographic situation. Rather, the reasons must be sought in underlying, indirectly observable social processes, in ideologies and symbol systems. When studying such topics the ethnoarchaeologist may not be able to resort to direct observation but will seek interpretations in particular cultures which 'make sense of' a wide variety of different types of data. Here again, a cross-cultural survey should not be the primary approach. It is difficult to identify underlying processes by a search through ethnographic files and atlases. Detailed contextual studies are needed.

Because the underlying processes for the explanation of material culture patterning include ideologies and frameworks of meaning, the materially constructed world is not a passive mirror of social organisation. In this Chapter the notion that homogeneity of cultural expression within a group varies directly with the homogeneity of group composition has been shown to be inadequate because pottery types are not simply by-products of behaviour. They are actively involved in social strategies. The patterning evident in pottery, burial and settlement is complementary to, and yet an effective part of, patterns in the social domain. Our analogue models must concern the underlying principles according to which the transformations are made.

The search for structural models makes nonsense of the compartmentalisation prevalent in archaeology (between bones, pots, economies, cultures, etc.) and still evident in the organisation of this book. Rather than build analogies which concern only settlement, or subsistence, or social organisation, the hypotheses used must be concerned with principles which underlie and cut across these various spheres. Indeed, in this Chapter, as in previous ones, discussion of contextual and relational analogies has necessitated a discussion of more than settlement, burial and exchange. It has been suggested that all aspects of society are ultimately social.

7   Ritual

This chapter is short, partly because the process of compartmentalis-ation of archaeology has pushed off ritual, and until recently art, design, culture and style as peripheral aspects of human behaviour. The core of adaptively active systems has been seen to lie in subsistence, production and social organisation. From a structural point of view, on the other hand, the underlying principles and frameworks of meaning are as evident and essential in ritual and art as they are in subsistence and production. Indeed it might even be claimed that an understanding of a society's rituals is of primary importance in revealing the models through which adaptive responses were made.

But whether one sees ritual as peripheral or central, there is a need to define clearly what is meant by the term. This is especially the case in archaeology where a wide range of activities are loosely labelled 'ritual'. An archaeologist might find a Mesolithic pebble painted with rectilinear designs and call it ritual, but the same name is given to burial procedures, strange cup-like engravings in stone blocks on the Yorkshire Moors, human skulls showing evidence of cannibalism, and pits intentionally filled with soil (*fig. 39* provides some examples). What do archaeologists mean when they call such evidence ritual?

While the word is used in a way similar to religion, there are differences. Unlike both religion and magic, ritual refers to perform-ance and the associated rules rather than to abstract concepts and beliefs. How then does ritual differ from custom which also includes prescribed rules of action and performance? While in our own society we may loosely call the shaking of a hand in greeting ritual, such an action might more appropriately be classed as custom. The difference again lies in the emphasis on performance. Ritual is usually odd and alerting; it attracts attention because it is special and not mundane.

The description of ritual as anything odd is very much part of standard archaeological procedure, although here the 'oddness' has particular meanings. Ritual is often taken to include things and acts which are not essential but are peripheral to the mainstream of human behaviour. In our particular western society, behaviour is often described as odd when it has little functional utility. Archaeologists use the same notion and they class as ritual that evidence which is not perceived as being directly and practically involved in the essential tasks of obtaining food and interacting with other individuals. Here archaeologists are imposing a modern notion of the separation of functional and non-functional pursuits on the evidence of the past.

a

39 Artifacts and behaviour termed 'ritual' by archaeologists. **a** 'Cup-mark' engravings on stones on the Yorkshire Moors, England. **b** Third millenium BC statue-menhirs from Provence, France (Phillips 1975)

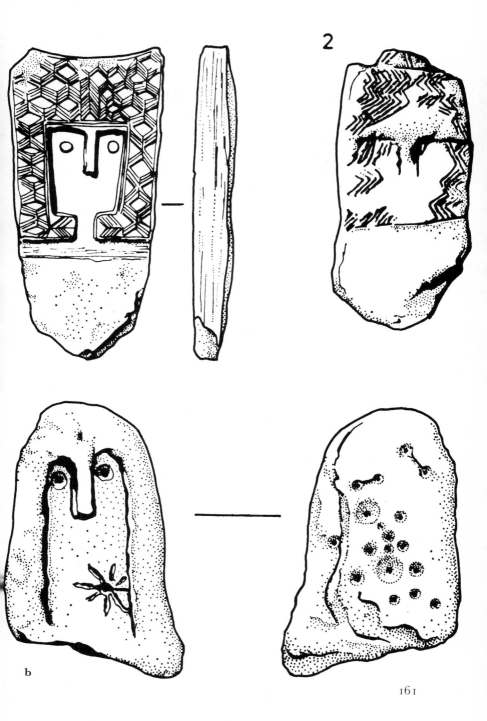

2

b

d

39 (cont'd) **c** The so-called 'ritual pit A' from the Danebury Iron Age hillfort (Cunliffe 1971). **d** Heap of broken potsherds covered in sticks at the edge of a circle of stones: Nuba rain-making ritual, Sudan

But when archaeologists say some evidence is odd or ritual they may not only mean that it does not have immediate functional value, but also that they do not understand it. It is a standard joke on archaeological sites that features and artifacts are called ritual when they are not understood. This lack of understanding may occur partly because there is insufficient evidence to allow interpretation. But it may also occur because the evidence is outside the archaeologist's range of experience and knowledge. For example, Neolithic causewayed camps in England are so called because their perimeter ditches are interrupted at frequent intervals by causeways (*fig. 40*). Such an arrangement makes no sense to us as a defence or enclosure because the interrupted ditches, often with discontinuous internal banks and palisades, would appear entirely ineffective. The interrupted ditches seem to have no sensible function, they are outside the archaeologist's understanding, and perhaps partly for this reason the causewayed camps are frequently called ritual.

Thus archaeologists use the term ritual for the two closely connected reasons that what is observed is non-functional and is not understood. In our own society the dominant ideology is that all behaviour should be directly accountable to some end. We are concerned with functional values and means-end relationships. As archaeologists we frequently try and use ethnographic evidence to make sensible and functional what initially appears ritual and odd.

An example of such a process is provided by work on prehistoric figurines. From the late nineteenth and early twentieth centuries onwards such objects from the Palaeolithic, Neolithic and Bronze Age of the east Mediterranean were taken as representing Mother Goddess worship and fertility ideology and thus not worthy of detailed stylistic and trait analyses. The Mother Goddess notion came largely from early archaeologists' contacts with classical literature. The idea of a great Earth Mother had been a continuing theme in the historically attested European cultural tradition (Ucko 1968, p. 410). The interpretation of figurines in this light persisted despite evidence which fits only uncomfortably. For example, the prehistoric figurines of the east Mediterranean include male figurines and figurines without sexual characteristics. Also, figurines are made of clay rather than more precious material which might, given twentieth-century values, be more appropriate for Mother Goddess depictions. Finally, the figurines often occur in occupational debris.

Ucko lists (1968, pp. 425–426) ethnographic cases in which small figurines occur and he mentions their use in the different societies. The descriptions are brief and there is little concern with context. However, the evidence does show the variety of uses of this artifact category. For example, in initiation ceremonies figurines may have pedagogic functions in the teaching of sexual matters. But there are also numerous ethnographic accounts of small human figurines being

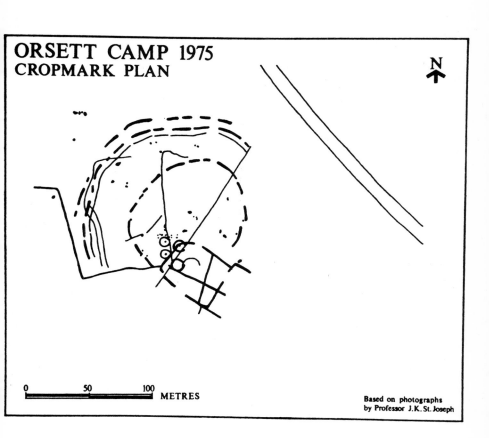

40 Neolithic causewayed-camp in the east of England (Hedges and Buckley 1978)

made and used as dolls. Such dolls usually serve one or two functions: (1) profane, as entertainment pure and simple, (2) sympathetic magic to ensure the well-being and/or presence of children for those who carry the dolls.

In ethnographic and historic accounts the use of figurines as dolls may be associated with female and male and sexless representations, and this is one of the reasons why Ucko prefers the doll interpretation to the Mother Goddess interpretation, for example for many of the figurines from Crete. This formal analogy is supported by increasing the number of points of comparison. Many ethnographic dolls are made of clay, as on Crete, and other relatively common material. In the archaeological examples, the decoration on sexless figurines with stump arms is seen as being unsurprising if the objects were dolls, while the predominance of female over male representations is also found in other periods and areas.

Rather more complete testing of such analogies would depend on a better understanding of the social and symbolic context of figurines. In what contexts and why do people model the human form (Douglas 1970)? There is a danger that the doll interpretation is seen as more satisfactory partly because it is less mysterious, less odd, than that based on the Mother Goddess. Ucko has provided clear functions for the figurines and has thus made them less 'ritual'.

There are other archaeological data which have been made less mysterious and alien by the application of ethnographic analogies. Renfrew (1973b) has sought to show that the construction of prehistoric 'temples' on Malta is not inexplicable if placed within a social process. The temples are to be given a social context and function. Renfrew achieves his end by comparing the Maltese constructions with the *ahu* and their associated chiefdoms on Easter Island (*fig. 41*). Similar parallels are made between Easter Island and the Neolithic burial tombs on Arran and Orkney in Scotland. The monumental architecture is seen as being produced within chiefdoms, the necessary labour being mobilised by the chiefs. The great stone and earth constructions of the Neolithic are 'at home' in the 'normal' competitive display between neighbouring social units.

As soon as behaviour is recognised as having functional utility it appears to be less 'ritual'. Just because we, as analysts, do not understand the behaviour (perhaps partly because it appears non-functional), we cannot assume that the behaviour is 'odd', a special category, within its own context. The Gnau men of New Guinea believe that if they let blood they will be as healthy as women, and the belief is effective (Lewis 1980). There is a function, in the New Guinea context. Neolithic causewayed camps and burial mounds in their own context may be perfectly understandable.

The tradition of making sense of ritual by finding it some function has a long tradition in social anthropology (see Durkheim 1915; Malinowski 1948). Ritual is seen as holding society together, making contradictions acceptable and often as a conservative influence in periods of change. Rappaport (1967) ascribes a wide range of functions to ceremonies, such as the maintenance of undegraded environments, limitation of inter-group raiding, adjustment of man-land ratios, permitting trade, redistribution of natural resources, and levelling of wealth differences. Ritual is thought to have a number of political functions (Burns and Laughlin 1979) in that it is a mechanism for the legitimation of social control, it helps to resolve conflicts, it maintains group solidarity and group identity, and it supports the power structure if ritual knowledge is limited to the elite.

All ethnographic analogy is concerned to make sense of the unfamiliar. There is, however, a danger that in deciding between analogies we choose that which best fits our own ideology of functional and material utility. Does a functional, adaptive approach adequately explain the form and content of ritual as opposed simply to its existence and do the explanations adequately capture its social effect? Perhaps there is a risk of making ritual too ordinary, of shying away from the oddness, and so missing the point. There is a need to define the particular and distinctive characteristics of ritual actions.

One widely recognised characteristic of ritual is the emphasis on formal and repetitive behaviour. Rules may be clearly prescribed and handed down, associated with special events, and within each formal act there is often considerable repetition of messages and actions. In certain cases the ritual may be a model of how to act in the world. For example, for the Gnau, ritual is a source of knowledge of how to do things, learned from the ancestors, and held in trust by senior men for their descendants (Lewis 1980, p. 71). In this way ritual may act as an ideal, often in contrast with the daily lived world. Bloch (1977) has emphasised that ritual may be out of time and out of place, a set of rules and concepts which exist beyond the lived world but complementary to it.

For Turner (1969) ritual is part of a continual relationship between structure and antistructure. Many ritual acts involve reversal of established patterns of life, of social structure. They reinforce the social relations by allowing their reversal or destruction in a liminal 'in-between' zone. The ideal that is present in ritual is often the inverse of patterns in daily life, giving those patterns meaning and coherence. The notion that ritual often involves contrast is implicit in many archaeological discussions. 'Vase supports' in the Neolithic Chassey culture of France stand out from other pottery types in their shape, in the fact that they are decorated, and in their contexts of find. Partly because of this contrast, this 'oddness' in a contextual sense, the objects are often described as ritual. But the concepts of structure and anti-structure in ritual are much more far-reaching than such examples allow. Ritual is a set of actions, in a particular context, which must be

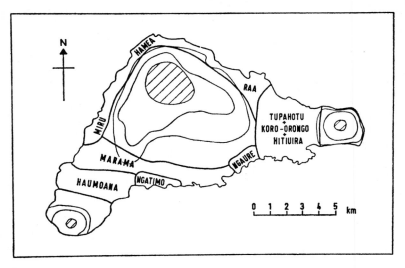

a

41 Easter Island as an analogy for chiefdoms and monumental
construction in prehistoric Europe. **a** The distribution of chiefdoms on
Easter Island compared with **b** the hypothetical territories around
Neolithic Maltese temples (Renfrew 1973b).

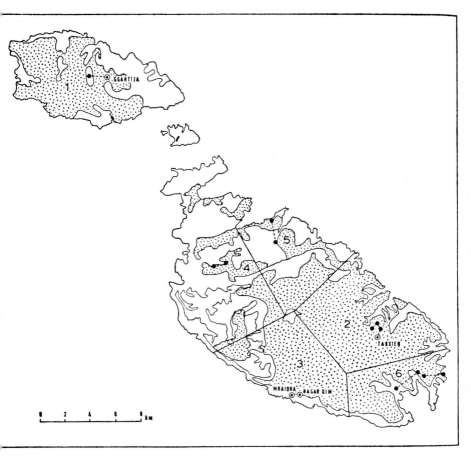

b

c

d

41 (cont'd) **c** Dressed and fitted masonry wall from Ahu Vinapu, Easter Island (Heyerdahl and Ferdon 1961). **d** Facade of Hagar Qim prehistoric temple, Malta (Evans 1971)

understood in relation to the structure of society as a whole.

If ritual can be described as the repetitive and formalised expression of social ideals, then we might expect that it could be studied as a language or code. It would be sufficient to 'read' what was being 'said' in the placing of artifacts in graves, shrines, temples in relation to the organisation of non-ritual activities. However, ethnographic studies suggest that many aspects of ritual are not analogous to language. Much ritual may be intended to be ambiguous, to be interpreted differently by different people, to mean all things to all people. Much ritual 'communication' has a message which is full of uncertainty, and this uncertainty, in the context of ritual, may actually be seen as desired (Lewis 1980).

As with the performance of a play, it may be better to think of ritual as stimulation rather than communication. It has an emotive effect or it sets the onlooker or participant thinking. Ritual is not made up of abstract tokens and images, but of real things experienced by people in a real context. It substitutes for and helps one to understand some alternative reality. The ritual can play an important and central part in life; it is not epiphenomenal.

Ritual is the formalised and repetitive basis for social action. Through its emotive and stimulating effects it restructures society. We have already seen in Chapter 6 how symbols play an active part in social strategies. The symbols used in ritual are in an active recursive relationship with the world which is their context. The ritual derives its meanings from society, but it also renews and gives significance to the social structure. Because of the emotive 'staging' of many rituals this renewal has special effect.

One type of active effect of ritual noted by Turner is termed by him 'communitas'. The upturning of established norms that is frequently associated with ritual releases a sense of community or commonality. The common feeling can be used to political advantage and Turner cites frequent examples where political figures or movements win support and enthusiasm through 'communitas'.

Conclusion

This brief discussion has been based less on particular ethnoarchaeological studies of ritual since these are few in number, and more on general anthropological accounts such as are found in the work of Turner, Bloch and Lewis. These modern studies throw a new light on traditional archaeological approaches to ritual. In particular, for many archaeologists ritual is used to mean 'odd' in the sense of 'not understood' and there are two possible sources of this lack of understanding. In the first, prehistoric features may be described as ritual because their function and use cannot be identified; no adequate explanation can be offered and so the features are termed ritual. In the second place, lack of understanding may occur because the interpretations do not add up to a picture of behaviour which makes sense in terms of functional utility. The behaviour appears unnecessary and inconsequential. Here the analyst is imposing a modern ideology which makes sense of the world in terms of material efficiency.

Ritual is odd, but in rather different ways to those often assumed by archaeologists. The characteristics of ritual such as repetition, stylisation, liminality and ambiguity often attract attention and stimulate by being different. The oddness here is one which is meaningful within a social context and which is central to any understanding of the structure of society. Ritual does have a function but it is a complex one, linked to ideologies, beliefs and values rather than to absolute levels of utility.

The contrast between ritual and non-ritual activities may be blurred and difficult to define, but in any particular context some aspects of behaviour can be placed at the more ritualistic end of the scale. In those contexts in which there are clear distinctions between daily mundane practices and behaviour which has ritual characteristics, the patterning of residues on ritual and non-ritual sites can be compared. By using the general models of anthropologists, as to the nature and functions of ritual, the contrasts and inversions identifiable in ritual can be used to explain the ideological basis of social life.

8 Art, decoration and style

Art

There are many similarities between the problems encountered in defining ritual and art. Archaeologists may call something art if they do not understand it. There may be problems in separating art from decoration and design in much the same way as ritual and non-ritual may merge. Art may be described as more formal representation which aims to alert or stimulate the observer. But there is a great deal of subjectivity in identifying formality in pictures and many would disagree that the definition of art must refer to this characteristic. Although we may use the word 'art' to mean almost anything, it is largely true that what is seen and defined as art is dependent on the particular social context. I will come back to this point and to the problems of defining art later in this chapter.

There are many ethnographic descriptions of traditional art from Africa (e.g. Thompson 1971 on Yoruba art) to the northern Tundra (e.g. Ray 1961). There are also attempts at synthesis and cross-cultural comparison (e.g. Otten 1971; Ucko 1977) which provide general statements usable by archaeologists in interpreting the past. Throughout this book the problem has been confronted of how generalisations can be made which hold true in widely different areas and time periods. Art provides one of the most exacting tests of the cross-cultural method since it is often assumed that art is ephiphenomenal – it is not seen as being directly linked into other aspects of social behaviour or at least the links are thought to be complex and tenuous. If art is creative and idiosyncratic, is it possible to identify statements which are generally true and which relate art to its context of production?

Certainly some have tried. In 1928 Honigsheim suggested a relationship between matrilineal kin groups and achievement in the plastic arts. Fischer (1961) related stylistic categories to social stratification, residence pattern and form of marriage. It is also claimed that design with a large amount of empty or irrelevant space should characterise egalitarian societies, as should art styles with simple repetitive forms. Cross-cultural psychological studies have identified other correlations. Kavolis (1965) suggests that a psychological attitude towards domination is associated with a preference for geometric outlines while resigned subjugation is congruent with a preference for flowing, smoothly rounded outlines (see also Barry 1957). Alschuler and Hattwick (1947) found that children who emphasised circles tended to be more withdrawn, more submissive, more subjectively orientated than children who mainly painted vertical, square or rectangular forms. Wolfe (1969) examined why

173

some societies produce more and better art than others and found an answer in the alienation of males from local lineage centres, brought about by matriliny. In all such generalisations the major difficulty lies in the tenuous nature of the links between the various components of the models. Unless some universal behavioural and cognitive response is supposed, which denies any active involvement of art and design in social strategies, the reasons for the relationships are ill-defined.

In addition to these supposed general relationships between society and art, there are even problems in identifying what is depicted in art across different cultures. Pager (1976) suggests that Palaeolithic European and Australian rock art includes depictions which elsewhere represent bees' nests and the ladders constructed to reach the hives. Jelinek (1974) equates scenes of coitus in Palaeolithic European and Australian Aboriginal art. But are these formal analogies really justified unless they can be supported in the various ways described in Chapter 1? Many archaeologists feel not, and some of the reasons will be examined below. If we cannot be sure what a depiction represents, how much more difficult it is to state general characteristics of art. For example, there have been many attempts to define schematic as opposed to naturalistic representations (Ucko 1977) within a cross-cultural perspective.

One could suggest that there are no secure universals in human abstraction. It can be claimed that what art is and how it is interpreted depend entirely on the particular social, cultural and historical context. The more extreme view can be taken (Macintosh 1977) that all attempts to interpret the significance of artistic representations are doomed to failure unless one can talk to people in the culture concerned. This highly relativistic position is founded on a conception of art as being based on idiosyncratic cognitive processes. For example, in different cultures people may draw animals differently because they pick out different characteristics of the animals as distinctive and depict them in ways which appear to us to be distorted. In Palaeolithic cave art, are the anthropomorphic representations (e.g. *fig. 42*) really people or what are they? When Macintosh checked a recorder's interpretations of ethnographic cave painting with informants who had some contextual understanding of the art, there was a 90 per cent failure by the recorder to diagnose correctly the individual painted items.

If such problems can be identified for the recognition of what is represented in art, how much more difficult must it be to interpret secondary symbolic aspects of the depictions in the art, and its general characteristics (schematic, naturalistic, etc.). Given these doubts it is hardly surprising that many have suggested that understanding of art

42 'The sorcerer': Palaeolithic cave painting of anthropomorphic animal from Les Trois Frères, Ariège (Clark 1967)

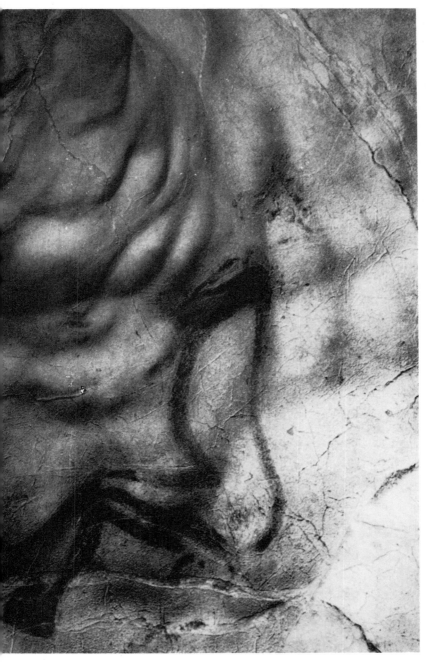

depends on being able to question informants familiar with the context in which the art is produced.

However, it is a common ethnographic experience, as well as one repeated many times in our own society, that individuals may not be articulate about their art. 'We may not know much about art, but we know what we like.' Deetz and Dethlefsen (1971) have shown that, unbeknown to the 'participants' of the American culture concerned, so-called 'death's head' motifs in their churchyards developed, by the addition of certain facial characteristics, into 'cherub heads'. No participant observer would have expressed verbally what was clear from the 'objective' analysis. While some societies, and some individuals in some societies, may be very explicit about their art and its meanings, verbal descriptions provide only one type of contextual evidence. What people say about their art may be different from what is observed and surmised by the analyst, but it is not necessarily more real or more valid. One essential aspect of the study of art might well be the correspondences and disjunctions between what is said and what is not said by the producers and 'consumers' of art. Because artistic expression is a non-discursive mode of communication it may be used to 'say' things which cannot be 'said' openly. A similar point can be made about all material culture (see Chapters 9 and 10). It is necessary, then, to go beyond Macintosh's 'cautionary tale' and ask why, and in what contexts, verbal and artistic expression do or do not correspond. The inability of archaeologists to talk to people in the past does not prevent them from studying and interpreting art, since art is an important form of expression in its own right.

How can one, then, suggest that a prehistoric drawing represents an animal species (*fig. 43*) or that a style of art if schematic? As with any analogy between the past (the cave drawing) and the present (modern living animals), the argument can be strengthened by increasing the number of points of comparison; do the past and present animals have many features in common? Reference can also be made to context in that the animal or other depiction may occur in a supporting environment or background paralleled in modern examples. In other cases the depiction may be interpreted both specifically (as an animal species) and generally (as naturalistic or schematic) by its contrast to others within and between sets. For example, at the Lepenski Vir prehistoric site there is evidence of naturalistic representations being placed opposite schematic versions. The interpretation of art thus depends on the careful use of formal and contextual analogies.

But an important element of the context of art is social structure. Art is a way of giving meaning to, and understanding the world. Fact and value may be indistinguishable at a fundamental level. It may be impossible to distinguish representation and concept. The values, meanings and effects of art depend on who is producing, encouraging

176

43   Bison engraved on clay from Niaux, Ariège. Palaeolithic (Clark 1967)

or viewing the representations. To avoid the pitfalls of the universal statements listed at the beginning of this Chapter the links between art and artist and the context of production and use must be examined more closely. It might be claimed that art and artist are historically and socially determined. But we should avoid a sociological approach which determines art from its social context. This amounts to little more than a refined universalist position. On the other hand, we should avoid an extreme relativism. Art is produced within social constraints to have social effect, and we can generalise about such processes. But the form of the art is built up within a specific historical context, carrying meanings particular to that context. The content and structure of the art are involved in social strategies such as emulation and legitimation. Meanings are created for art within social contexts, but the unique 'sentences' are 'legible' for they are based on widely found rules.

Thus a programme for the interpretation of prehistoric art must be based on ethnographic data concerning symbolic principles and dimensions. These principles are used creatively to produce unique cultural styles. But analogies are also required for determining how artistic expression might play a part in social strategies.

Many of the problems in interpreting prehistoric art with the aid of modern analogies are evident in studies of Palaeolithic cave art (*figs 42 and 43*). Ucko and Rosenfeld (1967) search for ethnographic parallels for the Palaeolithic art of Western Europe. But they only consider modern examples which occur on cave walls. There is no apparent reason why paintings on stone and on cave walls should somehow be different from those on mud walls or skin tents. This attempt to use a relational analogy is invalid if no reasons are provided to explain why the medium on which the painting occurs is relevant. 'Cave wall paintings' may be an arbitrary category and the similarities between the past examples and the present analogies may be illusory if based on the 'cave wall' characteristic. If caves are associated with a particular type of painting we need to know why.

As a result of limiting their search for analogies in this way, Ucko and Rosenfeld can find few ethnographic examples of parietal art where the painting process can still be observed. In fact they were forced to base their analogies largely on Australian Aboriginal art. The latter is produced for a number of different purposes. (1) Art is carried out purely for pleasure, as 'art for art's sake'. (2) Art may be totemic in that it illustrates statements or stories and records historical and mythical events. (3) Art is sometimes involved in sympathetic magic, in the context of sorcery or other rites. Since little information is provided on why art has these different functions in different situations and contexts it is impossible to use the analogy rigorously to interpret the past. In fact Ucko and Rosenfeld are forced to attempt subjective and imaginative fitting of the hypotheses to the Palaeolithic cave art. They argue almost entirely on *a priori* grounds.

A realisation of the need to situate art within its social and cultural context is clear in Vinnicombe's (1976) careful and sensitive study of prehistoric and recent rock paintings of the foothills of the Drakensberg escarpment in South Africa and Eastern Lesotho. The area was inhabited by Bushmen and parallels with those existing in the Kalahari allow interpretation of the Drakensberg art by direct historical analogy (*fig. 44*). Obviously art from different time periods may look the same but have different meanings. In comparing past and present Bushman depictions we must emphasise that the social context has not dramatically changed (see the historical evidence described in Chapter 5).

Vinnicombe's objective and quantitative analyses of the art showed that the rock paintings are not a realistic representation or reflection of the daily pursuits or environment of the artists. Certain subjects are emphasised (such as human figures with bows and arrows) while others are neglected (such as the plants which were an important source of Bushmen food). There is a coherence to certain conventions of posture. For example, human figures conform to the characterstic and formalised head, limb and buttock shapes, while a colour division in animals, especially the red body and white extremity of the eland, is a hall-mark of Bushman art.

How is one to interpret such art? Like Palaeolithic art, the main models used in the literature have been 'art for art's sake', and 'sympathetic magic'. Vinnicombe, however, came to realise that the highly selective aspect of the art might relate to a symbolic code. Bushmen had painted what was important for *them* symbolically within an ideological structure. There was a set of values centred on the relationship between man and eland (the most frequently depicted animal in Drakensberg art). To understand the art, then, it is necessary to comprehend something of the symbolism used in social strategies. The symbolic distinctions and relationships in the art have social meaning.

Thus, in studying Palaeolithic cave art from Western Europe we must first know something about how the art is symbolically organised; this is more useful than knowing if it is on stone walls or mud walls. For example, Alexander Marshak has identified the cumulative, participatory and sequential structure of Palaeolithic art. Other relevant aspects of context may include whether the caves were used for normal occupation or for ceremonies. In these ways a clearer idea can be built up of the nature of the art and its context. But before we can apply analogies from the present we need to have a good theoretical understanding of how symbolic codes are generated and transformed in different spheres of activity.

In examining how art represents symbolically the sphere of social relationships we are thrown back again on the problem of definition. Depending on what art is, the symbolism in the art will have different relationships with other aspects of life. It could be claimed that in our own society art is not closely linked into the major part of social interaction. It is peripheral and often irrelevant; or so the claim is made. A lack of relationship between art and its social milieu may occur because, within that social environment, art is separated and defined as a discrete category of behaviour linked to galleries and museums. Of course, attempts are made to bring 'art into the streets', but the main point to be made here is simply that our definition of art and the way it is linked symbolically to social strategies depend in turn on the overall place of artists and creative abstraction within society. The notion of 'art', and 'art for art's sake' may well be projections of our own preconceptions. The most successful studies of ethnographic 'art' (see below) have been those which have examined representation as representation within a social context and have not been concerned with imposing *a priori* categories.

Art, then, is not an idiosyncratic attitude of mind, a cultural quirk,

a

b

44 A direct historical analogy for a rock painting in South Africa (Vinnicombe 1976). **a** The Medicine Dance of the Kung Bushmen in the Kalahari desert. The seated women clap and sing while the men dance around them, sometimes cutting through the circular track made in the sand. Notice the typical dance posture of flexed hips and knees. **b** Site F6, Ndloveni Mountain. A line of male dancers, bodies leaning forward and legs bent at the knee, stamp with small steps towards a group of seated women who are clapping and singing the dance rhythm. This dance is apparently identical to the Medicine Dances among living Bushmen in the Kalahari desert (see a)

nor is it a behavioural response to social imperatives. Rather it is created uniquely within a social context to give meaning to the world and to have social effect. But in constructing the art widely found principles of composition and symbolism are used. Analogies can be used to inform both these symbolic principles and the place of art in society. In applying the analogies we must not impose our own categories but must locate 'art' and depictions in a social and symbolic framework.

Decoration

Decoration on a prehistoric pot may sometimes be described as art and in certain social contexts it may well be art in the way that we use the term in western society. But, as has been suggested, the same decoration, in another context, may have very different meanings. It is best to assume *a priori* as little as possible about the artistic nature of the pottery decoration. How, then, can one interpret the decoration and shapes of prehistoric artifacts? As with Bushmen painting, the symbolic codes in the pottery decoration and shapes may be related to codes within the social structure. But the relationships between the different codes depend very much on the position and function of decoration and pottery within the particular society concerned. Symbolic structure and social function must be considered side by side, as interdependent.

Decoration and design, whether on pottery, metal or other media, can be thought of as having two components; content and form. Ethnographic observations alerted archaeologists to the need to examine both these aspects of design although they have tended to concentrate on the second. Bunzel's early work (1929) amongst Pueblos in the American south-west determined that vessel form and decoration result in a design of which the essential part is a relationship. In other words, what is important are the rules, or grammar according to which the particular pot is put together. Friedrich's (1970) and Hardin's (1979) work with Tarascan potters also demonstrates that design grammar may have social implications which differ from the individual motifs or elements of design (such as circles, squiggles and blobs). For example, Friedrich found that design elements diffused rapidly through the village and were not good indicators of a pottery painting style. Washburn has suggested (1977; 1978) that the form and symmetry of design are better indicators of population group composition and interaction than individual design motifs.

An underlying assumption in such work, supported by ethnographic studies in the American south-west, is that different levels of design are generally linked to different types of social processes. Thus, at the higher level, design form is a good indicator of social units and their boundaries. At a middle level, the content of the individual motifs diffuses rapidly or may indicate matrilocal residence as discussed in Chapter 6. At the lowest level, the motor habits of individual potters can be recognised by studying details such as the angles at which parts of a design come together, distances between lines and their thickness (Hill 1977). In the latter case the distributions of individual designs indicate the movements of individual male or female potters and so are thought to be good reflectors of post-marital residence, population movements and exchange.

The notion that each level of design is related to different cultural variables and social units of different size (Redman 1977) partly derives from studies which suggest correlations with levels of consciousness. The middle-level design elements are often consciously chosen by potters (Bunzel 1929; Hardin 1979) so that the distributions of the motifs indicate self-conscious social units. Certainly, amongst the Nuba of Sudan, each design element, from zig-zags to rows of dots and triangles, is given a specific meaning such as snake, mountain or woman (Hodder 1982c).

Design form, on the other hand, has been noted in the American south-west and in Mexico to be sub-conscious. Potters may be unaware of the rules of the design grammar within which they work, in much the same way that we can speak good English without conscious knowledge of the rules. Similarly, individual motor habits which produce decorative lines of different thickness are thought to be sub-consciously controlled. If different levels of design relate to different levels of consciousness, then it may well be the case that the cultural variables which correlate with each level may also differ.

While it is certainly true that, in each cultural context, some knowledge is generally discursive and other information non-discursive there are problems in assuming a universal relationship between levels of design and levels of consciousness. No reason has been provided as to why the relationship should exist, and it seems likely that in certain societies the rules of design formation are as, or more, explicitly stated than the choice of motifs themselves. We cannot assume, *a priori*, that one level of design will always mean the same thing. In addition, even if for most members of society the formal rules are sub-conscious, it remains possible for individuals to penetrate the rules and their meaning, to give them renewed significance, to change them, invert them or prevent their diffusion. What each level of design means depends on the particular historical and cultural context and we must analyse design free from *a priori* assumptions of these sorts.

This is not to say that the relationship between discursive and non-discursive knowledge is not of central importance, because it is, as will be shown below. But in each context, pottery-design content and form must be studied in relation to other designs on other artifacts, and associations for designs must be sought on artifacts in burials, settlement contexts, hoards and so on. We must build up a picture of design variability and its correlates in each case rather than assuming universal relationships.

Similarly, we cannot assume that the 'etic' classifications of the archaeologist will always correspond with the 'emic' classifications of the individual making and decorating artifacts. Much energy has been expended to provide ethnographic corroboration of the fact that, whether one is talking of Tarascan potters in Mexico (Hardin 1979) or stone-tool producers in Australia (White and Thomas 1972), archaeological and 'native' classifications may differ. Such differences may partly occur because different levels of design are used as the basis of typologies in different contexts. But, as with art, the archaeologists should not conclude that their classifications are any less real or valid than those of the producers. The 'emic' typology may be just as mystifying and confusing as the 'etic'. Names and labels are provided for artifacts for social purposes within social contexts. The discursive and non-discursive levels may differ. The categories and contrasts which are not labelled verbally have social significance in their own right, perhaps complementary to the verbal groupings. We need, then, models which relate the form and content of design and decoration to a social context and which also examine the relationship between discursive and non-discursive levels of knowledge.

There are few convincing ethnographic studies of the relationship between design form and social structure, and this is partly because a static set of relationships is supposed rather than an on-going social process in which discursive and non-discursive levels interact. It is possible to show that in a particular society patterns of exchange, settlement and decoration are similar in form (e.g. Adams 1973), but it is important to know why the correspondences occur. It is not sufficient to suppose some determinacy of the mind. Korn (1978) identifies sets of rules for the production of Papua New Guinea paintings. According to Vastokas (1978) the rich designs of the Northwest Coast Indians in America demonstrate oppositions in the arrangements of bipartite and tripartite patterns. These formal tensions are linked by Vastokas to a general concern with conflicts between opposites in the whole culture and to social and economic tensions.

The archaeologist is unable to use these examples of *congruence* between decorative styles and other spheres of life to interpret material culture from past societies unless some idea is obtained of why, and in what contexts, congruence emerges. What are the social processes in which particular structural transformations and congruences occur? The above examples of correlations between different types of activity see design form and social structure as static replicas of each other. As Hardin (1979) has emphasised in her study of Mexican Tarascan potters, each decorative pattern on a pot is a problem-solving process, not a fixed typology in the mind of the potter. In order to understand this process of design generation, we need to comprehend what decoration is doing in society, how it functions and plays a part in the lives of individual social actors.

In many societies some things are decorated and other things are not. Why should this be the case? What is the social role of decoration on material items? Clearly, the answers to such questions are numerous. Decoration may increase the value of an artifact, it may give status and indicate social position, or it may show social affiliation. But most such models are general and may not explain why particular items are decorated and not others, or why decoration as opposed to shape or colour or texture is used in a particular context. Braithwaite (1982), however, in a study of potters and pottery in southern Sudan noted that pots are decorated which are involved in the transfer of food from one social category to another. For example, food prepared by women is served to men in decorated pots. Pots not involved in transfer between men and women, or between levels of the social hierarchy, are not decorated. The decoration marks out and draws attention to the transfer, maintaining and supporting the social dichotomy.

A related notion might be termed the 'chamber-pot model'. Amongst the Nuba of Sudan (Hodder 1982c), decoration occurs most frequently around activities in which dirt and symbolic pollution impinge on daily life (*fig. 45*). For example, decoration is placed around the flour in the grinding huts in order to keep the flour clean. It occurs around the washing places (*fig. 45c*). The areas in which the Mesakin women prepare food amongst filth and animals (see Chapter 3) are surrounded in rich decoration which in some sense purifies or guards the actions. Filled granaries are 'ritually' decorated. In the cattle camps, young men are associated with 'pure' cattle and cattle milk. When young girls bring drinks to the men in the camps, the calabash containers are intricately decorated (*fig. 45d*). In all these instances the decoration has multiple functions. At one level it prevents the potential pollution of dirt, women, insects, infection or whatever. But it also draws attention to the transfers and to the potential impurity. Since this impurity is frequently associated with women, it emphasises their subordinate status and the 'pure' male dominance. Yet the decoration also emphasises the threat of women and their ability to contradict male power. Discursive knowledge may centre on the rules of use and practice. Women may know what is 'right' to do. But, at a non-discursive level, the pot and other decoration *acts back* ideologically and silently as part of social processes.

Similar uses of decoration occur in Swahili communities on the E. African coast (Donley 1982) and it may not be too far-fetched to draw an analogy with Victorian chamber pots. These receptacles were often

a

b

c

45 Examples of Nuba decoration. **a** – **c** Decoration around the often dirt-covered compound (see also *fig. 15*). In 45c a granary is on the left and a washing area is on the right.

45 (cont'd) **d** Decorated calabash containers

richly decorated, especially those owned by more aristocratic English families. At one level the plants, flowers, trees and cherubs painted on the pots made the contents of the pots acceptable and respectable, especially to a society more and more concerned with the 'cleanliness is next to godliness' ethic. But as part of a social process the pots did much more. Individuals in Victorian society, especially its upper echelons, took great care that all bodily functions were private and personal and there was a concern with purity. In such a context, the handling, emptying and cleaning of chamber pots by servants presented a social problem. The difficulty could be countered not only by having special backstairs routes to be taken for the emptying of the pots, but also by having decoration which recalled things natural and pleasant on the one hand and fine dinner and tea services on the other. The decoration occurred on pots handled by other people more often than on pots filled and emptied in private. Ideologically, the designs supported the individual's own conception of herself or himself but the designs also acted back upon the stratification within society, drawing attention to the servant/master dichotomy and putting one group at a lower level of value than the other.

In the 'chamber-pot model' decoration draws attention to, and forms, social differences. At a discursive level it makes the contents of pots 'nice' and acceptable, but at a non-discursive level it acts back ideologically within social strategies. In other instances, a very different process may occur. Precisely because, in many societies, decoration on mundane objects such as pots is hardly noticed and is given little significance at the discursive level, it may be used to carry meaning that is hidden. For example, women in a subordinate position in relation to men may be able to form group solidarity and achieve social strategies through the silent discourse of their decorated pots (Braithwaite 1982) or calabashes (Hodder 1982c). In these cases the distributions and form of decoration may be inversions of and opposite to structures within society as a whole.

In these models the main concern has been with why some material items are decorated and not others. Archaeologists frequently excavate cemeteries containing inhumations around which artifacts are located – necklaces, rings on fingers and toes, brooches on shoulders, and so on. We can ask a similar question in relation to such evidence. Why are certain parts of the body decorated and not others? The human body is a natural 'map' onto which the social 'map' symbolised in clothing and jewellery is placed. The natural characteristics of the different parts of the body can be used symbolically and emphasised within social strategies by the appropriate choice of what is worn. An ethnographic study which makes these points clear is T. Turner's (1969) analysis of the bodily adornment of the Kayapo Indians in Brazil.

The complex body painting and decoration of the Brazilian tribe varies according to the age and sex of individuals. As one's role in life changes with age from child to adult, one changes appearance. Turner demonstrates that the parts of the body which are decorated at different stages in life are meaningfully chosen. A male infant wears an ear plug while a young man wears a small lip plug. When a man reaches the final stage of 'father' and is involved in the political affairs of the community in the men's house, he changes his lip plug for a flat plate, the diameter of which may reach 4in. and which is stuck in the lower lip. The contrast between ear and lip plug is significant. For the Kayapo, hearing and speaking have symbolic importance. Hearing is a passive activity and means understanding. For example, if a man has good relations with his father's side of the family, he may say 'I hear them strongly'. Speaking on the other hand is associated with social self-assertion and flamboyant oratory, one of the major activities of Kayapo men. The huge lip plates are consciously linked to this oral assertiveness. Infants are the reciprocal correlate of this. The relation of the infant to the father is analogous to that between hearing (in its Kayapo sense of passive affirmation of social relations) and speaking (considered as social assertiveness). The symbols of dress are thus appropriate within a given ideology which is the basis of adult male political power.

In an archaeological context a similar interpretation of the appropriate choice of ear and mouth decoration would have to be linked to other evidence (for example, from cemeteries) of adult male dominance over highly conformist younger males and females. Other aspects of context would also have to be verified. Overall, it might be thought that specific models of the Kayapo type are less likely to be applied successfully in prehistory than broad generalisations. Indeed, the main value of the Kayapo Indian case may simply be to make the general points that symbols are not arbitrarily chosen and that the natural human body can be used to represent and 'naturalise' social relations. But there is a danger with general models that the links between the various components are inadequately specified. This point can be made more clear in reference to decoration by considering some hypotheses suggested by Mary Douglas.

Up to this point decoration on particular types of artifacts (pots, calabashes) or parts of the body has been considered. Decoration distinguishes classes of artifact and helps to form different categories. Douglas has attempted to provide more general models for types of society in which there is an overall concern with categorisation and classification. She has suggested (1970) two independently varying aspects of society – group and grid. Membership of groups varies in that in some societies individuals are less subordinate to groups. Within a group, the grid describes the roles and networks of relationships centred on individuals. Within some societies, roles are undefined and ambiguous. In a context of strong group and weak grid,

Douglas suggests that the emphasis is on the purity of the group, and on the insider/outsider dichotomy. Danger is associated with boundaries, there are cleansing rituals, and the body interior is protected from pollution coming from the outside. There is an emphasis on classification, categorisation and logic-chopping exercises. In view of what we have seen so far in relation to decoration, we might also expect such societies to use designs to mark boundaries and to form categorical contrasts. (For another model suggested by Douglas (1966) linking male-female relationships to beliefs in sex pollution and decoration see Hodder (1982c, p. 160).)

The links between group and grid on the one hand and classification and categorisation on the other hand are not well described so that it is difficult to know what contextual links one should search for in applying the model to the past. The model appears to derive ritual behaviour and perception as passive by-products of social conditions. We can only understand why the general links occur if we know why in particular instances material culture is actively involved within ideologies and social strategies. Analogies such as the 'chamber-pot model' specify the relationships between variables more clearly and can be compared with evidence from the past more rigorously and with greater explanatory potential.

The major concern here has been with decoration as a marker of boundaries and as part of a process of categorisation. There are many other ways in which variability in types of category system can be noted. For example, shapes of pots may be used to set up contrasts between different individuals and the foods and activities associated with the pots. Similarly, in some societies stone tool assemblages are generalised with few distinct tool types, and with expedient working use of flake edges. In other societies each activity may be associated with one or more distinct tool types. This variation may be related at least partly to a symbolic process within strategies of social domination and within ideologies of purity and pollution. But very different models have been proposed for such patterning, as will be seen in the section which follows.

Style

In the discussion of art and decoration, ways of doing things have been described. These styles are made up of form and content and they are associated with individuals or social groups. Recently archaeologists have become interested in the social significance of style but they have followed a rather different route to that followed above. Style has been linked to information exchange (Washburn 1977; Conkey 1978; Wobst 1977). The underlying assumption is that symbolic communication between people is needed for them to interact and cooperation is necessary for their survival. Behaviour is more predictable if material symbols are given as clues beforehand, thus easing strain during social interaction.

Wobst's (1977) ethnographic study in Yugoslavia is aimed at clothing, especially headgear. It is argued that stylistic messages serve the greatest utility when they are directed towards a particular group. The target group should not be too close since the message usually would be known already or generally could be more easily transmitted in other communication modes. But it should not be too distant since decoding or encountering the message could not be assured. Thus it is for the socially not-too-distant that stylistic behaviour is targetted. People close to 'the transmitter' individual, in the immediate household, would receive only a few stylistic messages so that there would be little stylistic variation within a residence unit archaeologically.

The more members there are in the target group, the more efficient stylistic behaviour becomes relative to other communication modes. Thus, in the absence of other factors, the amount of stylistic behaviour should correlate positively with the size of the social networks in which individuals participate. In large and complex societies in which there is a large amount of repetitive and anticipated communication between socially distant but not-too-distant individuals, stylistic behaviour structures important aspects of artifact form.

In Wobst's model it is not always clear what is meant by stylistic behaviour, but here it will be assumed that decoration and shape elaboration is included in the term. But if style is the *way* that decoration and shape and other material and behaviour are organised, it is not at all clear that Wobst's model really explains style. The model concerns communication and information flow. As long as the symbols are visible and do what they are intended to do they are adequate. The way the symbols are put together, their form and content, is considered less than their function. We have hardly explained style at all. To understand style, as was shown in the previous section, it is necessary to examine the historical and meaning-laden context within which symbols are chosen and their organisation formed.

If the information processing model of style itself is limited, is it even an adequate explanation of the function of style? The model is concerned with the good of style for society as a whole, with its efficient running. Material items are simply passive bits of information in a communication system. They simply carry information from transmitter to receiver. This highly functionalist stance does not allow for symbols to act back upon society within an ideological framework. As was shown in the previous section, material symbols are actively involved in conflicting strategies within societies. They may be 'good' in some sense for some section of society, but not necessarily for all.

So, in returning to Wobst's hypothesis, it is clear that style and material culture elaboration are not directed at one target group.

Indeed a vaste area of stylistic behaviour occurs within the immediate residential unit around an individual. Here material symbols are often involved in questions of male and female purity, dominance and subordination and in the competing social strategies of older and younger members of the same sex. We have seen how rich decoration may surround areas of symbolic and social concern within the home. In explaining such stylistic behaviour at socially close distances, the information exchange model fails and it is necessary to consider ideologies and competing social strategies.

Equally, the amount of stylistic behaviour will not correlate directly with size of social unit. As has been indicated, such a hypothesis assumes that material symbols are passive 'words' of communication, allowing the efficient working of large complex societies. But in fact stylistic elaboration and a concern with classification, categorisation and decorative variability may relate to particular points in the historical development of social structures. We have seen how decoration and shape distinction may relate not so much to the existence of social categories but to a concern with those categories. The Nuba and Victorian decoration occur in contexts in which a dominant group is 'threatened'. The decoration marks off and keeps away. Material culture may often be involved in legitimating social groups – giving them meaning and supporting their position relative to other groups. Where social groups are threatened or contradicted, or are otherwise concerned with self-legitimation, 'stylistic behaviour', in the form of numerous contrasts and variations in pottery, stone, metal and other types, may be most marked. Stylistic behaviour is not linked directly to group size but to ideologies and strategies of legitimation.

With this more active social model, style should be studied as the surface appearance of structure. In other words, the style seen in artifact patterning should be linked to the rules and processes of the social structure as in the Nuba, Kayapo and Victorian examples. We can talk of the style of a whole society or culture, meaning the way that the surface appearance is organised by the underlying structural rules.

In considering the style of a whole social community one is close to the earlier archaeological use of style to define regional and temporal units. A set of pottery and other styles overlapping in the same area is called a culture, and the boundaries of the culture indicate the boundaries of a social unit, or so it was thought. Ethnographic and historical evidence (summarised in Hodder (1978a)) soon demonstrated that the boundaries of material culture and social units did not always coincide. Cultures have been identified in ethnographic data from the California Indians (Kroeber 1923) to Polynesia (Milke 1949). These material units sometimes correlate with linguistic divisions (Clarke 1968), but in many other cases material cultures are comprised of many non-coincident distributions and the correlations with social units are difficult to identify.

If archaeologists cannot answer the question, 'does this style or material attribute correlate with a self-conscious identity group?' they can tackle the rather different question, 'why do regional boundaries for different material types sometimes not coincide to produce distinct cultures but produce a palimpsest of overlapping distrubutions?' Ethnographic data from the Baringo district in Kenya (Hodder 1982c) suggested a link between the distinctiveness of cultural boundaries and economic competition between social units. Where there was more economic competition and raiding for gain, termed negative reciprocity, material boundaries were more distinct, and *vice-versa*. Negative reciprocity is based on a categorical distinction between 'us' and 'them'. 'They' are treated differently from 'us'; there is an attempt to gain something for nothing. Negative reciprocity is less possible among 'us', within a social unit, where taking and giving are balanced, at least in the long run. The one-sided attempt to gain is possible from those that are not 'us'. The material differences justify and define the negative relations. As competition and raiding increase, there is a premium on conformity within social units and differences between them.

This type of cross-cultural relationship between negative reciprocity and material culture or style boundaries is dangerous if it takes no account of the context within which boundary maintenance is chosen as a social and economic strategy. In the Baringo study it was suggested that the relationships between older and younger men within society played a part in maintaining the boundaries. It was to the advantage of older men to involve young men as warriors in inter-tribal raiding. In other social contexts, in which internal tensions of this type do not exist, raiding and material culture boundaries may not develop. The dry, poor environment of the Baringo area and the pastoralist adaptation are relevant components in the equation. It is difficult to generalise widely without bearing these points in mind.

In the examination of cultural boundaries it is not only the social context which must be considered but also concepts, beliefs and ideas. We are familiar with the fact that Puritanism and Catholicism are associated with particular styles of life which are in some sense incompatible. These cultural styles are historically determined and have an ideological and social basis. More generally it can be stated that styles and cultural groups with different underlying structures may develop side by side and the boundaries between them may be distinct because certain ways of doing things are not compatible to both groups. This type of difference has been noted amongst the Nuba tribes as was described in Chapter 3. The two processes which maintain distinct cultural boundaries, negative reciprocity and structural incompatability, are often linked since the structural differences may be developed within 'us-them' confrontations, and 'us-them' competition is in turn encouraged by structural and historical differences.

Conclusion

The styles of art and decoration can be linked to the rules which govern society as a whole, but only if the linkage is itself understood as a social process. How art and decoration are used and given meaning depends on ideologies and social strategies. It is insufficient then to link types of art and forms of design directly to types of society, as in the case of a link between repetitive design and egalitarian societies. Such models assume psychological universals and behavioural responses. Art and design are perceived as passive by-products of social processes and as passive bits of information. In reality, art and design, their content and form, have historically specific significance which is involved ideologically within social strategies. Our ethnographic models for art and design, to be used successfully in archaeology, must concern symbolism, social process and ideology.

9   Looking at ourselves

Throughout this book, but particularly in Chapters 7 and 8, the need for archaeologists to examine their own assumptions and preconceptions has become clear. For example, there is a danger that anything we find 'odd' is labelled ritual. Since most western archaeologists are white and have comfortable middle-class backgrounds their views as to what is 'odd' are likely to be similar and particular to their own context. Also, for this group, art has a particular meaning which has influenced reconstructions of prehistoric drawings, paintings and sculptures.

Two more general preconceptions which have been present in the discussions in this book will be examined in this chapter. The first concerns the way archaeologists have emphasised functional models and theories involving adaptive efficiency. For many archaeologists, style has function but the structure is little examined (Chapter 8). Refuse is cleared away for functional reasons and values are not considered of primary relevance (Chapter 3). Economies are adaptively efficient (Chapter 4). A rift has been formed between adaptive function and utilitarian value on the one hand, and cultural norms and historical contexts on the other. This notion of a gulf is at home in the value system of archaeologists themselves. In our own society functional efficiency is a primary dimension on which value is assessed. From knives and forks to houses, cars and the social order, streamlined efficiency is the key note. We are really into maximisation.

Another preconception which can be seen to have been imposed on the past is closely linked to the first. Material items, the bits and pieces of daily life, are simply tools, passive by-products, with little ideological or symbolic component. We have seen how burial and settlement patterns are thought by some archaeologists to be mirror images of social organisation. As such they may reveal the past to archaeologists, but they are of little importance in the formation and support of societies.

In our society it is generally thought that material artifacts are used and manipulated by people but that there is little reflexive relationship. Artifacts are trivia. Thus despite the materialist basis of western society there are remarkably few centres of research in which material culture is studied in its own right (see for example, the Centre for Contemporary Culture Studies in the University of Birmingham). Archaeologists have recently begun to emphasise the importance of material culture studies in our own society (e.g. Rathje 1979; Gould and Schiffer 1981), although it will be suggested below that many of

196

these analyses are inhibited by the same utilitarian preconceptions as have been detailed above.

One of the aims of looking at our own material culture is to understand the preconceptions and assumptions that we impose on the material residues from the past. But we need careful and self-critical analysis if we are to do more than confirm our own cultural beliefs. A second aim is to reach a deeper knowledge of material culture patterning in a context which we know well and understand. The difficulties of penetrating an alien culture were described in Chapter 2. It might be claimed that it is even more difficult to understand one's own culture because it is too familiar; it is difficult to remove the scales of assumptions and maintain a critical stance. Yet if a questioning self-analysis can be achieved it is likely to lead to deeper insights than brief participation in an unfamiliar world.

In many respects our own society is hugely at odds with a prehistoric past without industrialisation, high-speed communication, capitalism and the market economy, centralised state government and bureaucratic social care. Modern material culture studies can only contribute to an understanding of the past if the central concern is to examine directly the links between material and social variables and to ask searching 'why' questions about those links. As long as the contextual relationships are adequately researched then we can say something about the way material culture is involved in social strategies, about the nature of 'things', that will be relevant to reconstructions of a very different past. I hope to make this clear in the course of this Chapter.

However, most modern material culture studies conducted by archaeologists have not adequately examined the values which lie behind the production of material culture patterning. Wilk and Schiffer (1979) report an ethnoarchaeological study of vacant lots in Tucson, Arizona. The refuse, paths and vegetation patterns on these spaces clear of buildings were plotted. Several aspects of discard behaviour on the lots suggested more general statements to Wilk and Schiffer. For example, artifacts dropped during travel across the lots were randomly spaced along the paths. Material such as wrappers, containers and cigarette ends ceased being useful while walking and were dropped 'in transit'. Wilk and Schiffer suggested that this 'in transit' material may be of a general cross-cultural kind, affected by variables such as distance travelled and frequency of travel. Another observation was that beams, bricks and sand were stored on the lots but were in the end not wanted and were abandoned. It was suggested that this storage-abandonment process may be a general one relevant to hoards of coins and caches of chert blades.

In fact these different types of behaviour are specific to a social, cultural and economic context. That material of a particular kind is dropped in a particular way along certain paths (rarely on paths in nature parks for instance) is dependent on a complex set of interlinked variables. To mention a few, that we drop material in lots at all relates to overall values linking discard and land-types and to our conceptions of different types of environment. That we eat and drink meals 'on foot' may relate to our overall concern with maximising time and to the relatively small part played by eating ritual in our society. Similarly, the fact that items are stored on the lots and then abandoned is structurally linked to an economic system in which bulk buying saves money or in which 'do-it-yourself' contrasts with commercial building. We cannot adequately use such analogies to explain the past unless we know what variables in a social system are relevant to the behaviour observed. Wilk and Schiffer do not examine the relevant context.

Traces of children – playforts, tree houses, hearths, broken bottles, pits, clearings and bicycle tracks – were also found on the lots. 'These messy and often destructive activities occur in vacant lots rather than homes' (ibid., p. 532). Again, we would want to know why children played differently in two areas. Hammond (1981) has studied the effects of child play on refuse patterns in a context in which most of the relevant variables could be well understood since the subject of ethnographic enquiry was his son (*fig. 46*).

Whenever refuse is dropped it is not 'dead' but can be re-used and is actively given meaning and involved in social strategies (see Chapter 3). An extreme example of the same process occurs when children turn rubbish into toys. Non-biodegradable domestic refuse was dumped by Hammond Senior in a 1.0m diameter and 0.5m high pile on an area of sloping grassland. The child, 1.2 years old, moved in and around the refuse on four or three limbs for three 30-minute periods and the results of his activities were recorded during and after each session. Gradually the artifacts were picked up, tossed, transported, rolled and shaken until a highly dispersed artifact distribution was produced.

To what extent are we to conclude from this study that children may have been influential in causing dispersed artifact distributions on archaeological sites? To see whether the analogy is relevant for the past, we need to see why Hammond's child acted in the way he did. Presumably only Hammond, and his wife, could supply an adequate answer, but we may, with due timidity, hazard a guess. The last 30 years have seen a revolution in the way children are brought up in western, middle-class, Anglo-Saxon society. It is realised that the early months of life are crucial for social and mental development, children should learn through experience, they should be stimulated as much as possible, and they should be brought up liberally. Many young couples today allow their children to intrude fully into their lives, to be demanding and independent. 'Puppy power' has arrived. Needless to say, children in other cultures are brought up very differently. The offspring of several ethnic minorities in England are recognised to be generally less inquisitive and independent at an early age. It is likely, then, that not all children when faced with a pile of rubbish would have reacted in a similar way to Hammond's. It is also likely that in many societies children would not normally be allowed to carry out such activities. Before we can use this analogy for the past we must have a better understanding of how children are viewed and brought up in different cultures.

Some broad generalisations which are of relevance to discussions earlier in this book have resulted from modern studies of discard behaviour. In particular, Rathje (1978) has demonstrated the point made in Chapter 8 that verbal and material information may differ. What people say about what they do may itself be a gloss on reality and must be understood as part of a social process. Rathje found that the results of questionnaires concerning buying, eating and disposal habits were contradicted by detailed analysis of the contents of people's dustbins. Many of the predicted relationships between income, economy and discard behaviour were not corroborated by this objective analysis. Individuals may exaggerate or cover up their actions, often quite innocently, since responses to a questionnaire, especially about refuse, are an active process in which the respondant expects to gain or lose. Detailed examination of the links between verbal account and actual behaviour are not provided by Rathje, but some of the possible complexities of attitudes to refuse were discussed in relation to Gypsies in Chapter 3.

Just as individuals today think about and use refuse in different ways, so settlement space is organised differently in different industrialised countries. When archaeologists study a prehistoric or early historic settlement site they normally categorise each room or hut by function (kitchen hut, work room, storage room, etc.). But even this basic move may be no more than the imposition on the past of western twentieth-century concepts. The attitude of the West towards settlement space can be seen most clearly by making a contrast with modern Japan (Canter and Lee n.d.) The West operates on the idea that each function has its own space. In the Japanese house, however, rooms are named by location without direct reference to function. Japanese spaces, unlike our 'drawing room' or 'dining room', suit the function to the occasion and need. So the use to which a space is put varies with the time of day. The size of a space varies freely as the sliding screens are opened or closed. The notion of continuous and uninterrupted spatial flow pervades even the storage spaces, which are treated much like living areas. When a bed is needed in part of the house, the Japanese bring it in, and when a table is required, they bring that in too. This undifferentiated use of space certainly differs from the West. As archaeologists, we can examine to what extent rooms are functionally specific, but we must not assume, by assigning functional labels, that they should be.

All the above examples refer to the same general problem that the relationship between society and material culture is stylistic. How

46 Child play in refuse. **a** Day 1: the child and the pile of litter have been together 1 minute. **b** Day 1: after 23 mins. **c** Day 2: the refuse after a total of 60 minutes of play. **d** Day 3: the refuse after the total of 90 minutes play (By courtesy, N. Hammond)

burial, refuse and settlement relate to social organisation is part of an historical way of life, an ideology. That the way we treat things is appropriate to a way of life might be called the 'sandwich syndrome'. The English sandwich is thin, very thin, with finely cut bread and minute slices of cucumber. The mouth need hardly open, decorum is maintained. The American sandwiches are enormous, the mouth stretches wide, crunches, rips and tears. The nature of the contrast, its orientation, seems very right.

In a suburban high school in Detroit in the late 1970s, Penelope Eckert (n.d) noted two groups of kids who could be distinguished by the widths of their jean legs. A contrast was being set up here between children from different socio-economic backgrounds – the 'jocks' (also known as 'in-crowd', 'elite' or 'rah-rahs') from the upper end of the local socio-economic continuum and the 'burnouts' (also known as 'hoods', 'greasers' or 'freaks') from the lower end. Eckert actually measured the widths of the jean legs of kids in different parts of the school at different times and showed that a certain territoriality was being maintained. While the difference in dress was partly due to the ability of the better-off 'jocks' to keep up with changing fashions which were moving away from flared to peg trousers, the leg widths were also adhered to by each group as part of identity maintenance.

Table 3 Average jean leg width at lunch period in equal-sized areas of the cafeteria hall in a Detroit high school

WEST				EAST
Area 1 (jock territory)	Area 2	Area 3	Area 4 (burnout territory)	Area 5
2.6	2.9	3.6	3.7	3.5

The different leg widths were part of, and referred to, two different ways of life. The 'burnouts' were described by all (including themselves) as the kids who smoke, who take drugs, who hang out in the courtyard of the school, who are not interested in school, and who do not care a lot about clothing. 'Burnouts' did not eat in the cafeteria and did not involve themselves in school activity. The older style of flared jeans referred to alienation and anti-formalism. The 'jocks' did not smoke, were abstemious and preferred school to drugs, were involved in school activities, went to class and dressed well. In contrast to the 'burnouts', they wanted to conform and get on within the formalised school system. The jean widths did not just mark a difference, they also came to refer to particular ideals and outlooks and thus play an active part in forming and giving meaning to the lives of individual children.

In England, similar contrasts exist today in certain state schools between the 'lads', alienated male-centred youths, and the conformists and do-gooders (Willis 1977). To oversimplify, the 'lads' tend to get manual, semi-skilled working-class jobs. The 'do-gooders' tend to get qualifications and to move into a career which will take them into lower management. Already, in schools, individuals take sides in a class-ridden society. The polarisations manager/worker, middle class/lower class, public school/state school continue to play central roles in England. The affluent worker never really made it, despite the indications of the '60s. Young and old have been involved since the '50s and '60s in a series of 'style wars' (York 1980; Hebdige 1979) closely linked to class issues. By examining the dress and symbols of the post-war sub-cultures of Britain, we can learn something of the way material culture is used to mark out identity groups. What we find is once again that material symbols do not just identify or label. They also help to form ideologies, ways of life. They are chosen as meaningful and appropriate.

We can identify certain symbolic contrasts in England in the period since 1950 and then move on to consider the ideological, social and economic principles behind the visible contrasts. By the early '70s the hippy movement had developed into a diffuse mainstream consensus, centred on the middle class. The long hair, relaxed, floppy dress, informal life style, drugs or transcendental meditation, had developed into concerns with health food, ecology, body awareness, introspection and liberalism. Many of the '60s contrasts between hippies on the one hand and mods and rockers on the other began to be blurred by the early '70s when many mods became hippies.

The punks who emerged by 1976 hated hippies. They had hippies on the brain. To them, hippies were seen as 'self-indulgent decadent middle-class wankers'. Pictures circulated of Sid Vicious chain-whipping a hippy in 1976. The punk culture reacted against hippies by being, for example, aggressively and consciously working class and by wearing safety pins instead of delicate Eastern earrings. Punks were inner urban prole, photographed in front of council blocks with their zippers and chains. The heavy boots contrasted with hippy barefoot or sandals, the bin-liners with the leather and fur, the short dyed artificial hair with the long natural style of the Jesus freaks. Punks sniffed glue while hippies had taken marijuana. By the time punk had developed into punk rock or new wave, further contrasts were set up: styled narrow trousers against shapeless flared jeans, a thin formal tie and jacket against rags, patches and open necks. The punk music was jerky, monotonous and cruel. The white, mashed-potato faces were 'into' aggression and violence, 'into' symbols of Nazis (swastikas and the Iron Cross) and the IRA (berets, dark glasses and mackintoshes with turned-up collars).

These various dichotomies are not to be explained entirely in terms of contrast and opposition. Each symbol is appropriate within a particular set of ideas. Hippies were 'into' peace, love, informality and things natural. The various derivatives of the hippy movement emphasised mental and bodily health and purity, self-knowledge and liberal socialist consensus. Hippies were soft. Punks were hard. The hippy dream had failed. The only way forward was 'Anarchy in the UK' or 'Smash the System' (or somefink). The punk songs emphasised dolequeues, boredom, urban violence and perversity. The dichotomies that were set up began at the ideological and social level. The symbols were part of and supported this.

Punk culture was the most marvellously expressive of the post-war era. Each individual created on her or his body, through objects, clothes, face and body painting and hair dying, an original, fleeting work of art. This do-it-yourself emphasis, seen in the return to a grand proliferation of rock groups (the anyone-can-grab-a-guitar-and-form-a-group syndrome – lost since the early Beatles era) was a central part of the reaction against the mass commercialism of style and rock music in the late '60s and early '70s. But what strategies did punks follow in achieving the contrasts and in activating the ideology?

One aspect of the new style was 'cut-ups' and 'montage'. They took bits and pieces from their normal contexts and made a mockery of them, turning them inside out and upside down. They took the tie of the mods and of conformists and wore it without a shirt. The neat dress worn by new wave groups was associated with brutal sexual gestures, bright orange hair and vacant staring eyes. Everyday objects such as safety pins and bin liners were placed into new and Dada-like contexts. Swastikas and the Iron Cross were used, but Johnny Rotten said all his friends were blacks, gays and outcasts; punks were not sympathetic to the National Front. The Nazi symbols were used as being appropriately aggressive, but certain aspects of their meaning changed by being placed in a new context.

The effectiveness of the punk style was that it took things which were familiar and put them into new, unimagined sets which shocked and disturbed. Both the content of the symbols (for example, the swastika itself) and the way they were used (upsetting accepted relationships) were about violence. And this was part of their aim, to smash the system, to turn suburbia inside out, upside down. Many of their symbols were derived from the past. Punks were involved in 'style archaeology', digging up styles and fashions from recent decades. There were a number of reasons why this was an appropriate strategy. The past contained familiar symbols which could thus be mocked and inverted. Also, the punks lived in an era of nostalgia for the late '60s. '60s' music, '60s' clothes,' 60s' well-being were continually referred to

47 Johnny Rotten (York 1980)

THIS ROOF HAS RECENTLY
BEEN CLEARED AT CONSIDER
EXPENSE. IN VIEW OF
RISK OF FIRE, ETC, THE DUMPI
OF RUBBISH, UNWANTED FURNI
ETC, IS STRICTLY FORBIDDEN
THE LANDLORDS. THE CO-OPER
IF TENANTS IS REQUESTED.

in fashion and in the media. Punks smashed the nostalgia by giving new meaning to the old symbols, and be referring to the darker side of the '6os. Most of the symbolic references were to working-class sub-cultures of that era and to ethnic minorities. The symbolic ties to the paramilitary groups and the IRA and Nazis have been mentioned. Other references were to the '5os' bikeboys and early '6os' mods. The music was clearly influenced by Rasta and reggae, and new wave became 'camp', closely associated with gay movements.

Punk was a working-class look. It expressed the boredom and pointlessness of rising youth unemployment, it lay bare the simmering violence that broke out from time to time in inner urban areas, on holiday beaches, on football terraces and, in a different form, in industry. It was a reaction against the failed middle-class liberalism, epitomised by the hippy movement. Within all this, the material symbols played a central part, partly because few punks were articulate. But also because the silent ambiguity could say so much more, and much more effectively.

There are and were, of course, many other youth sub-cultures such as the mods, skins and teds which have scarcely been mentioned. Analysis would show that here too the material symbols chosen were appropriate and meaningful. There were also other middle- and upper-class groups so well described by York (1980). His Sloane Rangers and Mayfair Mercs are social types easily recognised in England. They are styles made meaningful by a series of related ideas, such as the upper middle class 'country' style in the horses, dress, cars and clubs of the Sloane Rangers. But a major characteristic of the late '7os was the segmentation and polarisation of styles. As soon as someone produced a new style it was played on and turned around by others. This resulted from processes of 'montage' already described, and emulation.

Punks had to strive continually to shake off the media and middle-class appropriation of their individuality. Coloured hair and the punk style became chic for the middle and upper classes. It could be exploited by the media. Plastic silver painted chains were marketed. Punks were pushed into starker and more blatant reaction, forced into extremes but continually frustrated by middle-class fascination and by a middle-class desire to be sympathetic to the working class.

This brief discussion of some aspects of stylistic change and variation in the last 20 years in England allows certain points to be made which are of relevance to archaeologists and to their understanding of material culture. First, it is apparent that a material symbol has meaning as part of a set and from its position within a set. A safety pin takes its meaning from its context of use in association with other items. Equally, it is from the transformation and inversion of sets that individuals can use symbols effectively.

Second, however, the symbol itself has certain meanings associated with it through previous use. The Iron Cross and Swastika are good examples; these are not arbitrary symbols. Their past associations affect the new context or structure of use, but the meaning of the symbol is immediately altered by being placed in a new set. There is thus an interplay between structure and content. As soon as a material thing is used, its meaning is added to.

Third, therefore, there is an inbuilt dynamism in certain types of symbolic process. The punk 'montage' procedure is an extreme example where the whole style was about ways of changing the meanings of things by putting them in new contexts. Archaeologists are familiar with the process by which a new prehistoric culture takes bits and pieces from earlier cultures and forms them into a new whole. In the punk case we can see this happening with particular speed and vitality. We can also see the social process involved – one of rejection of certain aspects of the past, and reference to others as part of a social and ideological statement.

Fourth, and most clearly, symbol structure, content and change must be understood as taking place within an ideological context. The mass media are only able to exploit particular artifacts, and those artifacts only become widely accepted, because they have an appropriate symbolic meaning within a framework of ideas, a way of life. As archaeologists we must pay greater attention to building models of the principles by which material symbols are organised.

Fifth, the principles may not be discussed readily. Material symbols can say things which words cannot or do not. Few punks could articulate verbally the meaning of their symbols, but individuals were nevertheless fluent and expressive in this material realm. As archaeologists we are not digging up what people said and thought, but we are digging up a particular type of expression which, through its ambiguity and subtlety, is powerful and effective.

Sixth, downward or upward emulations are processes whereby continual rapid change in material styles is ensured. As styles are copied across social categories their use as symbols for one group becomes devalued and that group has to invent or obtain new symbols in order to maintain material contrasts (Miller 1982). Also, the emulation may effectively mask and neutralise the social conflict. In the last 20 years in Britain upward emulation has occurred in many spheres. One after the other, blacks, women and gays have become OK out-groups, their symbols being appropriated. Despite further generation of variety by these groups, a general dissolving of overt contrasts has often occurred. But the symbolic change has rarely been associated with more than minor changes in the real status of blacks, women and homosexuals. Prejudices remain or increase. The power of the minority groups in the style wars is diminished, the effectiveness of their weapons reduced. So, also, their social statement is less easy to make.

Finally, however much material symbols are copied and 'disarmed', they remain important and central parts of individual strategies within social conflicts. Individuals create material culture, non-discursively, as a social strategy. Material symbols have multiple cross-cutting meanings which perhaps differ for each individual. The meanings are often like vanishing blurred images, evocative and inexplicit. With such emotive potential they may play a central role in social statements, not as peripheral, tangential by-products, but as important and key components.

As I write this Chapter in the summer of 1981, urban violence on an unprecedented scale has erupted in London, Manchester, Liverpool, Bristol and other major cities. For the first time cs gas has been used by the police on the British mainland and the Toxteth area of Liverpool is devastated. The nation is shocked, laying the blame on the breakdown of law and order, insufficient protection for the police, or the high level of unemployment in our inner cities. In certain cases, such as Brixton in London, the riots are seen as racial. In others, for example at Toxteth, the skinheads are blamed with their National Front ties, but a clear racist dichotomy seems difficult to identify; the youths in the mobs are black and white.

Few onlookers seem altogether surprised that the riots have taken and are taking place, given the level of unemployment in decaying inner city areas, but the ferocity, degree of organisation and scale were unexpected. Certainly there is no notion of how to cope, or even of the real causes of the civil disturbance. There is now a call for enquiries and solutions. The country has been caught unprepared.

Why were the clear warnings and statements in the youth sub-cultures largely ignored? In the music, self-decoration and material symbols the violence and rejection of all authority were clear to read. No serious analysis of them would have doubted the gravity of the problem. It is only because, in our society, we have come to see clothes, music and cultural arts as peripheral and unimportant that the signs were overlooked. This notion in archaeology has had the consequences described in Chapter 8. Deetz's (1977) 'small things forgotten' provide a language and a set of sentiments and intentions that we make no attempt to understand.

If archaeology can reawaken out attitudes to material things, then it will make a relevant contribution to the understanding of ourselves. Intentions and trends may often be seen in material culture before they erupt into serious social problems. Initially there are 'style wars' in which the distinctions are clarified, sides taken, abstract ideals objectified and intentions formulated. It is on these small things that the major civil disturbance is based. The 'little things' must be read in the early stages of crystalisation and movement. If archaeologists can contribute anything to an awareness of the importance of material culture in these early stages of social change, their contribution will not have been insignificant.

I have given seven reasons why I think that archaeologists could learn from more detailed study of post-war youth sub-cultures in Britain. There is archaeology all around us today and we should become aware of it, learning from it, living it. Although work on modern western styles has been undertaken recently in France (Bourdieu 1980), in England few scholars have paid much attention to this living archaeology. There is a potential for learning and for making relevant contributions to the society in which we live.

10 Conclusion: archaeological anthropology

Interpreting the past

In this book the reliance by archaeologists on the present as a model for the past has been demonstrated in many spheres from settlement and burial to ritual and art. As much as the past informs the present so the present informs the past. The proper use of analogy is the central issue of archaeological interpretation.

It has been shown that one approach to the search for a rigorous use of analogy is to consider the precise degree of similarity between source and subject. But it has also been indicated that this goodness of fit must be extended to include the context or environment of the primary attributes being compared. The contextual approach may amount to no more than increasing the number of similarities between the things being compared. But it should also involve an assessment of what similarities are relevant and what are not relevant for the successful fit of an analogy. To be able to assess relevance there must be a good theoretical knowledge of natural and social processes. We can only say that the organisation of decoration is relevant to the organisation of dirt if we have some knowledge of the reasons for the links between such variables in certain types of socio-cultural contexts.

Another strategy in argument by analogy is to identify cross-cultural regularities in the relationships between variables. But, once again, the successful use of this strategy depends on being able to demonstrate why the variables are linked. The natural or social processes involved need to be understood and a theory developed to allow meaning to be given to the cross-cultural statistics. Also, the use of such statistics is not explanatory unless allied with theoretical discussions concerning the reasons for relationships.

It is easier to assess relevance within the use of relational analogies when reference can be made to natural, physical and chemical laws. Here we can identify which aspects of the data from the past are relevant to the present situation because it can be assumed that basic principles of water, wind and earth have remained more or less constant. The linking processes can be described and experimented with. The underlying rules of the properties of elements and chemicals explain the visible patterning. If interpretation of past economies and technologies is thought to be easier than the interpretation of social organisation and ritual it is because the former involve more natural processes about which generalisation is easier.

As regards the relationships between material culture and society, the underlying rules are highly complex and must include contextual meanings and ideologies. Relational analogies must seek below the surface appearance of settlements and burials for the underlying processes (see the comparison of Binford's and Woodburn's work in Chapter 5). There is a need for a general understanding of material culture within social processes so that the relevance of present analogies for the past can be assessed. On the other hand, the particular historical context has to be understood as unique and meaningful in its own right. Throughout this book there has been a tension between cross-cultural generalisations and the particular context. Both seem necessary for an adequate understanding of a particular moment in the past. Yet how can the archaeologist hope to reconstruct this particularity associated with contextual meanings?

The answer must lie once again in the realm of general theory. Although each cultural context is unique, it is created historically through the use of widespread rules. The point can be made by reference to language. It is inadequate to explain a particular language (English, French, Russian) at the surface level, for example by linking the language to other variables such as environments. The language must be understood as a particular historical product. But in the build-up towards that product, widely found principles or rules of language formation are used. There is a particular language in a particular place but the rules of grammar, word construction and language use may occur widely.

The use of analogy does not lead to a final solution, a definitive interpretation. Assumptions, logic and conclusions may be wrong. Other arguments may be more pursuasive. Alternative explanations may fit the data equally well. Any interpretation is just a stage in a process of argumentation. Some have tried, however, to 'test' their interpretations by embracing a logico-deductive procedure. Implications are deduced logically according to a 'law' or generalisation. Binford's deductions in reference to smudge pits were described in Chapter 2. Unfortunately, such deductions often involve the imposition of the analyst's own values and assumptions. Whenever an archaeologist refers to the hypothetico-deductive method or logical argument, care should be taken to ascertain whose logic is involved. There is a difference between a logic based on a good theoretical understanding of the context of social and ideological action and a logic based on twentieth-century middle-class backgrounds.

The only rigorous archaeology is a self-aware archaeology. If archaeologists want to be explanatory they must include the meaningful and ideological in their models of social process and material culture production. Archaeologists have been prone to disregard their own assumptions and have imposed their own ideologies on the past. A range of such preconceptions has been identified in this book. For example, it has frequently been assumed that the primary values according to which social institutions and material items are to be assessed concern function, utility and maximisation (see Chapter 3). A related assumption is that different spheres of activity can be discussed as distinct. Thus, as in the organisation of this book, burial, settlement, subsistence and exchange are discussed separately. But as soon as structural or relational analogies are considered, for traditional small-scale societies, the distinctions become less clear. For example, the discussion of Gypsies in Chapter 3 brought in many 'different' types of behaviour. It may be the case that economy and culture and social relations, function and style, are only distinct in societies organised structurally as our own.

The marked modern concern with hygiene, health and purity was recognised in the attitudes of archaeologists to the organisation of refuse (Chapter 3). The general low standing of material culture in the central problematic areas of archaeological discourse also reflects the lack of attention given to its symbolic and ideological dimensions in middle-class lives. Material things are desired and consumed, but the artifacts themselves have only utilitarian and social functions. They are the passive objects of human control. As was suggested in Chapter 9, studies of material culture in its own right are little developed.

In our attempts to become aware of the preconceptions that we might impose on the past, we must 'live' archaeology, not in the sense of Gould's (1978a) 'living archaeology', but in the more radical sense of gaining knowledge and experience from the world in which we live our daily lives. There is a danger, though, that if we only look at ourselves we may be blind to the relativity of our own logic. Contrasts with other cultures and with the results obtained by social anthropologists encourage awareness of our own cultural bias. The proper purpose of archaeology may be to contribute to this critical self-awareness.

A theory of material culture

In the discussion above the need for theories of social and ideological processes and of interrelationships with material culture was described. It is only through an adequate set of general theories that the relevance of particular analogies can be assessed and the validity of cross-cultural correlations can be acknowledged. Since archaeologists infer all aspects of the past from material culture their main concern is with the material world. The theories developed must be about material culture. The search for such theories in the modern world is called archaeological anthropology. Unlike ethnoarchaeology, described in Chapter 2 as a field method, archaeological anthropology is part of a generalising science of human culture.

While archaeologists and anthropologists have considered material culture as functionally useful or as a language, few have tried to identify it as a disinct realm with distinct theories relevant to it. At first sight it might seem a hopeless task to say anything valid yet interesting about objects as far apart as a Rembrandt painting, a kitchen fork and a left football boot. While all these artifacts have functional values (social, ideological and utilitarian), and are all structured by binary and other codes as in a language, they are also more than tools or speech. In this book some further attributes of material culture have been glimpsed, and in discussing the possibility of a theory of material culture, or at least of theories of material culture, these distinctive aspects can be summarised.

In the first place, material symbols are value-laden. They do not simply indicate status and role. They are not so much saying 'this person is of a certain category' as in much verbal signalling, but they are also forming the quality of that person and category. The symbols are 'saying' things about underlying beliefs and values which are constituted by the symbols through analogies of form and through associations of use. Material symbols are models of, and models for, behaviour. Because of the value-laden, qualitative characteristic of material symbols, they are not chosen arbitrarily. In Chapter 9, the appropriate production and use of material items within a set of cultural values was termed the 'sandwich syndrome'. The meaning of symbols can be identified by archaeologists through comparisons of form within past cultural contexts and through examinations of the association and use of material items.

As a result of the first point, it is necessary to understand symbols by reference to the particular historical situation within which artifacts have been used and forms have become associated with particular values. Of course, it can be claimed that it is not necessary to understand the total history of a nursery rhyme or of the raising of hats in greetings in order to understand their present use and meaning. But the history of a cultural trait is not irrelevant to its use in any cultural context. While the distant origin of a particular trait may be of little significance in a present context, the more immediate history is relevant. The total history of swastikas is less relevant to the present meaning of this sign than its more recent associations. In general, the choice of a symbol as part of a present strategy must be affected by at least its immediately previous use. But as soon as a symbol is used in a new context its meaning and its history are altered.

Spoken messages tend to avoid ambiguity in many circumstances. While certain material symbols, in certain contexts, are also un-ambiguous, material items and the organisation of the constructed world often mean very different things to different people. They can often be re-interpreted at will and their implications reassessed. This great ambiguity of the visual image, which was used as a central part of much twentieth-century fine art, is the third component of material culture theory.

The fourth component concerns the possibility for do-it-yourself 'montage' and quick change identified in Chapter 9. Since material symboling is more than language, and since ambiguity is rife, and the rules of procedure are less strict than in speech, there is a greater potential for dissembly and reassembly. While in modern Britain such processes are accelerated, they may be characteristic of many types of social strategy.

Fifth, material culture may, in certain respects and like ritual, be more like a performance or play than an abstract code or language. It may stimulate, shock or disturb; it is not a passive component of social action. The ambiguity can be used to have emotive effect, as can the ideal, unreal character.

Sixth, therefore, material items often express an ideal world, rather than passively mirroring reality. While we may emphasise the functional nature of many of our own material symbols, they often represent our aspirations. Nowhere is this more clear than in the 'dream-world' furnishings of many modern houses. The 'chamber pot syndrome' described in Chapter 8 is about making something appear what it is not. The decoration and moulding of birds, flowers and fountains on the chamber pots made what was distasteful to the Victorians acceptable. The 'ideal' nature of certain burial ritual and other types of ritual were discussed in Chapters 6 and 7. But the material world is not simply ideal and unrelated to practical activity. Amongst the Nuba of Sudan, ash is placed on cattle to protect them from flies. Because of this practical association the ash has the potential symbolic meaning of protection, and ash is used with this meaning in burial ritual. The 'ideal' ritual association affects the placing of ash on cattle and protects them symbolically. In such a case the practical world forms the material patterning and its ideational significance. But we could also argue that the reason the Nuba are concerned to protect their cattle from flies, and the reason they do it with ash, lie in a set of prior ideas about the significance of cattle and the meaning of ash. Much of the significance of artifacts derives from their practical and social use. But ideas and values are always involved.

The seventh point is that the symbolic meaning of many material items, in our own and in other societies, may not be discussed readily. Clearly which, if any, material items are surrounded in discursive knowledge is dependent on various attributes of the social context. For example, where status and social control are based on restricted access to knowledge about the meaning of things (for example, see Barth 1975) there may be an elaborate body of discursive knowledge. But in many situations individuals may know how to act in relation to material culture but they may not be able to articulate the reasons for those actions with any ease. Much material expression can be covert, unnoticed. A similar point can be made about spoken language, but where the emphasis is on the message itself, and its decoding, the meanings must be clear and the potential for covert significance is less substantial.

Eighth, it may be the case that as the participant in a culture finds that it is difficult to be articulate about material behaviour, so the analyst may, in attempting to provide a scientific verbal description and analysis of material symbols, confound adequate understanding and interpretation. The rigidly structured, dry descriptions and verbal formulations of scientific archaeology may not capture the evocative and emotive content of material discourse. A more appropriate and productive analytical and interpretive procedure may be the use of a poetic and elliptical language.

Finally, the notion that many material symbols are value-laden, ambiguous, multi-focal and are often not organised at a conscious or discursive level, leads to the implication that they have particular importance in ideological and social strategies. They provide qualities of social relations. Material organisation does not equal social organisation. Rather, the material world is involved in the interpretation of social actions. Artifacts mean different things to different people and can carry contradictory meanings, so they can be used to reveal social distinctions and to hide them at the same time, to represent and misrepresent.

A last ethnographic example might help to clarify certain of the above aspects of material culture theory. British culture today is an appropriate illustration since British youth often stresses its separation from the adult world by its devotion to the visual rather than the verbal. A highly articulate symbol for which all verbal descriptions and explanations have proved inadequate is the safety pin as used as an item of dress by punks. Punks themselves, interviewed about wearing safety pins, claimed it was started 'for a larf', 'it didn't mean nothing particularly' followed by the perpetual refrain 'know what I mean?' Their songs, poetic and evocative, were articulate enough, but in daily speech the symbols could not be analysed by participants in the punk way of life. But this did not prevent non-punk participants in British society offering meanings, trying to provide an explanation for the widespread adoption and visual success of the safety pin. The meanings which have been given include the aggression and anger associated with sticking a pin in one's face and nose. This quality of the use of a safety pin was seen as appropriate to the general aggression of the punk style of behaviour. However, others have seen the pins as seeking pity through the primary association with babies and babies' nappies (diapers). The punks were anti-hippies and the pins, often worn in the ears, could be seen as a mockery of the delicate Eastern earrings worn by many hippies. The safety pins were cheap and anyone could get one. This leads to a further value associated with punks – that anyone could do it themselves. Finally, the pins, associated with chains, symbolised bondage, a recurrent theme of punk youth. These five meanings which have been given to safety pins in one context illustrate the ambiguity and multi-focality of material symbols and show that the various meanings are appropriate within a set of values, a way of life. Such characteristics of the material world (ambiguity, multi-focality, etc.) have been identified widely in ethnographic contexts. But by considering a symbol within our own culture, the points can be clearly made. In particular, it becomes possible to see that the very attempt to capture the meaning of material symbols in normal verbal description may be inadequate. None of the five interpretations may be right and none wrong. The aim of describing and seeking correct verbal accounts of symbols such as the safety pin may be misguided. The more articulate the material evocations and shadowy images, the less articulate may be the descriptions in speech. Social actors 'know how to go on'. They know how to use objects and situations to achieve ends. But this practical knowledge need not be associated with any theoretical, analytical understanding. On the other hand, actions on material leave an objective trace. Material culture objectifies social relationships and so can be manipulated to change the quality and structure of those relationships.

A set of questions, problems and areas of analysis has been identified in relation to artifacts. But beyond these general aspects of a theory of material culture, there is the need to develop specific hypotheses. In this book ideas about decoration, dirt, settlement organisation and the use of animal bones have been suggested. In all these hypotheses certain of the general characteristics of material culture theory (for example, meaning, ideology, non-passive role) have been evident. As such theories are developed within archaeological anthropology the use of analogy to interpret the past can become more secure. The two-pronged result will be a more rigorous archaeology and a more relevant one, contributing to understanding of the material world we construct around us.

Bibliography

ADAMS M.J.   1973   'Structural aspects of a village art', *American Anthropologist* 75, 62–79

ALSCHULAR R.H. and HATTWICK L.W.   1947   *Painting and personality: a study of young children*, U.C.P., Chicago

ANDERSON K.M.   1969   'Ethnographic analogy and archaeological interpretation', *Science* 163, 133–8

ARNOLD D.E.   1978   'Ceramic variability, environment and culture history among the Pokom in the valley of Guatemala' in Hodder I. (ed) *Spatial organisation of culture*, Duckworth, London

ASCHER R.   1962   'Ethnography for archaeology: a case from the Seri Indians', *Ethnology* 1, 360–69

AUDOUZE F and JARRIGE C.   1980   'Perspective et limites de l'interpretation anthropologique des habitats en archéologie, un example contemporain: les habitats de nomades et de sedentaires de la plaine de Kachi, Baluchistan' in Barrelet M.T. (ed) *L'archéologie de L'Iraq*, C.N.R.S., Paris

BAKELS C.C.   1978   *Four Linearbandkeramik settlements and their environment*, Analecta Praehistorica Leidensia 11

BALFET H.   1966   'Ethnographic observations in North Africa and archaeological interpretation: the pottery of the Maghreb' in Matson F.R. (ed) *Ceramics and man*, Viking Fund Publication in Anthropology 4

BALFET H.   1980   'A propos du metier de l'argile: example de dialogue entre archeologie et ethnologie' in Barrelet M.T. (ed) *L'archéologie de l'Iraq*, C.N.R.S., Paris

BARRELET M.T.   1980   'A propos du metier de l'argile: example de dialogue entre archéologie et ethnologie' in Barrelet M.T. (ed) *L'archéologie de l'Iraq* C.N.R.S., Paris

BARRY H.   1957   'Relationships between child training and the pictorial arts', *Journal of Abnormal and Social Psychology* 54, 380

BARTH F.   1956   'Ecologic relations of ethnic groups in Swat, North Pakistan', *American Anthropologist* 58, 1079–89

BARTH F.   1975   *Ritual and knowledge among the Baktaman of New Guinea*, Yale University Press, New Haven

BATES D.   1973   *Nomads and farmers: a study of the Yoruk of south-eastern Turkey*, Museum of Anthropology, University of Michigan, Anthropological Paper 52, Ann Arbor

BENDER B.   1978   'Gatherer-hunter to farmer: a social perspective', *World Archaeology* 10, 204–22

BERSU G.   1940   'Excavations at Little Woodbury, Wiltshire', *Proceedings of the Prehistoric Society* 6, 30–111

BIBLIOGRAPHY

BINFORD L.R. 1967 'Smudge pits and hide smoking: the use of analogy in archaeological reasoning', *American Antiquity* 32, 1–12

BINFORD L. 1971 'Mortuary practices: their study and their potential' in Brown J.A. (ed.) *Approaches to the social dimensions of mortuary practices*, Society for American Archaeology Memoir, 25

BINFORD L.R. 1972 *An archaeological perspective*, Seminar Press, New York

BINFORD L.R. 1976 'Forty-seven trips: a case study in the character of archaeological formation processes' in Hall E.S. (ed.) *Contributions to anthropology: the interior peoples of Northern Alaska. Archaeological Survey of Canada* 49, 299–351, Ottawa National Museum of Man, Ottawa

BINFORD L.R. 1978 *Nunamiut ethnoarchaeology*, Academic Press, New York

BINFORD L.R. 1980 'Willow smoke and dogs' tails: hunter-gatherer settlement systems and archaeological site formation', *American Antiquity* 45, 4–20

BINFORD L.R. 1981 *Bones: ancient men and modern myths*, Academic Press, London

BINFORD L.R. and CHASKO W.J. 1976 'Nunamiut demographic history: a provocative case' in Zubrow E.B.W. (ed.) *Human demography*, University of New Mexico Press, Alburquerque

BINFORD L.R. and S.R. (eds) 1968 *New perspectives in archaeology*, Aldine, Chicago

BLACKMORE C., BRAITHWAITE M and HODDER I. 1979 'Social and cultural patterning in the late Iron Age in southern England' in Burnham B. and Kingsbury J. (eds) *Space, hierarchy and society*, British Archaeological Reports, International Series 59

BLOCH M. 1971 *Placing the dead*, Seminar Press, London

BLOCH M. 1977 'The past and present in the present', *Man*, 12, 278–292

BONNICHSEN R. 1973 'Millies' camp: an experiment in archaeology', *World Archaeology* 4, 277–91

BOSERUP E. 1975 *The conditions of agricultural growth*, Aldine, Chicago

BOURDIEU P. 1977 *Outline of a theory of practice*, Cambridge University Press, Cambridge

BOURDIEU P. 1980 *La distinction*, Minuit, Paris

BRAITHWAITE M. 1982 'Pottery as silent ritual discourse' in Hodder I. (ed.) *Symbolic and structural archaeology*. Cambridge University Press, Cambridge

BRIM J.A. and SPAIN D.H. 1974 *Research design in anthropology*, Holt, Rinehart and Winston

BUNZEL R. 1929 *The Pueblo potter, a study of creative imagination in primitive art*, University Press, New York

BURNS T. and LAUGHLIN C.A. 1979 'Ritual and social power' in D'Aquili E.G., Laughlin C.A. and McManus J. (eds) *The spectrum of ritual – a biogenetic structural analysis*, Columbia University Press, New York

CAMPBELL J. 1968 'Territoriality among ancient hunters: interpretations from ethnography and nature' in Meggers B.J. (ed.) *Anthropological archaeology in the Americas*, Anthropological Society of Washington

BIBLIOGRAPHY

CANTER D. and HOI LEE K.   n.d.   'A non-reactive study of room usage in modern Japanese apartments', Circulated mimeograph

CARNEIRO R.L.   1970   'A theory of the origin of the state', *Science* 169, 733–38

CARNEIRO R.L.   1979   'Tree felling with a stone axe' in Kramer C. (ed.) *Ethnoarchaeology*, Columbia University Press, New York

CHAPMAN R.   1981   'Archaeological theory and communal burial in prehistoric Europe' in Hodder I., Isaac G. and Hammond N. (eds) *Pattern of the past*, Cambridge University Press, Cambridge

CHAPPELL J.   1966   'Stone axe factories in the highlands of East New Guinea', *Proceedings of the Prehistoric Society* 32, 96–121

CHERRY J., GAMBLE C. and SHENNAN S.J. (eds)   1978   *Sampling in contemporary British Archaeology*, British Archaeological Reports, British Series 50

CHILDE V.G.   1931   *Skara Brae*, Kegan Paul, London

CHILDE V.G.   1950   *The dawn of European civilisation* (5th ed.), Routledge, London

CHISHOLM M.D.I.   1962   *Rural settlement and land use: an essay in location*, Hutchinson, London

CHRISTY H. and LARTET E.   1875   *Reliquae Aquitanicae*

CLAMMER J. (ed.)   1978   *The new economic anthropology*, Macmillan, London

CLARK J.G.D.   1952   *Prehistoric Europe: the economic basis*, Methuen, London

CLARK J.G.D.   1954   *Excavations at Star Carr*, Cambridge University Press, Cambridge

CLARK J.G.D.   1965   'Traffic in stone axe and adze blades', *Economic History Review*, 2nd series, 18, 1–28

CLARK J.G.D.   1967   *The Stone Age hunters*, Thames and Hudson, London

CLARK D.L.   1968   *Analytical Arhcaeology*, Methuen, London

CLARKE D.L.   1972   'A provisional model for an Iron Age society and its settlement system' in Clarke D.L. (ed.) *Models in archaeology*, Methuen, London

COLES J.   1973   *Archaeology by experiment*, Hutchinson, London

COLES J.   1979   *Experimental archaeology*, Academic Press, London

CONKEY W.   1978   'Style and information in cultural evolution: toward a predictive model for the Paleolithic' in Redman C. *et al* (ed.) *Social Archaeology*, Academic Press, New York

COPI I.M.   1954   *Introduction to logic*, Macmillan, New York

CRADER D.C.   1974   'The effects of scavangers on bone material from a large mammal: an experiment conducted among the Bisa of the Luangwa Valley, Zambia' in Donnan C.B. and Clewlow C.W. (eds) *Ethnoarchaeology*, University of California, Los Angeles, Institute of Archaeology, Monograph 4

CRANSTONE B.A.L.   1971   'The Tifalmin: a 'Neolithic' people in New Guinea', *World Archaeology* 2, 134–42

CUNLIFFE B.W.   1971   'Danebury, Hampshire: first interim report on the

BIBLIOGRAPHY

excavation, 1969–70', *Antiquaries Journal* 51, 240–52

DALTON G. 1969 'Theoretical issues in economic anthropology', *Current Anthropology* 10, 63–102

DALTON G. 1981 'Anthropological models in archaeological perspective' in Hodder I., Isaac G. and Hammond N. (eds) *Pattern of the past*, Cambridge University Press, Cambridge

DANIEL G.E. 1950 *A hundred years of archaeology*, Duckworth, London

DAVID N. 1971 'The Fulani compound and the archaeologist', *World Archaeology* 3, 111–131

DAVID N. 1972 'On the life span of pottery, type frequencies and archaeological inference', *American Antiquity*, 37, 141–2

DE BRY T. 1590 *America, part 1*, Frankfort

DEETZ J. 1965 *The dynamics of stylistic change in Arikara ceramics*, Illinois Studies in Anthropology 4, University of Illinois Press, Urbana

DEETZ J. 1977 *In small things forgotten*, Anchor Books, New York

DEETZ J. and DETHLEFSEN E. 1971 'Some social aspects of New England colonial mortuary art' in Brown J.A. (ed.) *Approaches to the social dimensions of mortuary practices*, Society for American Archaeology Memoir 25

DE MONTMOLLIN O. 1980 'The archaeological record of an Alaskan whale hunting community' in Smiley F.E. *et al.* (eds) *The archaeological correlates of hunter-gatherer societies: studies from the ethnographic record*, Michigan Discussions in Anthropology, 5

DIVALE W.T. 1977 'Living floor area and marital residence: a replication', *Behaviour Science Research* 12, 109–116

DONLEY L. 1982 'Space as symbolic marker' in Hodder I. (ed.) *Symbolic and structural archaeology*, Cambridge University Press, Cambridge

DONNAN C.B. and CLEWLOW C.W. (eds) 1974 *Ethnoarchaeology*, University of California, Los Angeles, Institute of Archaeology, Monograph 4

DOUGLAS M. 1966 *Purity and danger*, Routledge and Kegan Paul, London

DOUGLAS M. 1970 *Natural symbols*, Barrie and Rockliff, London

DUGDALE W. 1856 *The antiquities of Warwickshire illustrated*

DURKHEIM E. 1915 (transl. 1964). *The elementary forms of religious life*, Allen and Unwin, London

DYSON-HUDSON N. 1972 'The study of nomads' in Irons W. and Dyson-Hudson N. (eds) *Perspective on nomadism*, Brill, Leiden

EARLE T. 1978 *Economic and social organisation of a complex chiefdom: the Halelea district, Kaua'i, Hawaii*, Anthropological Papers, Museum of Anthropology, University of Michigan 63

EBERT J. 1979 'An ethnoarchaeological approach to reassessing the meaning of variability in stone tool assemblages' in Kramer C. (ed.) *Ethnoarchaeology*, Columbia University Press, New York

ECKERT P. n.d. 'Clothing and geography in a suburban high school', Circulated mimeograph

ELLISON A. 1981 'Towards a socio-economic model for the Middle Bronze Age in southern England' in Hodder I., Isaac G. and Hammond N. (eds) *Pattern of the past*, Cambridge University Press, Cambridge

BIBLIOGRAPHY

ELLISON A. and DREWETT P.   1971   'Pits and post-holes in the British early Iron Age: some alternative explanations', *Proceedings of the Prehistoric Society* 37, 183–194

EMBER C. and M.   1972   'The conditions favouring multilocal residence', *South-western Journal of Anthropology* 28, 382–400

EMBER M.   1967   'The emergence of neolocal residence', *Transactions of the New York Academy of Sciences* 30, 291–302

EMBER M.   1973   'An archaeological indicator of matrilocal versus patrilocal residence', *American Antiquity* 38, 177–82

EMBER M. and C.   1971   'The conditions favouring matrilocal versus patrilocal residence', *American Anthropologist* 73, 571–94

EVANS J.   1860   'Reigate flints', *Proceedings of the Society of Antiquities*, January 1860

EVANS J.D.   1971   *The prehistoric antiquities of the Maltese Islands: a survey*, Athlone Press, University of London

FEWKES J.W.   1893   'A-wa-to-bi: an archaeological verification of a Tusayan legend', *American Anthropologist* 6, 363–75

FIRTH R.   1927   'Maori hill-forts', *Antiquity* 1, 66–78

FISCHER J.L.   1961   'Art styles as cultural cognitive maps', *American Anthropologist* 63, 79–93

FLETCHER R.   1981   'People and space: a case study of material behaviour' in Hodder I., Isaac G. and Hammond N. (eds) *Pattern of the past*, Cambridge University Press, Cambridge

FOLEY R.   1981   'Off-site archaeology: an alternative approach for the short sited' in Hodder I., Isaac G. and Hammond N. (eds) *Pattern of the past*, Cambridge University Press, Cambridge

FORD J.A.   1954   'The type concept revisited', *American Anthropologist* 56, 42–57

FORGE A.   1972   'Normative factors in the settlement size of Neolithic cultivators (New Guinea)' in Ucko P., Tringham R. and Dimbleby G. (eds) *Man, settlement and urbanism*, Duckworth, London

FRANKENSTEIN S. and ROWLANDS M.   1978   'The internal structure and regional context of early Iron Age Society in south-west Germany', *Bulletin of the Institute of Archaeology* 15, 73–112

FREEMAN C.G.   1968   'A theoretical framework for interpreting archaeological materials' in Lee R.B. and De Vore I. (eds) *Man the hunter*, Aldine, Chicago

FRIED M.   1967   *The evolution of political society*, Random House, New York

FRIEDL E.   1975   *Women and men*, Holt, Rinehart and Winston, New York

FREIDMAN J.   1975   'Tribes, states and transformations' in Bloch M. (ed.) *Marxist analyses and social anthropology*, Malaby Press, London

FRIEDRICH N.   1970   'Design structure and social interaction: archaeological implications of an ethnographic analysis', *American Antiquity* 35, 332–43

BIBLIOGRAPHY

GALLAGHER J.P.   1972   'A preliminary report on archaeological research near Lake Zuai', *Annaler d'Ethiopie* 9, 13–18

GALLAGHER J.P.   1977   'Contemporary stone tools in Ethiopia: implications for archaeology', *Journal of Field Archaeology* 4, 407–14

GELLNER E.   1973   'Introduction to nomadism' in Nelson C. (ed.) *The desert and the sown*, Institute of International Studies, Research Series 21, Berkeley

GIFFORD D.P.   1977   *Observations of modern human settlements as an aid to archaeological interpretation*, PhD dissertation, University of California, Berkeley

GIFFORD D.P. and BEHRENSMEYER A.K.   1978   'Observed depositional events at a modern human occupation site in Kenya', *Quaternary Research* 8, 245–66

GIMBUTAS M.   1974   *The gods and goddesses of old Europe*, Thames and Hudson, London

GIMBUTAS M.   1977   'Gold treasure at Varna', *Archaeology* 30, 44–51

GOLDSTEIN L.   1976   *Spatial structure and social organisation: regional manifestations of Mississippian society*, PhD dissertation, North-western University

GOODY J.   1971   *Technology, tradition and the state in Africa*, Oxford University Press, London

GOULD R.   1974   'Some current problems in ethnoarchaeology' in Donnan C.B. and Clewlow C.W. (eds) *Ethnoarchaeology*, University of California, Los Angeles, Institute of Archaeology, Monograph 4

GOULD R.   1977   *Puntutjarpa Rockshelter and the Australian Desert Culture*, American Museum of Natural History, Anthropological Papers 54, New York

GOULD R.   1978a   'Beyond analogy in ethnoarchaeology' in Gould R. (ed.) *Explorations in ethnoarchaeology*, University of New Mexico Press, Albuquerque

GOULD R. (ed.)   1978b   *Explorations in ethnoarchaeology*, University of New Mexico Press, Albuquerque

GOULD R.   1980   *Living archaeology*, Cambridge University Press, Cambridge

GOULD R. and SCHIFFER M. (eds)   1981   *Modern material culture*, Academic Press, New York

HAALAND R.   1980   'Man's role in the changing habitat of Mema during the Old Kingdom of Ghana', *Norwegian Archaeological Review* 13, 31–46

HAALAND R.   1981   *Migratory herdsmen and cultivating women*, Archaeological Museum, University of Bergen

HALL S, and JEFFERSON T. (eds)   1976   *Resistance through rituals*, Hutchinson, London

HALSTEAD P.   1981   'From determinism to uncertainty: social storage and the rise of the Minoan palace' in Sheridan A. and Bailey G.N. (eds) *Economic archaeology*, British Archaeological Reports, International Series 96

HALSTEAD P.   1982   'The animal bones' in Hodder I. (ed.) *The excavation of an Iron Age and Romano-British settlement at Wendens Ambo, Essex,* Passmore Edwards Museum, London

HAMMOND G. and N. 1981 'Child's play: a distorting factor in archaeological distribution', *American Antiquity* 46, 634–6

HARDIN M.A. 1979 'The cognitive basis of productivity in a decorative art style: implications of an ethnographic study for archaeologists' taxonomies' in Kramer C. (ed.) *Ethnoarchaeology,* Columbia University Press, New York

HARPENDING H.C. 1976 'Regional variation in !Kung populations' in Lee R.B. and De Vore I. (eds) *Kalahari hunter-gatherers,* Harvard University Press, Cambridge, Mass.

HARPENDING H. 1977 'Some implications for hunter-gatherer ecology derived from the study of spatial structure of resources', *World Archaeology* 8, 275–86

HAWKES K., HILL K. and O'CONNELL J.F. 1982 'Why hunters gather: optimal foraging and the Aché of eastern Paraguay', *American Ethnologist* 9, 379–98

HEBDIGE D. 1979 *Subcultures: the meaning of style,* Methuen, London

HEDGES J. and BUCKLEY D. 1978 'Excavations at a Neolithic causewayed enclosure, Orsett, Essex 1975', *Proceedings of the Prehistoric Society* 44, 219–308

HEIDER K.G. 1967 'Archaeological assumptions and ethnographical facts: a cautionary tale from New Guinea', *South-western Journal of Anthropology* 23, 52–64

HESSE M.B. 1974 *The structure of scientific inference,* MacMillan, London

HEYERDAHL T. and FERDON E.N. (eds) 1961 *Archaeology of Easter Island,* V.I.I. Monographs of the School of American Research and the Museum of New Mexico 24, Allen and Unwin, London

HILL A. 1980 'A modern hyaena den in Amboseli National Park, Kenya' in Leakey R.E. and Ogot B.A. (eds) *Proceedings of the 8th Pan-African Congress of Prehistory and Quaternary studies Nairobi, September 1977,* The International L. Leakey Memorial Institute for African Prehistory, Nairobi

HILL J. 1965 *Broken K: a prehistoric community in Eastern Arizona,* PhD Dissertation, University of Chicago

HILL J. 1970 *Broken K Pueblo,* Anthropology Papers of the University of Arizona 18

HILL J. 1977 'Individual variability in ceramics and the study of prehistoric social organisation' in Hill J. and Gunn J. (eds) *The Individual in Prehistory,* Academic Press, New York

HITCHCOCK R.K. 1980 'The ethnoarchaeology of sedentism: a Kalahari case' in Leakey R.E. and Ogot B.A. (eds) *Proceedings of the 8th Pan-African Congress of Prehistory and Quaternary Studies, Nairobi, September 1977,* International L. Leakey Memorial Institute for African Prehistory, Nairobi

HIVERNEL F. 1978 *An ethnoarchaeological study of environmental use in the Kenya highlands,* PhD dissertation, University of London

HODDER I.   1975   'The Spatial distribution of Romano-British small towns' in Rowley T. and Rodwell W. (eds) *Small towns of Roman Britain*, British Archaeological Reports, Oxford

HODDER I.   1977   'The distribution of material culture items in the Baringo district, Kenya', *Man* 12, 239–69

HODDER I. (ed.)   1978a   *The spatial organisation of culture*, Duckworth, London

HODDER I. (ed.)   1978b   *Simulation studies in archaeology*, Cambridge University Press, Cambridge

HODDER I.   1979a   'Pre-Roman and Romano-British tribal economies' in Burnham B. and Johnson H. (eds) *Invasion and response*, British Archaeological Reports British Series 73

HODDER I.   1979b   'Pottery distributions: service and tribal areas' in Millett M. (ed.) *Pottery and the archaeologist*, Institute of Archaeology, London

HODDER I.   1981a   'Towards a mature archaeology' in Hodder I., Isaac G. and Hammond N. (eds) *Pattern of the past*, Cambridge University Press, Cambridge

HODDER I.   1981b   'Society, economy and culture: an ethnographic study amongst the Lozi, West Zambia' in Hodder I., Isaac G. and Hammond N. (eds) *Pattern of the past*, Cambridge University Press, Cambridge

HODDER I.   1982a   *Excavation of an Iron Age and Romano-British settlement at Wendens Ambo, Essex*, Passmore Edwards Museum, London

HODDER I.   1982b   'Theoretical archaeology: a reactionary viewpoint' in Hodder I. (ed.) *Symbolic and structural archaeology*, Cambridge University Press, Cambridge

HODDER I.   1982c   *Symbols in action*, Cambridge University Press, Cambridge

HODDER I. and HEDGES J.W.   1977   '"Weaving combs"; their typology and distribution with some introductory remarks on date and function' in Collis J. (ed.) *The Iron Age in Britain, a review*, Sheffield University, Sheffield

HODGE F.W.   1897   'The verification of a tradition', *American Anthropologist*, 10, 299–302

HOLE F.   1978   'Pastoral nomadism in western Iran' in Gould R. (ed.) *Explorations in ethnoarchaeology*, University of New Mexico Press, Albuquerque

HOLE F.   1979   'Rediscovering the past in the present: ethnoarchaeology in Luristan, Iran' in Kramer C. (ed.) *Ethnoarchaeology*, Columbia University Press, New York

HOLE F.   1980   'The prehistory of herding: some suggestions from ethnography' in Barrelet M.T. (ed.) *L'archéologie de l'Iraq*, C.N.R.S., Paris

HONIGSHEIM P.   1928   'Gesellschaftbeddingtheit der sogennanten primitiven Kunst', *Verhanlungen des Deutschen Soziologentages* 6

HUGHES I.   1977   'New Guinea Stone Age trade', *Terra Australis* 3

BIBLIOGRAPHY

HUGH-JONES C. 1979 *From the milk river*, Cambridge University Press, Cambridge

HUMPHREY C. 1974 'Inside a Mongolian tent', *New Society* 31, 273–5

INGERSOLL D., YELLEN J.E. and MACDONALD W. (eds) 1977 *Experimental archaeology*, Columbia University Press, New York

INGOLD T. 1980 *Hunters, pastoralists and ranchers*, Cambridge University Press, Cambridge

ISAAC G. 1967 'Towards the interpretation of occupation debris: some experiments and observations', *Kroeber Anthropological Society Papers* 37, 31–57

ISBELL W.H. 1976 'Cosmological order expressed in prehistoric ceremonial centres', Paper given in Andean Symbolism Symposium, Part 1: space, time and mythology, International Congress of Americanists, Paris

JACKSON R. 1972 'A vicious circle? – the consequences of von Thünen in tropical Africa', *Area* 4, 258–61

JARRIGE C. and AUDOUZE F. 1980 'Etude de'une aire de cuisson de jarres au IIIe millenaire: comparaison avec des techniques contemporaines de la plaine de Kachi, Baluchistan' in Barrelet M.T. (ed.) *L'archéologie de l'Iraq*, C.N.R.S., Paris

JELINEK J. 1974 '"Ethnographical" contributions to the interpretation of the Laussel Palaeolithic relief', *Anthropologie* 12, 227–29

JOCHIM M.A. 1976 *Hunter-gatherer subsistence and settlement. A predictive model*, Academic Press, New York

JOHNSON D. 1969 *The nature of nomadism*, Department of Geography Research Paper 18, University of Chicago

KAVOLIS V. 1965 'The value-orientations theory of artistic style', *Anthropological Quarterly* 34, 1–19

KLEINDIENST M. and WATSON P.J. 1956 'Action archaeology: the archaeological inventory of a living community', *Anthropology Tomorrow* 5, 75–8

KLINDT-JENSEN O. 1976 'The influence of ethnography on early Scandinavian archaeology' in Megaw J.V.S. (ed.) *To illustrate the monuments*, Thames and Hudson, London

KORN S.M. 1978 'The formal analysis of visual systems as exemplified by a study of Abelam (Papua New Guinea) paintings' in Greenhalgh M. and Megaw V. (eds) *Art in Society*, Duckworth, London

KRAMER C. (ed.) 1979 *Ethnoarchaeology. Implications of ethnography for archaeology*, Columbia University Press, New York

KRAMER C. 1980 'Estimating prehistoric populations: an ethnoarchaeological approach' in Barrelet M.T. (ed.) *L'archéologie de l'Iraq*, C.N.R.S., Paris

KROEBER A.L. 1916 'Zuni potsherds', *Anthropological Papers of the American Museum of Natural History* 18, 1–37

KROEBER A.L. 1923 *Anthropology: culture patterns and processes*, Harrap, London

BIBLIOGRAPHY

KUPER A.   1980   'Symbolic dimensions of the Southern Bantu homestead', *Africa* 50, 8–23

KUS S.   1982   'Matters material and ideal: the Merina of Madagascar' in Hodder I. (ed.) *Symbolic and structural archaeology*, Cambridge University Press, Cambridge

LANGE F.W. and RYDBERG C.R.   1972   'Abandonment and post-abandonment behaviour at a rural central American house-site', *American Antiquity* 37, 419–32

LEE R.B.   1972   'Population growth and the beginning of sedentary life among the !Kung Bushmen' in Spooner B. (ed.) *Population growth: anthropological implications*, MIT Press, Cambridge, Mass.

LEE R.B. and DE VORE I. (eds)   1968   *Man the hunter*, Aldine, Chicago

LEE B.B. and DE VORE I. (eds)   1976   *Kalahari hunters and gatherers*, Harvard University Press, Cambridge

LEWIS G.   1980   *Day of shining red*, Cambridge University Press, Cambridge

LHWYD E.   1713   Letters published in *Philosophical Transactions of the Royal Society* 1713, 93ff.

LONGACRE W.A.   1964   'Sociological implications of the ceramic analysis', *Fieldiana Anthropology* 55, 155–170

LONGACRE W.A.   1970   *Archaeology as anthropology*, Anthropological papers of the University of Arizona 17, Tucson, Arizona

LONGACRE W.A. and AYRES J.E.   1968   'Archaeological lessons from an Apache Wickiup' in Binford S. and L. (eds) *New perspectives in archaeology*, Aldine, Chicago

LUBBOCK Sir J.   1865   *Prehistoric times*

MCBRYDE I.   1978   'Wil-im-ee Moor-ring. Or where do axes come from?', *Mankind* 11, 354–82

MACINTOSH N.W.G.   1977   'Beswick Creek cave two decades later: a re-appraisal' in Ucko P. (ed.) *Form in indigenous art*, Duckworth, London

MCINTOSH R.J.   1974   'Archaeology and mud wall decay in a West African village', *World Archaeology* 6, 154–171

MCNETT C.W.   1979   'The cross-cultural method in archaeology' in Schiffer M. (ed.) *Advances in archaeological theory and method 2*, Academic Press, New York

MALINOWSKI B.   1948   *Magic, science and religion, and other essays*, Doubleday Anchor, New York

MEGGARS B.J. (ed.)   1968   *Anthropological archaeology in the Americas*, Anthropological Society of Washington, Washington, D.C.

MEILLASSOUX C.   1973   On the mode of production of the hunting band' in Alexandre P. (ed.) *French perspectives in African studies*, Oxford University Press, London

MESSER E.   1979   'Cultivation and cognition: plants and archaeological research strategies' in Kramer C. (ed.) *Ethnoarchaeology*, Columbia University Press, New York

MILKE W.   1949   'The quantitative distribution of cultural similarities and

BIBLIOGRAPHY

their cartographic representation', *American Anthropologist* 51, 237–52

MILLER D. 1982 'Structures and strategies: an aspect of the relationship between social hierarchy and social exchange' in Hodder I. (ed.) *Symbolic and structural archaeology*, Cambridge University Press, Cambridge

MOORE H. 1982 'An ethnoarchaeological study of discard amongst the Marakwet of Kenya' in Hodder I. (ed.) *Symbolic and structural archaeology*, Cambridge University Press, Cambridge

MUELLER J.W. 1975 *Sampling in archaeology*, University of Arizona Press, Tucson

MUNSEN P.J. 1969 'Comments on Binford's "Smudge pits and hide smoking: the use of analogy in archaeological reasoning"', *American Antiquity* 34, 83–5

MURDOCK G.P. and PROVOST C. 1973 'Factors in the division of labour by sex. A cross-cultural analysis', *Ethnology* 12, 203–225

MURRAY P. 1980 'Discard location: the ethnographic data', *American Antiquity* 45, 490–502

NADEL S.F. 1947 *The Nuba*, Oxford University Press, Oxford

NAROLL R. and COHEN R. (eds) 1973 *A handbook of method in cultural anthropology*, Columbia University Press, New York

NEEDHAM R. 1962 'Genealogy and category in Wikmunkan society', *Ethnology* 1, 223–64

NELSON N.C. 1916 'Flint-working by Ishi', *Holmes Anniversary Volume*

NICKLIN K. 1971 'Stability and innovation in pottery manufacture', *World Archaeology* 3, 13–48

NILSSON S. 1863 *The primitive inhabitants of the Scandinavian North*, English edition, Lubbock (ed.)

OCHSENSCHLAGER E.L. 1974 'Modern potters at Al-Hiba with some reflections on the excavated early Dynastic pottery' in Donnan C.B. and Clewlow C.W. (eds) *Ethnoarchaeology*, University of California, Los Angeles, Institute of Archaeology, Monograph 4

OKELY J. 1975 'Gypsy women: models in conflict' in Ardener S. (ed.) *Perceiving women*, Malaby Press, London

OKELY J. 1979 'An anthropological contribution to the history and archaeology of an ethnic group' in Burnham B.C. and Kingsbury J. (eds) *Space, hierarchy and society*, British Archaeological Reports, International Series 59

ORME B. 1973 'Archaeology and ethnography' in Renfrew, C. (ed.) *The explanation of culture change*, Duckworth, London

ORME B. 1974 'Twentieth-century prehistorians and the idea of ethnographic parallels', *Man* 9, 199–212

ORME B. 1981 *Anthropology for archaeologists: an introduction*, Duckworth, London

OSWALT W.H. and VAN STONE J.W. 1967 *The ethnoarchaeology of a Crow Village*, Alaska, Bureau of American Ethnology Bulletin 199, Washington

OTTEN C.M. (ed.) 1971 *Anthropology and art*, Natural History Press, New York

BIBLIOGRAPHY

PAGER H.   1976.   'Cave paintings suggest honey hunting activities in Ice Age times', *Bee World* 57, 9–14

PASTRON A.G.   1974   'Ethnoarchaeological observation on human burial decomposition in the Chihuahua Sierra' in Donnan C.B. and Clewlow C.W. (eds) *Ethnoarchaeology*, University of Claifornia, Los Angeles, Institute of Archaeology, Monograph 4

PEEBLES C. and KUS S.   1977   'Some archaeological correlates of ranked societies', *American Antiquity* 42, 421–8

PETERSON N.   1968   'The pestle and mortar: an ethnographic analogy for archaeology', *Mankind* 6, 567–70

PETERSON N.   1971   'Open sites and the ethnographic approach to the archaeology of hunters and gatherers' in Mulvaney D.J. and Golson J. (eds) *Aboriginal Man and Environment in Australia*, Australian National University Press, Canberra

PHILLIPS P.   1971   'Attribute analysis and social structure of Chassey-Cortaillod-Lagozza populations', *Man* 6, 341–52

PHILLIPS P.   1975   *Early farmers of West Mediterranean Europe*, Hutchinson, London

PIRES-FERREIRA J.W. and FLANNERY K.V.   1976   'Ethnographic models for formative exchange' in Flannery K.V. (ed.) *The early Mesoamerican village*, Academic Press, New York

PLOT R.   1686   *The natural history of Staffordshire*, Oxford, printed at the theatre

POLANYI K.   1957   'The economy as instituted process' in Polanyi K., Arensberg C.M. and Pearson H.W. (eds) *Trade and markets in the early empires*, Free Press, Glencoe

PRYOR F.L.   1977   *The origins of the economy*, Academic Press, New York

RAPOPORT A.   1969   'The Pueblo and the Hogan' in Oliver P. (ed.) *Shelter and society*, Barrie and Jenkins, London

RAPPAPORT R.   1967   *Pigs for the ancestors*, Yale University Press, New Haven

RATHJE W.L.   1978   'Archaeological anthropology . . . because sometimes it is better to give then to receive' in Gould R.A. (ed.) *Explorations in ethnoarchaeology*, University of New Mexico Press, Albuquerque

RATHJE W.L.   1979   'Modern material culture studies' in Schiffer M.B. (ed.) *Advances in archaeological method and theory Vol. 2.*, Academic Press, New York

RAY D.J.   1961   *Artists of the tundra and the sea*, University of Washington Press, Seattle

REDMAN C.   1977   'The "analytical individual" and prehistoric style variability' in Hill J. and Gunn J. (eds) *The Individual in Prehistory*, Academic Press, New York

RENFREW C.   1973a.   'Monuments, mobilisation and social organisation in neolithic Wessex' in Renfrew A.C. (ed.) *The explanation of culture change: models in prehistory*, London, Duckworth

BIBLIOGRAPHY

RENFREW C.   1973b   *Before civilisation; the radiocarbon revolution and prehistoric Europe*, Cape, London

RENFREW C.   1977   'Alternative models for exchange and spatial distribution' in Earle T.K. and Erikson J. (eds) *Exchange systems in prehistory*, Academic Press, New York

RICE P.M.   1981   'Evolution of specialised pottery production: a trial model', *Current Anthropology* 22, 219–240

ROBBINS L.H.   1973   'Turkana material culture viewed from an archaeological perspective', *World Archaeology* 5, 209–214

ROBBINS M.   1966   'House types and settlement patterns: an application of ethnology to archaeological interpretation', *Minnesota Archaeologist* 28, 3–35

RODEN D.   1972   'Down-migration in the Moro hills of S. Kordofan, Sudan', *Sudan Notes and Records* 53, 79–99

ROUSE I.   1972.   *An introduction to prehistory*, McGraw-Hill, New York

ROWLANDS M.J.   1971   'The archaeological interpretation of prehistoric metal working', *World Archaeology* 3, 210–24

ROWLANDS M.J.   1976   *The organisation of middle Bronze Age metal working in southern Britain*, British Archaeological Report, 31, Oxford

ROWLANDS M.J.   1980   'Kinship, alliance and exchange in the European Bronze Age' in Barrett J. and Bradley R. (eds) *The British Later Bronze Age*, British Archaeological Reports British Series 80

MCLEOD M.D.   1978   'Aspects of Asante images' in Greenhalgh M. and Megaw V. (eds) *Art in society*, Duckworth, London

SAHLINS M.D.   1965   'On the sociology of primitive exchange' in Banton M. (ed.) *The relevance of models for social anthropology*, ASA monograph 1, Tavistock, London

SAHLINS M.D.   1968   *Tribesmen*, Prentice-Hall, Englewood Cliffs, N.J.

SAHLINS M.D.   1972   *Stone Age economics*, Aldime, Chicago

SAXE A.A.   1970.   *Social dimensions of mortuary practices*, PhD dissertation, University of Michigan

SCHIFFER M.B.   1976   *Behavioural archaeology*, Academic Press, New York

SCHIFFER M.B.   1978   'Methodological issues in ethnoarchaeology' in Gould R. (ed.) *Explorations in ethnoarchaeology*, University of New Mexico Press, Albuquerque

SCHIRE C.   1972   'Ethnoarchaeological model and subsistence behaviour in Arnhem land' in Clarke D.L. (ed.) *Models in archaeology*, Methuen, London

SCHMIDT P.R.   1980   'Steel production in prehistoric Africa: insights from ethnoarchaeology in West Lake, Tanzania' in Leakey R.E. and Ogot B.A. (eds) *Proceedings of the 8th Panafrican Congress of Prehistory and Quaternary Studies, Nairobi, September 1977*, International L. Leakey Memorial Institute for African Prehistory, Nairobi

SERVICE E.   1962   *Primitive social organisation*, Random House, New York

SHARP L.   1952   'Steel axes for stone-age Australians', *Human Organisation* 11, 17–22

SHERRATT A.G.   1976   'Resources, technology andtrade' in Sieveking G., Longworth I. and Wilson K. (eds) *Poblems in economic and social archaeology*, Duckworth, London

SHERRATT A.G.   1981   'Plough and pastoralism: aspects of the secondary products revolution' in Hodder, I., Isaac G. and Hammond N. (eds) *Pattern of the past*, Cambridge University Press, Cambridge

SMILEY F.E., SINOPOLI C.M., JACKSON H.E., WILLS W.H. and GREGG S.A. (eds)   *The archaeological correlates of hunter-gatherer societies: studies from the ethnographic record*, Michigan Discussions in Anthropology 5

SPAULDING A.C.   1953   'Statistical tests for the discovery of artifact types', *American Antiquity* 18, 305–313

SPEED J.   1611   *The history of Great Britaine*

SPRIGGS M. and MILLER D.   1979   'Ambon-Lease: a study of contemporary pottery making and its archaeological relevance' in Millett M. (ed.) *Pottery and the archaeologist*, Institute of Archaeology Occasional Publication, 4

STANISLAWSKI M.B.   1974   'The relationships of ethnoarchaeology, traditional and systems archaeology' in Donnan C.B. and Clewlow C.W. (eds) *Ethnoarchaeology*, University of California, Los Angeles, Institute of Archaeology, Monograph 4

STANISLAWSKI M.B.   1978   'Hopi and Hopi-Tewa ceramic tradition networks' in Hodder, I. (ed.) *Spatial organisation of culture*, Duckworth, London

STEENSBERG A.   1980   *New Guinea gardens*, Academic Press, London

STEWARD J.H.   1942   'The direct historical approach to archaeology', *American Antiquity* 7, 337–43

STILES D.   1977   'Ethnoarchaeology: a discussion of methods and applications', *Man* 12, 86–99

STRATHERN M.   1969   'Stone axes and flake tools: evaluations from two New Guinea Highlands societies', *Proceedings of the Prehistoric Society* 35, 311–29

STRONG W.W.   1935   *An introduction to Nebraska archaeology*, Smithsonian Miscelleneous Collections, 93:10, Washington, D.C.

SUMNER W.M.   1979   'Estimating population by analogy: an example' in Kramer C. (ed.) *Ethnoarchaeology*, Columbia University Press, New York

TAINTER J.A.   1978   'Mortuary practices and the study of prehistoric social systems' in Schiffer M.B. (ed.) *Advances in archaeological method and theory*, Vol. *1*, Academic Press, New York

TAYLOR W.W.   1948   *A study of archaeology*, Memoir series of the American Anthropological Association 69, Menasha

THOMAS C.   1894   *Report of the mound explorations of the Bureau of Ethnology. Washington, D.C.*

THOMPSON F.   1971   *Black gods and kings*, University of California, Los Angeles

THOMPSON R.H.   1958   *Modern Yucaten Maya pottery making*, Society for American Archaeology, Memoir 15

BIBLIOGRAPHY

THOMSON D.F. 1939 'The seasonal factor in human culture', *Proceedings of the Prehistoric Society* 5, 209–221

TRETYAKOV P.N. 1934 'I Istorii doklassovogo obsh'chestva verkhnego Povolzhya' (On the history of pre-class society in the area of the Upper Volga), *Gosudarstavannaia Akademiia Istorii Material'noi kul'tury (Moscow)*, 106, 97–180

TRINGHAM R. 1978 'Experimentation, ethnoarchaeology and the leapfrogs in archaeological methodology' in Gould R. (ed.) *Explorations in ethnoarchaeology*, University of New Mexico Press, Albuquerque

TURNER T.S. 1969 'Tchikrin: a central Brazilian tribe and its symbolic language of bodily adornment', *Natural History* 78, 50–70

TURNER V.M. 1969 *The ritual process*, Routledge and Kegan Paul, London

TYLOR E. 1865 *Researches into the early history of mankind*

UCKO P.J. 1968 *Anthropomorphic figurines*, Andrew Szmidla, London

UCKO P.J. 1969 'Ethnography and archaeological interpretation of funerary remains', *World Archaeology* 1, 262–77

UCKO P.J. (ed.) 1977 *Form in indigenous art*, Duckworth, London

UCKO P.J. and ROSENFELD A. 1967 *Palaeolithic cave art*, Weidenfeld and Nicolson, London

UMEOV A.I. 1970 'The basic forms and rules of inference by analogy' in Tavenec P.V. (ed.) *Problems in the logic of scientific knowledge*, Dordecht, Holland, D. Reidel Publishing Company

VASTOKAS J.M. 1978 'Cognitive aspects of North Coast art' in Greenhalgh M. and Megaw V. (eds) *Art in society*, Duckworth, London

VINNICOMBE P. 1976 *People of the eland*, University of Natal Press, Pietermaritzburg

VITA-FINZI C. and HIGGS E.S. 1970 'Prehistoric economy in the Mount Carmel area of Palestine: site catchment analysis', *Proceedings of the Prehistoric Society* 36, 1–37

WASHBURN D. 1977 *A symmetry analysis of Upper Gila Area ceramic design*, Papers of the Peabody Museum of Archaeology and Ethnology 68, Cambridge

WASHBURN D. 1978 'A symmetry classification of Pueblo ceramic designs' in Grebinger, P. (ed.) *Discovering past behaviour, experiments in the archaeology of the American southwest*, Gordon and Breach, New York

WHALLON R. 1965 *The Owasco period: a reanalysis*, PhD dissertation, University of Chicago

WHITE J.P. and MODJESKA N. 1978 'Acquirers, users, finders, losers: the use of axe blades among the Duna', *Mankind* 11, 276–87

WHITE J.P. and PETERSON N. 1969 'Ethnographic interpretations of the prehistory of West Arnhem land', *South Western Journal of Anthropology* 25, 45–67

WHITE J.P. and THOMAS D.H. 1972 'What mean these stones? Ethno-taxonomic models and archaeological interpretations in the New Guinea

BIBLIOGRAPHY

Highlands' in Clarke D.L. (ed.) *Models in archaeology*, Methuen, London

WHITING J. and AYRES B. 1968 'Inferences from the shape of dwellings. in Chang K.C. (ed.) *Settlement archaeology*, National Press, Palo Alto

WEISSNER P. 1974 'A functional estimator of population from floor area', *American Antiquity*, 39, 343–9

WILK R. and SCHIFFER M. B. 1979 'The archaeology of vacant lots in Tucson, Arizona', *American Antiquity* 44, 530–36

WILLEY G.R. and SABLOFF J.A. 1974 *A history of American archaeology*, Thames and Hudson, London

WILLIAMS B.J. 1974 'A model of band society', *American Antiquity* 39, Memoir 29

WILLIS D. 1977 *Learning to labour: how working class kids get working class jobs*, Gower Press, London

WILLS W.H. 1980 'Ethnographic observation and archaeological interpretation: the Wikmunkan of Cape York Peninsula, Australia' in Smiley F.E. *et al* (eds) *The archaeological correlates of hunter-gatherer societies: studies from the ethnographic record*, Michigan Discussions in Anthropology, 5

WILMSEN E.N. 1979 *Prehistoric and historic antecedants of a contemporary Ngamiland community*, Boston University African Studies Centre Working Paper 12

WILMSEN E.N. 1980 *Exchange, interaction and settlement in North Western Botswana: past and present perspective*, Boston University African Studies Centre Working Paper 39

WOBST M.H. 1977 'Stylistic behaviour and information exchange' in Cleland C. (ed.) *Papers for the director: research essays in honor of James B Griffin*, Anthropology Papers of the University of Michigan, 61, Ann Arbor

WOBST M.H. 1978 'The archaeo-ethnology of hunter-gatherers or the tyranny of the ethnographic record in archaeology', *American Antiquity* 43, 303–9

WOLFE A.W. 1969 'Social structural bases of art', *Current Anthropology* 10, 3–44

WOODBURN J. 1980 'Hunters and gatherers today and reconstruction of the past' in Gellner E. (ed.) *Soviet and western anthropology*, Duckworth, London

WRIGHT H.T. and ZEDER M.A. 1977 'The simulation of a linear exchange system under equilibrium conditions' in Earle T.K. and Erikson J.E. (eds) *Exchange systems in prehistory*, Academic Press, New York

WYLIE M.A. 1980 'Analogical inference in archaeology', Paper presented at the Society for American Archaeology conference, Philadelphia

YELLEN J.E. 1977 *Archaeological approaches to the present. Models for reconstructing the past*, Academic Press, New York

YORK P. 1980 *Style wars*, Sidgwick and Jackson, London

Index

Aborigines (Australian) 34, 93, 97, 98,
    101, 152, 174, 178
Adams, M.J. 184
Africa 11, 18, 33, 39, 50, 54, 61, 70, 84,
    86, 106, 107, 110, 133, 153, 173, 178,
    181, 185
agriculture 56, 64, 94, 96, 97, 104, 105,
    106–111, 151, 152, 154
Alaska 93
Alschular, R.H. 173
Ammerman, A. 110, 111
analogy 11–27, 9, 28, 29, 31, 33, 34, 35,
    36, 37, 38, 40, 41, 47, 50, 54, 56, 60,
    67, 68, 72, 79, 80, 92, 94, 97, 104,
    107, 108, 111, 117, 122, 125, 139,
    147, 152, 153, 157, 158, 164, 167,
    171, 176, 178, 181, 182, 191, 198,
    199, 210, 211, 212, 213, 216
analogy, formal 16, 18, 19, 20, 32, 33,
    68, 70, 174
analogy, relational 16, 19, 20, 23, 25,
    27, 37, 38, 47, 54, 61, 64, 67, 68, 72,
    89–92, 104, 117, 156, 157, 158, 210,
    211, 212
ancient Britons 31, 32, 39, 122
Anderson, K.M. 37
anthropology 24, 27, 28, 31, 33, 34, 35,
    38, 40, 41, 42, 43, 44, 46, 93, 104,
    114, 133, 147, 154, 171, 172, 212
anthropological archaeology 9, 36, 37,
    47, 139, 210–216
Arabs 65
Ardrey, R. 54
Arnold, D.E. 86
arrowheads 68, 69
art (see: Palaeolithic art) 138, 159,
    173–195 (Chapter 8), 196, 204, 208,
    210, 213
art, schematic 176
Arussi-Galla 90
Ascher, R. 37
Asia 11, 123
Audouze, F. 72, 105, 124
Australasia 147, 150
Australia (see: Aborigines)
Australopithecine 54
Ayres, J.E. 38, 126
axe 11, 12, 32, 34, 59, 79, 80, 146, 147,
    149, 150

Bakels, C.C. 108
Balfet, H. 72, 86, 87
Baluchistan 72, 105, 106, 124
bands 152, 154, 156
Baringo district 41, 42, 47, 49, 57, 73,
    81, 82, 84, 85, 87, 88, 89, 194
Barrelet, M.T. 72
Barry, H. 173
Barth, F. 42, 104, 214
Bates, D. 104
Behrensmeyer, A.K. 54
Bender, B. 107, 150
Berber 86
Bersu, G. 16, 117, 120
Binford, L.R. 14, 20, 21, 23, 24, 38, 42,
    54, 58, 59, 60, 95, 100, 101, 104, 111,
    126, 128, 129, 140, 141, 146, 211
Bloch, M. 43, 145, 167, 171
bones 54, 55, 56, 59, 65, 67, 92, 95,
    111–113, 158, 216
bones, human 120, 140, 159
bone distributions 54, 56
Bonnichsen, R. 58, 122
Boserup, E. 107
Botswana 95, 126
boundaries 194
Bourdieu, P. 139
Braithwaite, M. 26, 185, 189
Brazil 11, 189
Brim, J.A. 41
Bronze Age 153, 164
Bunzel, R. 182, 183
burial 11, 14, 19, 25, 36, 40, 43, 88, 92,
    113, 117, 120, 123, 134, 138, 139,
    140, 141, 142, 143, 144, 145, 146,
    154, 155, 156, 157, 158, 159, 166,
    171, 184, 189, 190, 196, 202, 210,
    211, 212, 214
Burjat 68
bushmen 38, 43, 54, 95, 96, 97, 123,
    126, 178, 179, 182

'Caches' 20
Caesar 31
calabashes 56, 76, 91, 142, 185, 188,
    189, 190
Campbell, J. 96
Canter, D. 199

Caribou Eskimos 13
Carneiro, R.L. 79, 80, 154
Carpathos 112
caste 90
causewayed camps 164, 165, 166
central place theory 19
chalcolithic 72
Chapman, R. 151, 155
Chappell, J. 147, 149
charcoal 78, 79
Chasko, W. 126
Chassey 167
Cherry, J. 45
chiefdoms 88, 147, 152, 153, 154, 155, 156, 166, 168
Childe, G. 33, 34, 89, 107
children 198
Chisholm, M.D.I. 108
Christy, H. 33
Clark, G. 12, 13, 14, 16, 18, 19, 34, 68, 69, 107, 134, 147, 150, 174, 176, 193
Clarke, D. 89
Clewlow, C.W. 38, 140
climate 45, 54, 67, 100, 105, 123, 134, 140, 151, 155
Cohen, R. 41
Coles, J. 29
combs 68, 70
computer simulation 29–30, 157
conical clan 154, 156
Conkey, M. 191
context 13, 21, 22, 23, 24, 25, 26, 27, 29, 33, 34, 35, 37, 38, 40, 41, 43, 47, 56, 58, 59, 60, 61, 62, 65, 67, 70, 72, 84, 87, 89–92, 95, 96, 97, 101, 107, 108, 110, 111, 113, 114, 116, 117, 120, 122, 124, 125, 126, 128, 133, 134, 138, 139, 140, 147, 151, 152, 157, 158, 164, 167, 171, 173, 174, 176, 179, 182, 183, 184, 190, 191, 194, 196, 197, 198, 204, 206, 207, 210, 211, 213, 214
Copi, I.M. 16
Crader, D.C. 54
craft production (see also: specialist production) 86, 87, 88, 89, 90
Cranstone, B.A.L. 58
cremation 19
Crete 166
cross-cultural generalisation 24, 40, 67, 68, 91, 108, 127, 128, 132, 140, 141, 142, 158, 197, 210, 211, 212
cross-cultural laws 18, 27, 38, 60, 61, 85–89, 90, 126, 132, 154, 157, 194
Cunliffe, B.W. 163
curation 59, 60

Dalton, G. 14, 147, 151
Daniel, G.E. 32, 33
Dart, R. 54
Dassanetch 56
David, N. 34, 58, 59
decoration 173, 182–191, 216
Deetz, J. 61, 62, 112, 128, 176, 208
De Montmollin, O. 93
Denmark 11, 68, 69, 80
deposition 47, 56, 56–65, 92, 117, 122
Dethlefson, E. 176
De Vore, I. 37, 94, 96, 108, 122
direct historical approach 18, 36
dirt (see also: refuse, discard) 60, 61, 62, 63, 64, 65, 67, 91, 126, 144, 145, 185, 187, 210, 216
discard (see also: refuse, dirt) 24, 59, 60, 61, 62, 64, 65, 67, 117, 197, 198, 199
discursive knowledge 42, 43, 46, 183, 184, 189, 214, 215
Divale, W.T. 127, 128
Donley, L. 139, 185
Donnan, C.B. 38
Dorobo 96
Douglas, M. 64, 166, 190, 191
Drakensberg 178, 179
Drewett, P. 118, 120
Dugdale, W. 32
Dugum Dani 58
Durkheim, E. 166
Dyson-Hudson, N. 104

Earle, T. 154, 155, 156
Easter Island 84, 166, 168, 170
Ebert, J. 95
Eckert, P. 202
ecology 37, 38, 101, 145, 154, 155, 203
economy 13, 14, 16, 18, 24, 26, 27, 29, 39, 56, 62, 64, 67, 84, 88, 90, 91, 92, 93, 96, 97, 104, 108, 109, 110, 111, 113, 123, 124, 138, 142, 145, 146, 147, 151, 152, 153, 154, 156, 157, 158, 194, 196, 197, 198, 199, 203, 210, 212
egalitarian societies 67, 133, 152, 155, 173, 195
elite 90, 151, 156, 167
Ellison, A. 118, 120, 155
Ember, C. and M. 127, 128
endogamous 90
England 31, 34, 35, 52, 62, 63, 68, 71, 120, 160, 164, 165, 189, 202, 203, 206, 209
environment 13, 16, 18, 24, 44, 54, 56, 67, 68, 94, 95, 100, 101, 104, 105, 107, 120, 124, 134, 138, 139, 155,

156, 157, 167, 176, 178, 179, 198, 210, 211
Eskimos (see also: Nunamiut) 14, 16, 19, 34, 42, 59, 60, 68, 93, 94, 95, 100
Ethiopia 90
ethnic groups 26, 28, 35, 64, 67, 90, 105, 198, 206
ethnoarchaeology 28–46, 47, 54, 56, 67, 72, 79, 93, 95, 96, 104, 114, 116, 123, 124, 125, 128, 157, 158, 171, 212
ethnocentrism 30, 39
ethnohistory 35
ethnology 12, 27, 28, 33, 35
Europe 11, 28, 31, 32, 33, 35, 36, 38, 61, 79, 86, 96, 107, 110, 150, 155, 164, 168, 174, 178, 179
Evans, J. 33, 170
evolution 151, 152, 153, 154, 156
exchange 11, 117, 146–152, 153, 157, 183
experimental archaeology 29–31, 72, 79, 80, 157

Faki 90, 91
farming 26, 31, 104, 105, 106, 107, 110, 120, 151
Fewkes, J.W. 28, 35, 37
field methods 40, 41–46
figurines 164, 166
Firth, R. 34
Fischer, J.L. 173
Flannery, K. 147
Fletcher, R. 123, 124
flint knapping 39, 40, 67, 89, 90
Foley, R. 100, 122
food 59, 61, 63, 64, 65, 93, 94, 95, 97, 99, 100, 101, 106, 107, 113, 114, 115, 117, 120, 123, 134, 150, 151, 154, 185, 191, 203
food distribution 43, 150
Ford, J.A. 41
Forge, A. 125
fowling 68
France 31, 160, 167, 209
Frankenstein, S. 150
Freeman, C.G. 14
Frere, J. 32
Friedl, E. 108, 152, 153
Friedman, J. 156
Friedrich, N. 182
Fulani 58
functional explanation 20–24, 27, 33, 37, 40

Gallagher, J.P. 90
Galton, G. 61

Gamble, C. 45
gathering (see hunter-gatherers)
Gellner, E. 104
Germany 19, 31, 33
Gifford, D.P. 54, 56, 111
Gnau 44, 166, 167
Goldstein, L. 141
Goody, J. 107
Gould, R. 14, 20, 26, 28, 38, 40, 41, 43, 100, 196, 212
granary 16, 18, 20, 118, 120, 121, 143, 185, 187
Greenland 13
Gurage 90
Gypsies 24, 25, 62, 63, 64, 65, 67, 90, 113, 144, 145, 199, 212

Haaland, R. 79, 90, 108
Hadza 94, 101
Halstead, P. 111, 112, 150
Hammond, G. and N. 198, 199, 200
Hani 50
Hardin, M.A. 38, 41, 182, 183, 184
Harpending, H.C. 96, 126
Hawaii 154, 155, 156
Hebdige, D. 203
Hedges, J. 68, 165
Heider, K.G. 58
Herero 96
Hesse, M.B. 16
Heyerdahl, T. 84, 170
hide smoking 20, 21, 22, 23
hierarchical societies 88, 105, 123, 133, 144, 152, 153, 154, 155, 185
Higgs, E.S. 108
Hill, J. 54, 128, 183
hillforts 16, 84, 120
hippies 24, 25, 62, 64, 203, 204, 206, 215
Hitchcock, R.K. 126
Hivernel, F. 106
Hodge, F.W. 35
Hogan 137, 138
Hole, F. 104, 105, 106
Hopi 70, 129
Hottentot 54
houses 45, 58, 67, 91, 98, 99, 100, 105, 114, 115, 121, 122, 127, 128, 133, 134, 137, 138, 141, 214
house collapse 47, 49
house construction 47, 80, 81, 82, 84, 105
house, round 11, 15, 47, 117, 132
Hugh-Jones, C. 114, 115, 116, 134
Hughes, I. 150, 151
Humphrey, C. 134, 139

hunter-gatherers 13, 38, 39, 58, 64,
93–104, 107, 108, 109, 111, 122, 126,
152
hunting 13, 31, 56, 59, 68, 85, 93, 94,
95, 96, 97, 106, 108, 126, 151
huts (see: houses) 47, 50, 58, 60, 81, 82,
126, 139
hypothetico-deductive method 20, 21,
38, 211

ideology 11, 24, 27, 29, 40, 41, 43, 101,
104, 133, 134, 140, 141, 144, 145,
152, 156, 158, 164, 167, 172, 179,
189, 190, 191, 192, 193, 194, 195,
196, 202, 203, 204, 207, 208, 211,
212, 213, 215, 216
Indians (Canada) 32, 34
Indians (North America) 11, 18, 31, 34,
35, 39, 120, 184, 193
Indians (South America) 114
Indonesia 92
industrialisation 28, 29, 197
Ingersoll, D. 38
Ingold, T. 104
Iran 123, 125
Iraq 58
iron 72, 78, 79, 88, 89
Iron Age 15, 16, 17, 18, 26, 34, 52, 68,
70, 71, 72, 78, 117, 120, 122, 163
Isaac, G. 54, 55
Isbell, W.H. 139
Italy (Southern) 108, 110, 113

Jackson, R. 110
Japan 199
Jarrige, C. 72, 105, 124
jeans 202
Jelinek, J. 174
Jochim, M.A. 94, 95
Johnson, D. 104
Jones, G. 112

Kalahari 97, 178, 181
Kavolis, V. 173
Kayapo 189, 190, 193
Kenya 15, 17, 26, 39, 41, 47, 49, 56, 57,
71, 73, 80, 81, 84, 85, 87, 88, 89, 90,
96, 118, 194
Khuzistan 105
kilns 29, 86
kinship 117, 151, 153
Kleindienst, M. 37
Klindt, O. 32
Korn, S.M. 184
Kraft, J. 32
Kramer, C. 38, 123, 124

Kroeber, A.L. 35, 193
!Kung bushmen (see bushmen) 43, 94,
96, 101, 108, 113, 181
Kuper, A. 133, 134
Kus, S. 88, 139, 154, 155

Lafitau, J.T. 32
Lange, F.W. 58, 122
Lee, R.B. 37, 54, 94, 95, 96, 108, 122,
126, 199
Lewis, G. 44, 166, 167, 171
Lhwyd, E. 32
Linearbandkeramik 107
Little Woodbury 117
logico-deductive method (see also:
hypothetico-deductive) 21, 22, 211
Longacre, W.A. 37, 38, 128
Lozi 56, 57, 61, 69, 88, 120, 121, 129, 132
Lubbock, Sir J. 33
Lund, P.W. 11, 12

Maasai 96
Madagascar 43, 143, 145
Maglemosian 68
Maghreb 86
Malinowski, B. 166–167
Malta 166, 168, 170
Maori 34, 84, 120
marriage 134
Marshak, A. 179
matrilineal 108, 142, 143, 173, 174
matrilocal 127, 128, 129, 183
maximisation 58
McBryde, I. 147, 150
McIntosh, N.W.G. 50, 51, 174, 176
McNett, C.W. 61
Meggers, B.J. 37
Meillassoux, C. 104, 107
Merina 145
Mesakin 65, 66, 91, 141, 142, 143, 185
Mesolithic 12, 13, 16, 68, 69, 159
Messer, E. 113
metal production (see also: iron) 72, 79,
86, 182
Mexico 140, 183, 184
migratory groups 60
Milke, W. 193
Miller, D. 92, 151, 207
Mississippian sites 20, 155
Modjeska, N. 59, 147, 150
monogamous 126
monuments, construction of 84
Moore, H. 139
Moro 91, 141
Mueller, J.W. 45
Munsen, P.J. 23

Murdock, G.P. 94, 108
Murray, P. 60, 61

Nadel, S.F. 142
Naroll, R. 41, 123
Navajo Indians 134, 137, 138, 139
Needham, R. 101
Nelson, N.C. 39
Neolithic 34, 39, 80, 107, 108, 147, 150, 153, 164, 165, 166, 167, 168
New Guinea 30, 34, 41, 44, 58, 59, 79, 80, 107, 147, 149, 151, 166, 184
New Zealand 84, 120
Nicklin, K. 85, 86, 87
Nilsson, S. 11, 32, 33
Nitra 150
Njemps 73, 85
nomadic societies 105
Nuba 64, 65, 66, 91, 92, 112, 139, 141, 142, 143 144, 163, 183, 185, 187, 193, 194, 214
Nunamiut Eskimos 95

obsidian 90
Ochsenschlager, E.L. 56
Ojibwa 95
Okely, J. 62, 64, 144
Olorgesailie 54
optimal foraging theory 95
Orme, B. 33, 35
Oswalt, W.H. 37

Pager, H. 174
Palaeolithic 32, 54, 97, 164, 174
Palaeolithic art 177, 178, 179
pastoralists 56, 84, 96, 97, 104, 104–106, 108, 111, 194
Pastron, A.G. 140
patrilineal 65, 108, 114, 152
patrilocal 114, 127, 128, 129, 132, 143, 152
Peebles, C. 88, 154, 155
Peterson, N. 96
Phillips, P. 85
Pira-parana 114, 115, 116
Pires-Ferreira, J.W. 147
pits (see also: smudge-pits) 50, 52, 61, 78, 117, 120, 122, 123, 159, 198
Pleistocene 93, 96, 97
Plot, Dr. R. 32
Polanyi, K. 147, 151
politics 45, 125, 150, 153, 156, 167, 190
pollen 107
pollution (see also: purity) 90, 91, 144, 145, 185, 191
polygamous 126, 132

Popper, K. 22
population 60, 61, 107, 123, 124, 125, 126, 132, 153, 154, 156, 157, 182, 183
positivist explanation 21
post-deposition 47, 65, 67, 92, 117, 122
post-holes 11, 15, 16, 17, 47, 58, 117, 120, 122
post-hole patterns 18, 19, 47, 80, 117
pottery 21, 23, 41, 42, 43, 45, 56, 57, 58, 59, 76, 85, 86, 87, 88, 105, 106, 128, 130, 132, 142, 143, 146, 158, 163, 167, 193
pottery decoration 68, 87, 91, 132, 133, 167, 182–191
pottery manufacture 40, 43, 72, 73, 74, 76, 85, 86, 87, 88, 89, 90, 91, 92, 108, 128, 129, 155
Powell, Major J.W. 35, 37
Pryor, F.L. 150, 151
Pueblo 134, 136, 139, 182
punks 203, 204, 206, 207, 215, 216
purity, concept of (see also: pollution) 65

rainfall patterns 26
ranked societies 88, 117, 153, 154, 155
Rapoport, A. 184, 136, 137, 138
Rappaport, R. 150, 167
Rathje, W.L. 41, 196, 199
Ray, D.J. 173
redistribution (centric transfers) 146, 147, 151, 153, 154, 156
Redman, C. 183
refuse (see also: dirt, discard) 24, 41, 42, 52, 59, 60, 61, 62, 63, 64, 65, 66, 67, 92, 116, 126, 196, 197, 198, 199, 200, 202, 212
religion 33, 42, 92, 134, 137, 159
Renaissance 31
Renfrew, A.C. 88, 147, 153, 166, 168
Rice, P. 87, 88
ritual 91, 116, 125, 134, 139, 141, 143, 144, 145, 153, 155, 157, 159–172, 173, 191, 196, 210, 214
Rivers, P. 32, 33, 120
Robbins, M. 56, 105, 126
Roden, D. 142
Roman Britain 19
Rosenfeld, A. 178
Rouse, I. 28
Rowlands, M.J. 34, 86, 89, 150, 151
Rydberg, C.R. 58, 122

Sabloff, J.A. 37
Sahlins, M.D. 94, 147, 151, 152, 153
sampling 45

Saxe, A.A 141, 142
Scandinavia 107
scavengers 54, 55, 56, 62
Schiffer, M.B. 18, 24, 38, 39, 43, 47, 59, 60, 196, 197, 198
Schire, C. 96
Schmidt, P.R. 72, 78, 79
Scotland 71, 166
Scott, K. 54
sedentary groups 60, 61, 62, 94
sedentism 93, 125, 126
seeds 111–113, 142
Service, E. 152, 153
settlement mobility 45, 56, 95, 125
settlement pattern 86, 92, 93, 117, 126, 133, 134, 138, 139, 141, 143, 156, 196
settlement plan 45, 122, 138, 157, 216
settlement size 122, 123, 124, 125, 155, 157, 158
Sharp, L. 150
Shennan, S. 45
Sherratt, A.G. 107, 150
shifting agriculture 107
Sidamo 90
site catchment analysis 95, 108, 110, 111
Skara Brae 34
skins 13, 14, 16, 18, 68, 73, 90, 178
Smiley, F.E. 93
smiths 89, 90
smudge-pits 20–23, 36, 211
social anthropology 39, 152, 157, 166, 212
social organisation 117–158, 159, 196, 210, 215
social relations 11, 42, 117, 133, 134, 144, 145, 147, 151, 157, 167, 179, 190, 212, 215, 216
soil 76, 86, 105, 107, 110, 111, 159
Spain 138
Spaulding, A.C. 41
spears 87, 88, 142, 146
specialist production (see also: craft production) 86, 87, 88, 89, 155
Speed, J. 31
Spriggs, M. 92
standardisation 87, 88
Stanislawski, M.B. 28, 129
Starr Carr 12, 13, 14, 16, 18, 19, 34
states 88, 147, 152, 153, 154, 156
status 90, 125, 144, 150, 151, 154, 155, 156, 185, 213, 214
Steensberg, A. 79, 80, 107
Steward, J.H. 36
Stiles, D. 28, 38, 41
stone tools 24, 30, 31, 32, 33, 41, 59,

60, 79, 85, 90, 95, 108, 123, 184, 191
storage (see also: pits, granaries) 150
Strathern, M. 147
Strong, W.D. 36
style 88, 91, 191–194, 196, 199, 204, 206, 207, 208, 209, 212
subsistence 93–116, 117, 153, 154, 155, 156, 158, 159, 212
Sumner, W.M. 123, 125
Swahili 185
Swazi 133, 134
Sweden 68
swidden cultivation 108, 109
symbolism 25, 26, 62, 64, 65, 90, 91, 101, 111, 112, 113, 116, 125, 133, 134, 139, 151, 152, 158, 166, 171, 174, 177, 179, 182, 185, 189, 190, 191, 193, 195, 196, 203, 204, 206, 207, 208, 212, 213, 214, 215, 216

Tacitus 31
Tainter, J.A. 141
Tallensi 133
Tanzania 72, 78, 101
taphonomy 54
Taylor, W.W. 36
technology 16, 24, 29, 68–92, 93, 104, 138, 157, 210
Thomas, C. 30, 31, 35, 41, 184
Thomson, D.F. 34, 37, 97, 98, 100, 173
Tollius 32
tools 68, 79, 80, 86, 90, 101, 106, 126, 196
trade 85, 87, 155, 167
trampling 56
transhumance 105
Tretyakov, P.N. 128
tribes 97, 152, 154, 156
Tringham, R. 14, 20
Tugen 17, 89
Turner, T. 189, 190
Turner, V. 167, 171

Ucko, P.J. 14, 19, 35, 164, 166, 173, 174, 178
Umeov, A.I. 16
use-life 59, 60

Vastokas, J.M. 184
Venezuela, 79
Vinnicombe, P. 178, 179, 181
Virginia 31
Vita-Finzi, C. 108

wall construction 50
warfare 84, 155, 156

warring 120
Washburn, D. 54, 182, 191
Watson, P.J. 37
wealth 124, 125, 126, 133, 151, 153, 154, 167
weaving 70, 71
Whallon, R. 128
White, J.P. 30, 31, 41, 59, 147, 150, 184
Whiting, J. 126
Wiesnner, P. 123, 124
Wikmunkan 34, 97, 98, 100, 101, 103
Wilk, R. 197, 198
Willey, G.R. 37
Williams, B.J. 96
Willis, D. 203
Wills, W.H. 100, 101
Wilmsen, E.N. 38, 96, 104
Wittfogel, K. 151, 154
Wobst, M.H. 39, 43, 96, 191, 192
Wogul 68

Wolfe, A.W. 173
wood 79, 87, 88, 89
Woodburn, J. 94, 95, 101, 104, 114, 211
Wright, H.T. 150
Wylie, M.A. 16

Yankton 118, 120
Yellen, J.E. 18, 38, 42, 58, 59, 96, 97, 111, 126
Yir Yoront 150
York, P. 203, 204, 206
Yoruba 173
Yugoslavia 192

Zagros Mts. 123, 124
Zambia 47, 50, 52, 56, 57, 61, 68, 69, 88, 118, 120, 121, 129
Zapoteck Indians 113
Zeder, M.A. 150
Zu/oasi 96